MILES JUPP was born in London in 1979, and is an actor, writer and comedian. In 2003 he was nominated for the Perrier Best Newcomer Award at the Edinburgh Festival. He has been a frequent guest on Radio 4's *The News Quiz*, and BBC TV's *Have I Got News For You* and *Mock The Week*. He plays Nigel in the sitcom *Rev*, and John Duggan in *The Thick Of It*. He has also appeared (to be fair sometimes extremely briefly) in a number of feature films such as *Harry Potter And The Order Of The Phoenix*, *Made In Dagenham* and *Johnny English:Reborn*. He's done all sorts of stuff, really. Even proper theatre; *A Day In The Death Of Joe Egg* at the Glasgow Citizens, *The Way Of The World* at the Northampton Royal, and Alan Bennett's *People* at the National Theatre. He's made several documentaries about literature for Radio 4. None of this seems to matter though. He could have spent six months manning the international space system, or been kidnapped by guerilla fighters, or pioneered a new method of losing weight using sound alone; any description of him would still be likely to focus on the fact that he used to play Archie The Inventor in the childrens' programme *Balamory*.

FIBBER IN THE HEAT

MILES JUPP

EBURY
PRESS

1 3 5 7 9 10 8 6 4 2

This edition published 2013
First published in 2012 by Ebury Press, an imprint of Ebury Publishing
A Random House Group company

The Random House Group Limited Reg. No. 954009

Addresses for companies within the Random House Group can be found at
www.randomhouse.co.uk

A CIP catalogue record for this book is available from the British Library

The Random House Group Limited supports the Forest Stewardship
Council® (FSC®), the leading international forest-certification organisation.
Our books carrying the FSC label are printed on FSC®-certified paper. FSC is
the only forest-certification scheme supported by the leading environmental
organisations, including Greenpeace. Our paper procurement policy can be
found at www.randomhouse.co.uk/environment

MIX
Paper from
responsible sources
FSC® C016897

Designed and set by seagulls.net

Printed and bound by CPI Group (UK) Ltd, Croydon, CR0 4YY

ISBN 9780091943134

To buy books by your favourite authors and register for offers visit
www.randomhouse.co.u

For my father, who rang me up one day
and told me to write a book.

Chapter One

I love cricket. But I can still remember a time, very clearly, when I didn't. I was ambivalent about cricket. It was just another sport, like all the other sports that I also felt ambivalent about. I must have first played it when I was about six or seven at school. I had a copy of the tabletop game Test Match, which featured Ian Botham and David Gower on its box. I played the real game, albeit badly, for my school under-10s team. I even, for a time, went to afternoon nets in the indoor school at Lord's.

All the time, however, I was just going along with it. It was part of the timetable, like football or athletics. It was just one of those many things that you did at that age, simply because you had to.

But one day all of that changed. One fateful morning during the summer holidays in 1991, bored, back from boarding school and looking for something to do, I pushed open the study door of my father; a former church minister, he now had a mysterious academic career writing about death. 'Come in,' he called without registering that I hadn't actually knocked. His study was a long, narrow room with steep, crammed bookcases on each side. The shelves were piled high with the academic tomes that provided the bibliography and footnotes to his work. A number of tall, grey filing cabinets were arranged haphazardly about the place, giving the room a feeling not unlike a carelessly thrown together sculpture garden. Each one had been placed exactly where they stood by a delivery man. 'Just put it down where you like,' my father had told the first delivery man, 'I haven't decided quite where to put it yet.' He would then give the cabinet not another moment's thought until a day came when he realised that it was full and so ordered a second one to be delivered, whereupon the pattern repeated itself.

I dodged my way in and out of the metallic standing stones and made my way to the far end of the room where my father's desk was placed, under a huge window through which bright sun was streaming down onto the many piles of notepads, newspaper cuttings and files that covered most of the desk. Only a small proportion of the desk seemed to have been set aside for working on, but in the summer months that position was usually coveted by a large tabby cat who liked to sprawl and bask, eyes shut, for as much of the day as possible. 'I've just stopped working to have a cup of something for elevenses,' said my father, who then immediately began to reorganise a pile of files on the floor by the desk.

I sighed. I wasn't really sure what the work was that my father claimed to have just stopped doing. All I knew for sure was that it involved lots of paper and lots of books, and that when we went on family holidays we seemed to spend a lot of time visiting cemeteries. I knew what my mother did for a living – she worked in London in order, she said, to finance whatever it was that Daddy did. But the truth was that I wasn't remotely curious about what my father did all day in his study; I wasn't very curious about anything. This made it all the more surprising to my father when I suddenly posed him a question.

'Daddy,' I said, 'what's happening in the cricket at the moment?'

To this day I have no idea where the question came from. I lingered over the words 'the' and 'cricket', as if I was repeating a phrase that I had heard somebody else use, and wanted to make sure that I was pronouncing the phrase correctly. Of course, I had talked occasionally about cricket in the past. But never before would I have dreamt of referring to it as 'the cricket', as if it was a region of Africa that people had suddenly started mentioning because there was a civil war there.

My father was both delighted and stunned. It was probably the first question that he had heard me utter all holiday, other than endlessly saying, 'What can I do to stop me being so bored?'

'Well,' he said, breaking off from attempting to decipher some handwritten notes he had once made on an index card, 'at the moment England are playing a Test series against the West Indies. There is one game of the series remaining, which starts in a week's time, and if England win it they will draw the series.'

And that was that. In a single moment of intimate paternal connection, I became obsessed. There was something so beauti-fully clear about this equation. So much of what my father usually tried to explain to me was well beyond my comprehen-sion, but here I had been furnished with an answer the essence of which I could grasp immediately. My interest in cricket went from almost nothing to an obsession in an instant, lurching into action in the same way that a sleepy dog might when it hears a key turning slowly in a lock. My father passed me a copy of that day's *Times* still warm from another cat, this time a large, ginger one, who had been sleeping on it. I sat down on the floor of my father's study and read all of the cricket reports and articles in it. I then went to the pile of back issues that teetered on a creaking chair in the kitchen and wormed my way through all of them, ignoring the headlines on the front pages that must have been concerned with unrest in the Gulf, and instead turned to one of the back pages where I could read about 'bowlers in good rhythm' or batsmen 'struggling to convert their county form into Test runs'. Cricket, I soon realised, had its own language, and it was one with which I instantly fell in love. Outside of articles on cricket, one could never conceive of people being described as 'wristy', or happen upon a sentence that read:

'Although proving adept at playing inside out, he was less sure sweeping against the turning ball and eventually perished as he top edged to a leg gully that had been moved finer.' The fact that at first I didn't understand a single word of it did nothing to dampen my new-found fervour.

As well as its language, I also found great pleasure in analysing the statistics that were carefully laid out in each day's edition. I realised that if I attacked the last week's papers in order, and spread them all out on the kitchen table, I could follow the course of each county game day by day. Each game was a self-contained story. I would read the preview that was printed on the morning of a game's start, and then monitor the scorecards and reports that appeared in the next four days' editions, thus feeling that I myself was involved in each game's ebb and flow. In some games one side would dominate through-out. In other games the initiative would be seized and re-seized in unexpected, brilliant moments and thus the balance of power would swing back and forth wildly, like a lunatic on the end of a rope. I spent entire days just doing this.

I tried to share some of my new knowledge with my older brother Edmund, who liked to spend all his waking hours read-ing novels and listening to music. Several times I bounded up the stairs to his room at the top of the house armed with some bits of newspaper that I thought contained interesting tales, but he could never really demonstrate any interest in what I was telling him. He would merely wait until I had finished my prepared speech and then say, 'Call me Ed.' He had, in fairness, just commenced the messy business of being a teenager, and so who knows what sort of thing was going on inside that body or head of his. Instead I would report my observations to my father, who would say things like, 'Yes, cricket can be like chess sometimes.' I thought that cricket seemed nothing whatsoever like chess. Whenever had a chess player been praised for being 'strong off his legs'? Alongside such insane utterances, my father was also able to impart more practical advice. This included showing me how to use the Teletext service on the television, so that I could check for cricket news and scores throughout each day.

It was through this medium that I eventually learnt that England's squad for the last Test of our series against the West Indies had been announced. I recognised many of the names from the county scores that I had been reading in *The Times*. G. Gooch and H. Morris played for Essex and Glamorgan, I knew, and M. Atherton played for Lancashire. A man called A. Stewart had been recalled, whom I knew to be a Surrey player. Another player had also been recalled, with a name far more recognisable than all the other names put together: I.T. Botham.

*

In the event, I was unable to watch any of the match's coverage on television. My father, as had long been agreed, had taken my brother and me away on a holiday to Ireland. My mother, though too busy to commit to any substantial time away herself, felt that the three of us would benefit from a camping trip. People that knew us thought that camping seemed a strange thing to attempt by a family that hadn't ever really managed to master simple domestic life. We were, after all, a family that sometimes sat down together for supper when my mother had returned exhausted from London, only to discover that none of us had actually thought to prepare anything to eat. Thus we would sit around the dinner table discussing our respective days and eating nothing but cheese and tinned fish. We were all very excited about the idea of camping though, and had gone and rented an enormous tent, as well as a portable cooking stove and gas canisters.

But being excited about the idea of something and actually having any aptitude for it are very different things. In the end, of the 18 nights that we spent away from home, a mere six were spent sleeping in the tent that been hired for this purpose. We had a terribly depressing experience in a place called Spiddle that was so wet and gloomy that my brother and I decided that camping was not for us. Privately, I suspect my father had realised very early on in the holiday that we simply were not up to its demands. All that I really liked about this way of life, it turned out, was starting fires – an activity that was forbidden at most campsites. On one disastrous evening I was stung on the ankle by a wasp, and in a state of confused shock all that I was capable of doing was jumping up and down whilst shouting 'my head, my head', which meant that the source of my panic took far longer for my father to uncover than it should have done.

Ed, meanwhile, had a habit of letting his mind wander at crucial points during our frequently fraught attempts to put up the tent. Just as my father was saying something along the lines of, 'Now we all need to pull at the same time,' he would realise that Ed had let go of his end, and was instead practising chords on an imaginary guitar. 'The rest of us are trying to put a tent up, Ed. What are you doing?' my father would ask through gritted teeth. Ed, once shaken from his reverie, would always calmly reply, 'I am awaiting further instruction.'

My father began to find this ritual rather tiresome, although he could never admit to this. And so he told us that he didn't like camping for an altogether different reason. He told us that he was appalled by how much it had changed since he was a boy scout, and was horrified by how prissy it had become. If you were going to stay in something called a campsite that actually had electricity, gas hobs and working lavatories then you might as well be staying in a bed and breakfast. And so we did.

Much of our time away was spent travelling to what the guidebooks described as 'places of interest'. We kissed the Stone Of Eloquence at Blarney Castle in Cork and climbed the stairs of Thoor Ballylee, where the poet Yeats had lived. In Dublin we visited the house in Upper Dorset Street where Sean O'Casey had been born, and late one afternoon we clambered over the rocks of Sandycove to see the Martello Tower where Oliver St John Gogarty was said to have fired a shot at James Joyce. My father and Ed were both utterly entranced by it all.

I, however, was less entranced. None of these things, I am ashamed to say, meant a great deal to the 11-year-old Jupp. Being away from home didn't represent a wonderful opportunity to see new things and places. It simply meant that I was unable to watch the cricket on the television or check county scores on Teletext. I mentioned this to my father in the car, though, and for my troubles I was rewarded with a wonderful discovery: BBC Radio 4's *Test Match Special*. This represented some sort of heaven to me: a radio show in which jolly men with jolly-sounding names and even jollier voices told listeners exactly what was happening in the cricket and filled in the gaps with chatter of more general interest, such as their best recent experiences involving cakes, or a discussion about whether or not hedgehogs should be given milk. At one point during this game, and I had no idea what had caused it, two of the men on this show collapsed into hysteria and for a minute and a half no sound emanated from the car's radio but that of their barely muffled shrieking and the occasional fragment of a croaked sentence. Ed and I, sitting in the back of the car, found ourselves giggling too, whilst in the driver's seat my father let out a series of snorts and laughed so hard that he had to punch the horn four times in order to get a grip on himself.

Sadly, the luxury of *Test Match Special* was taken away from me as suddenly as it had been delivered when one afternoon my father, perhaps whilst explaining French verbs to Ed, became a victim of the power of association and found himself driving on the wrong side of the road. No one was hurt, but the family car had to be towed away and was replaced with a hire car that –

horror of horrors – had no radio. Cricket news would now have to be sourced via the telephone.

And so it was that one day, whilst staying in a town called Clifton, the three of us rang home, and my mother's friend Karen, who was visiting for the afternoon, told me that England had won. Botham had hit the winning runs and immediately became my hero. I was elated. From that moment on my moods began to run more or less in tandem with the fortunes of the England cricket team. My adolescence, for instance, was perfectly in sync with England's horrendous spell throughout the nineties.

*

As I grew older, my obsession deepened. At school, I would absent-mindedly play batting strokes as I walked along the corridors. For my twelfth birthday I asked for a tiny radio so that I could surreptitiously check the score during lessons. I once chose to be late for a maths lesson so that I could watch David Gower make his 1992 comeback on the television in the common room, and then skipped the rest of it to witness him become England's highest run scorer of all time. I was given an absolute rocketing and a detention by a man called Mr Wridgeway, but I didn't regret it for one moment.

In the early months of 1993, I would wake at four in the morning in order to listen to *Test Match Special* on my tiny radio, and would then feign sickness during the day so that I could regain my lost sleep. England were playing India at that time, and it was a disastrous series in which the England team's averages took as much of a battering as their intestines, which were frequently turned to soup by a combination of bad prawns and ignorance. Most of the England team were ill at one stage or another and an even greater number of them played abysmally. They lost each one of their three Test matches, and their leading wicket taker was Graeme Hick, with his part-time off-spin. Their leading batsman, David Gower, hadn't even been selected for the tour. Despite these failures, I loved listening to the games from India. To me it didn't matter how much England struggled, because the quality of our performances at the games seemed somehow incidental to the carnival of noise created by the crowds present at them. There was a constant cacophony in the background from Indian fans, and whenever the frequent wickets fell during each of England's brief innings it was a full minute before the commentators' voices could be heard over the roar of the Indian crowd. 'Here,' I thought, 'is a country where the people are as obsessed with cricket as I am.' Lying in a bunk bed in a boys' dormitory in a Berkshire preparatory school, wearing both tartan pyjamas and a woollen dressing gown just to keep warm, I genuinely imagined that I had a lot in common with those Indians whose shouts I could hear so clearly.

But cricket did not always bring joy. Later that same year I suffered my first cricketing heartbreak when Ian Botham retired from the first-class game. His last match, fittingly, was against the touring Australians. That week the Jupp family, none of us genetically inclined to great athletic endeavour, were on an extremely stressful cycling holiday in the Loire Valley. A sense of direction is essential to the long-distance cyclist, but so too is the judgement to pack only that which is truly necessary and the ability to ride a bike confidently when being squeezed off the road by heavy goods vehicles. Day after day, our convoy of four, which sometimes stretched out over a kilometre, would find itself lost or out of water or out of patience. Tempers flared, thighs were chafed and a family vowed never to go on holiday together ever again.

I had calculated the exact time when Botham's last game would come to its conclusion, and at that precise moment I took the time to shed a tear for the end of an era. It was a rare moment of respite from an otherwise continuous barrage of screaming and grumpiness into which our ill-advised vacation had descended. Ian Botham had been my first cricket hero and I was close to bereft. But not entirely. Because before he retired from the game, I had already found another one. A demi-god in fact. And his name was Michael Atherton.

*

Michael Atherton became my favourite cricketer at some point in 1993, a tough year for English cricket during which we played a disastrous series against Australia. Throughout that summer Atherton was a lone beacon for England and by the end of the series I was obsessed with him and grateful for his scores of 19, 25, 80, 99, 11, 9, 55, 63, 72, 28, 50 and 42.

I always believed there was something trustworthy and honest about him. He was stubborn yet unassuming, and he was quiet. It didn't matter to me that he had limitations as a player. The great thing about Atherton was that he knew exactly what his limitations were, and so played within them.

He was such a hero that when I was 13 or 14 at school other boys would say things like 'Michael Atherton? He's your boyfriend.' I suppose this was classic schoolboy misnomenclature – perhaps understanding the definition of 'boyfriend' to be 'someone that you've never actually met, who has no idea of your existence, and whom you merely admire from afar'. Which, as every schoolboy of 13 or 14 knows, would actually make him a 'girlfriend'.

Late in the summer of 1993, Atherton became England captain. In 1994 he was accused –wrongly – of ball-tampering at Lord's. This was a tough moment for me – it probably hit me harder than it hit him. He was fined by his own team manager and hounded by the media. He withstood calls to resign, never even went back to his house between the Lord's game and the next Test at Headingley, and then when he came out to open the batting he got an amazing response from the crowd, and batted doggedly and brilliantly for most of the day. But then, after batting for 360 minutes, he prodded the 224th delivery he faced back to the bowler Brian McMillan who caught it and he was out. For 99 runs. 99. For the second time in his career. I switched off the television, lay on my bed and howled and howled and howled.

For much of the 1990s Michael Atherton *was* English cricket. He led from the front; he scored the most runs. Once he was out, we were usually all out, as if he was some sort of inadvertent trade unionist accidentally leading a strike. Other people did great things in that era for us, but no one, as far as I was concerned, could hold a candle to him. I worshipped him.

I encountered him once in 1995. I went with a friend to see England play West Indies at the Oval in south London. I was an enthusiastic autograph collector in those days, and someone had told me that all of the England players parked their cars in the playground of Archbishop Tenison's School, just along Oval Road. So my friend and I went along to this car park and waited for as long as we had to. In dribs and drabs, various players came back to the car park and signed autographs for us and chatted pleasantly. There was a small crowd of us, and we waited and waited until I had the autograph of every other member of the England team, the twelfth man, both umpires, the match referee, and two national broadsheets' cricket correspondents. But still no Atherton.

Then eventually a smaller boy shouted, 'There's Atherton', and we all looked back along the road towards the ground. There he was, laden down with cricket equipment, slowly making his way towards the car park, all the while besieged by a group of fans and autograph hunters who had followed him from the ground. Patiently, we waited and by the time he got to us he maybe had a group of just six people around him. He stopped, and again signed autographs diligently and graciously.

Just at that moment a couple of cocky, confident, probably slightly drunk, teenage girls came walking in the other direction. When they clocked that Atherton was signing things, they stopped and one of them said, 'Who are you?'

And he said, in his delightful Lancastrian lilt, 'Why? Who are you?'

And one of the girls said, 'It doesn't matter who we are. You're the one signing autographs, you must be someone.'

And Michael Atherton said to them, 'No. I'm not anyone. I'm just a cricketer.'

The captain of the England cricket team, who had just scored a match-saving 95 against the West Indies: 'I'm just a cricketer.'

He rocketed yet further in my estimation.

When I grew up and became the captain of the England cricket team, then I would definitely behave as modestly as that.

Chapter Two

I never did become the England cricket captain. I never even became good at cricket. The 11-year-old who was mad about the game seemed to be no better a player than the 10-year-old who didn't care a damn for it. As an under-10 player I could usually be guaranteed a passenger berth somewhere in the team. By the time I was in the under-11 age group I was being asked to operate the scoreboard. It was not a big school, however, and so as a 12-year-old I was given a slot in the second XI as a reward for nothing other than enthusiasm. As one of the few players in the team with any interest in the game, I was asked to open the batting. On one occasion I batted for an hour and four minutes and made just one run.

I did have one amazing day, though, when having made single-figure scores in every other match, I suddenly came good in our last fixture of the season. Chasing, as I remember, a total of 77, I went out to face the first ball and, out of nowhere, found form. I had never before been in 'the zone' – as professional batsmen might term it – in my life. Nor have I ever been in it since. But that day people kept bowling at me, and I kept on hitting it, and the ball kept screaming across the outfield. I brought up my half-century with a four driven through mid-on. If you took into account the number of seconds that I raised my bat to the crowd (about 20) compared to the number of people that crowd contained (about seven) then, proportionally speaking, it was probably one of the biggest celebrations any cricket ground has ever witnessed.

I played a bit at my public school, always enthusiastically but never successfully. I represented the school in various B teams and eventually captained the school Third XI. Played one. Drew one. So I was not in a position, when I left school, to embark on a dazzling career as an international sportsman.

Instead, possibly predictably, I went on to Edinburgh University to read Theology. Whilst there, possibly less predictably, I had started performing stand-up comedy. At the end of the Edinburgh Festival in 2001, I won a long-running newcomer competition called So You Think You're Funny? The final was held on 25 August, the same date that Michael Atherton played his final innings for England. In my victory speech, I dedicated my prize to him.

Getting more professional, I found myself an agent, and started travelling to London to do gigs at weekends. And then suddenly I was asked to be in a BBC Scotland comedy programme called *The Live Floor Show*. It was a completely nerve-racking experience. I was a 22-year-old undergraduate who had been doing stand-up less than two years and I was completely, and hopelessly, out of my depth.

At some point during this exhilarating and terrifying period I went to an audition. A few weeks later I was offered the part of 'Archie The Inventor' on a new children's show called *Balamory*. It wasn't quite what I had imagined myself doing with my life, but I was going to get 22 weeks of filming work on it. Besides, it would be on a digital channel, and therefore not many people would even see me pratting about in a pink kilt and jumper.

And so I did it. We had two weeks of filming on the Isle of Mull doing various bits of dancing about, and then we went back to Glasgow and filmed the rest of it. When it started being shown on the CBeebies channel a handful of people watched it. For a while it looked like *Balamory* might die a slow death as so many things do. But then Alan Yentob, or whoever was in charge of these things, decided that this wonderful piece of work deserved to be put out on a terrestrial channel and that, I think, is when it started going bonkers. There were articles in the newspapers, and in the *Radio Times*. There were impressions of the show on *Dead Ringers*. People would shout 'Archie' at me in the street or in pubs. It was suddenly a big, slightly out of control, deal.

In 2003 I went back to university for two terms and then did a solo stand-up show at the Edinburgh Festival. I muddled through to the end of the year with some writing work and a presenting job for E4, to which I was not at all well suited. 2004 was spent almost entirely filming more episodes of *Balamory*. And then, over Christmas, we did an arena tour.

As 2004 turned into 2005, I didn't know which way to turn. Already another arena tour was planned for the end of the year, but until then I had no idea what I would do with myself. I couldn't really be bothered doing any stand-up gigs on the comedy circuit, and I wasn't offered any other acting work, so I just sat about a bit. I wrote one long essay, which was enough for me to finally finish my degree. But I completely lacked any ambition. The *Balamory* juggernaut had somehow killed all that in me.

In an attempt to get things going again I decided to do not one but two daily shows at that August's Edinburgh Festival. But by the time the festival came around, I had no wish to be involved in it. All I wanted to do was to sit in my flat and watch cricket on the television. Not just any cricket, though. This was the gripping Ashes series of 2005, and in August alone there were three Test matches, of which we won two and drew the other. This was one of the most amazing series ever played on English soil. I found it impossible to concentrate on either of my shows. My girlfriend Rachel, after she had recovered from the shock of watching my emotional response to the Edgbaston Test, decided that I had to pull myself together. 'You'll just have to get yourself a job that enables you to watch even more cricket,' she told me. 'Oh hang on, you're an actor. There isn't one.'

And yet in many ways it is here that this story begins. When the beastly month-long festival was finally over, England were leading the Australians 2–1, with one game still to play. That fifth and final Test got under way at the Oval on 8 September. England, who had fielded an unchanged team throughout the series, had had to make a change in their team owing to an injury to the Welsh fast bowler Simon Jones. Paul Collingwood came into the team as his replacement, and having won the toss, England chose to bat. At that exact moment I was a little over five miles away, as the crow flies, in the London rehearsal rooms of the National Youth Theatre. This was where the cast of *Balamory* were rehearsing the latest live show, and we were spending that particular day learning the choreography for the various musical numbers. Just as Glenn McGrath was running in to bowl the first ball of the game to Marcus Trescothick, I was struggling to keep up with a rather tricky salsa sequence that for reasons I could never quite establish involved the use of pom-poms.

At the first available opportunity I snuck out onto the fire escape to try and check England's progress on my mobile phone. As it happened, there was no need for the phone, as on the fire escape I found Rich, an Australian crew member who had a portable radio clamped to his ear. I had spent much of the last week telling Rich that Australia were going to be given a hammering, and on each occasion, much to my annoyance, Rich had always smiled and then calmly agreed with me.

'What's happening, Rich?'

'England are going well, mate. For the moment at least. Love your dancing, by the way.'

Rich was being far too calm for an Australian that genuinely thought that they might be about to lose the Ashes. And as

England slumped from 82 without loss to 115–3 by lunch, Rich still kept calmly claiming that we would definitely win. I found his attitude extremely irritating.

Not nearly as irritating, however, as the rest of the cast found my behaviour. They were all well aware that I was not giving the rehearsals the concentration that they required. Whereas the others were all terrified that the remaining three days were not going to be enough time to get the show bashed into order, for me the rehearsals really couldn't be over soon enough. Much to everyone's annoyance, I ducked out of the room to check the score at every opportunity.

By the evening the atmosphere was fraught. The production was encountering rather a lot of difficulties, and in an effort to combat this trend, everybody was doing their utmost to pull the show into some sort of shape. I had spent the day, however, concentrating on England's fortunes, which had brightened considerably since lunch. They had made it to 300 thanks to a century from Andrew Strauss and 70 from Andrew Flintoff. I learnt this news from a text message, and was in a cheery mood as the director Martin and his choreographer wife Beth presented the cast with a series of long and detailed notes. The others all wore long, drawn faces carved with agony and worry. The director finished what he had to say and then explained in grave detail how he was personally going to brutalise anyone who caused him any further stress today and then asked if anybody else had anything to add.

'Australia have just taken the new ball!' I announced cheerily, looking up from my mobile.

This news was greeted with silence by the rest of the group, and so I attempted to explain this announcement. I had got as far as saying, 'In Test matches, the bowling side can ask for a new ball after eighty overs…' before sensing that no one wanted to hear the rest.

'If you don't shut up about cricket,' said Martin. 'I'm going to go out and buy a cricket bat just so I've got something to stuff up your stupid, lazy arse.'

'Right,' I said. 'Sorry. We're 315-7, by the way.'

We added four more runs by the close of play, and as it was my birthday I went out for dinner with friends from university, and then we returned to a flat near Victoria and drank whisky until the last of us had passed out. I awoke in an armchair at nine in the morning still fully clothed, and with no possibility of nipping back to the cast's Bloomsbury hotel before getting to my rehearsal. I arrived a quarter of an hour late to find the rest of the cast splayed out on the floor doing a series of extreme stretches under the supervision of the choreographer. I found a spot near the back next to Juliet Cadzow, who played Edie McCredie, the bus driver, and lay down next to her.

'Yesterday's clothes, darling?' she asked with a laugh.

'I can't speak,' I replied. 'I can't do anything.'

I have no idea what our rehearsals achieved that day, but England managed to make 373 before they were all out. Australia had reached 112 for no wicket in reply by teatime when rain washed out the rest of the day's play. Our rehearsals ended at lunchtime the next day when Martin headed up to the National Indoor Arena in Birmingham to supervise the finishing touches that were being made to the set. Everybody else headed back to their homes for two days' rest before we reconvened in Birmingham. I took the tube back to the hotel in Bloomsbury and spent the afternoon sitting in the Irish pub next door, watching the action on a big screen. Eventually England took a wicket, but by that stage Australia's opening pair had put on 185. Australia then looked like batting on and on. Numerous appeals were turned down, but England only had one more success in the day and at six o'clock I returned to my hotel room with Australia having finished the day on 277–2. There were two days remaining in the game. It was incredible stuff.

*

That evening I met my friends Dougie and Nigel for some drinks in Camden. As I stood waiting for them at the entrance of the tube station, repeatedly turning down offers from men who were trying to sell me drugs, I assessed my options. After the frustrating time that I had had in Edinburgh, I was so thrilled to have actually made it to a city where one of the Ashes games was being played. I didn't want to hear about any more of it via text message or the radio or the television though. I wanted to watch it live. The only hope I had, I realised, would be to buy a ticket from a tout outside the ground. And that, I decided, would be astronomically expensive and not even worth considering.

But, of course, when I was standing outside Camden tube station having those thoughts, I was stone cold sober. Six hours later, things had changed somewhat. Clambering out of a taxi in Russell Square, I was determined that the next morning I would buy a ticket from a tout and so headed straight to a cash machine to withdraw as much as I could.

And so it was that I woke up with a sore head and four hundred pounds in cash sitting on the bedside table. I showered, shovelled down one of the hotel's obscene breakfasts, and then dashed to a tube station. It was only nine in the morning when I arrived at the Oval – an hour and a half before play was due to start – but already the place was heaving with cricket fans. Above the noise, I could just make out my mobile phone ringing. It was Rachel, demanding to know why she had not received any call the previous night.

'Where were you? Were you rehearsing until late?'

'No, we finished at lunchtime.'

'Lunchtime? And you couldn't find time to call?'

'I was too engrossed in the cricket, Rachel. And then I met up with some friends who really frown upon the use of mobile phones in social situations.'

'Who was that?'

'Dougie and Nigel. You don't know them, they're quite staunch on the issue. I can't really talk at the moment, Rachel.'

'Where are you?'

'I'm at the Oval about to try and buy a ticket.'

'I hope you're not going to try and buy one from a tout. That really would be a stupid waste of money.'

'Of course I wouldn't.'

'Then what's your plan?'

'I don't really have one, Rachel. I'm just hoping that some-thing will arise...organically.'

'Give me a ring when you've stopped talking nonsense.'

'Will do. Love you.'

Touts immediately started proffering tickets, but I found myself carried past them by the crowd surging towards the gates. A sixth sense guided me to turn right at the busy turnstiles and then I walked until I came across a queue that included only 20 people or so. I asked the chap at the head of it what it was for.

'Returns. If you join this queue, you'll probably get a ticket in an hour.'

I was staggered, and so instantly joined the back of the queue. It hadn't even occurred to me that such a thing existed. I asked the man in front of me how likely it would be that we would all get in.

'Very,' said the man, with a strong Sunderland accent. 'I've got in like this every day so far. Today won't be any different.'

'Why are there so few people queuing here?'

'Nobody seems to know about it. Or it doesn't occur to them.'

But an hour and a half later we were all still standing in the queue. It was the start of play and a hush had fallen around the ground. In this moment of quiet I considered the situation of the game. If I did get into the ground, it would be to watch Australia batting and it was definitely them who held the upper hand. With two days of cricket still to go it was entirely conceivable that they could go on to win the Test and thus retain the Ashes. It was a truly horrible thought. For ten whole minutes the queue fell silent. Some of them listening to their radios through earpieces; others, like me, were trying to listen to the noise of the crowd for any hint of what was going on. There were 23,000 people inside the ground and each of them was just as quiet. But then, suddenly, there was a great roar from within.

'Martyn's gone,' said a voice. 'Caught Collingwood, bowled Flintoff.'

There was a huge cheer from the queue.

Then a steward poked his head out of the little entrance at the head of our queue.

'Okay, everyone, that's some more tickets just released.'

There followed an even bigger cheer from the queue, and we filed into the booth to buy them. Fifty-six pounds bought me a ticket.

*

I made my way around to Block Ten and took a seat at the very back of the stand. It was the first time I had been in a packed cricket stadium for years. My first thought as I looked out over the scene before me was that it was strange to finally be watching some of this incredible series at the ground itself. I had watched so much of it on the television on my own or with Rachel, that every emotional moment of it up to now seemed personal to me, and only me. Sitting in a crowd of thousands I now realised that it wasn't like that at all. And for a brief moment I felt almost cheated. As if some other people had just stumbled upon my secret. Now that I had to share it with all these people, it suddenly wasn't so much fun any more.

Next ball those thoughts were immediately dismissed from my mind. Flintoff swung one into Hayden's pads, and he was given out leg before. Hayden's almost seven-hour vigil was over and watching cricket had never felt so good. The crowd rose as one, arms aloft, and I found myself yelling, 'COME ON!' as loud as I possibly could. A man who had looked incapable of getting out for two days was now trudging back to the pavilion, and past the England team who were celebrating in a huddle. The crowd that morning had seemed so apprehensive, and yet these 11 men seemed to have more belief than all of us together.

Flintoff and Hoggard were bowling superbly well in tandem, and who knows where they found the energy reserves that they were drawing on. The fortress that Australia had spent two days defending was razed to the ground in a two-hour siege by the pair. Katich was the next to go, also leg before to Flintoff, and then Gilchrist, after flourishingly briefly, was adjudged LBW to Hoggard. At lunch Australia, having started the day on 277–2, were 356–6. England still possessed a slender lead of 17, and the crowd had gone from a state of anxiety to one of elation.

They added only another 11 runs before they were all dismissed. Hoggard took three of the remaining four that fell, the last of which was a catch by Ashley Giles sprinting around the long-on boundary just in front of where I was sitting. The moment that the catch was pouched the fielder, still at full pelt, turned to the crowd behind him, punched the air and proffered up a war cry that was lost amidst the crowd's own raucous response. But dark clouds gathered up above, and brought about an early end to the day's proceedings after a brief and nervous stint at the crease by England. We had made it to 36 for the loss of Andrew Strauss, prodding at a big spinning delivery from Warne and getting an inside edge to Katich at short leg. The crowd, anxious only that England secure a draw, were delighted by the sight of their team leaving the field, and applauded their decision to do so with uncharacteristic warmth. It is rare to see a full house celebrate the fact that there is no more cricket for them to watch that day, but the less play that was possible, the more chance England had.

All around me, other fans were rising from their seats and collecting their possessions. Newspapers were picked off the floor and folded into bags to sit alongside flasks that had been emptied long ago. The detritus from their day out was left where it had fallen, or kicked under seats. There was just one day remaining of this fascinating and absorbing series, and I was determined that I was going to return to witness it.

Of course, I knew that tickets for the final day were as scarce as hen's teeth. And so the next morning I arrived at the Oval even earlier. The sight that greeted me was disheartening beyond belief: the returns queue was already 200 deep.

'Do you reckon there'll be enough tickets for everyone in the queue?' I asked a passing steward.

'No way,' he told me. 'There probably won't be any.'

Brilliantly, though, I had another plan. I still had much of the £400 in my pocket, and so set off to find a tout. It did not take long. As soon as I had headed into the throng by the turnstiles, someone grabbed my shoulder and bellowed into my ear.

'Want to buy a ticket, mate?'

I turned round to see an incredibly meaty-looking man, with a hard stare, a shaved head and a huge anorak. Had I encountered such a man in a pub, I would probably have left. Had I seen him in a tube station, I would probably have run outside and hailed a taxi. I had no idea what to say to this gruesome creature.

'Possibly,' I ventured.

'Follow me,' he said. He took me by the arm and marched me through the crowd.

'Where are we going?' I asked nervously.

'Behind a van,' he growled. 'I don't want the police to see us.'

Oh God.

We reached a red van parked on Oval Road, and he dragged me behind it. There an even meatier man with fat, fat hands was waiting. This had been a terrible idea.

'This lad says he wants to buy a ticket,' said Meaty Man 1, positioning me between himself and Meaty Man 2.

'Oh yeah?' said Meaty Man 2. 'How much have you got on you?'

'Two hundred and fifty pounds,' I heard myself say. Quite the wheeler-dealer.

Oh no. What had I done? Maybe these men weren't ticket touts at all, but muggers. Perhaps one of them was going to take a hammer out of his anorak and knock me out cold with it. Who knew what they'd do when they discovered that I was carrying a hundred pounds more than I had claimed. Maybe they'd drug me, and pass me around their meaty mates for sex?

I racked my brains for a way out of the situation. I couldn't fight these men; I had no combat skills whatsoever. The only moves I had in my head were the ones for the salsa sequence that we'd just been taught for *Balamory: Live!* At best that would only ever buy me time. I didn't even have any pom-poms on me.

I waited for the hammer blow. Instead I heard Meaty Man 1 say, 'Wait here then, I'll just go and get your ticket.'

As he headed off into the crowd again, I was instantly relieved. It appeared that these men really did want to sell me a ticket. But although relieved, I also found the situation a little sordid. These men were criminals, after all, and not particularly clean ones. They had a definite air of menace about them and were probably wanted by the police. Even so, I thought it would be only polite to try and strike up a conversation.

'Will he be long, do you suppose?' I asked my new companion, a fan of spiders if his facial tattoo was anything to go by.

'Don't know. Just wait here with me and you'll be fine.'

'Right. Are you a cricket fan yourself?'

'I prefer football,' said the man. I was not remotely surprised.

'I suppose it must have been a busy year for you touts?' I asked.

'Mm.'

I gave up on the conversation and peered around the side of the van to see if Meaty Man 1 was making any progress. To my surprise he was only about 30 yards away, wandering about and asking if anyone had a ticket to sell for £100. The penny suddenly dropped. They didn't even get the tickets until you had promised them the money. I watched him approach a number of people, all of whom turned him down. In the meantime, I was expected to quietly excuse the matter of a cheeky £150 mark-up and make small talk with a terrifying spider-loving lunatic with sausages for fingers and the conversational skills of a beef patty.

'Right, that's it,' I said to myself with a sudden firmness. 'He hasn't even got a bloody ticket to sell me. I'm going.' I stormed off, angry with the touts for trying to rip me off so brazenly, and furious with myself for nearly falling into their trap. The only option that remained, however, was to go back to the returns queue and join the back of it. Since I had first seen it that morning it had easily swelled in size by another 50 or so people. Getting in was now looking decidedly unlikely. Even so, the queue did occasionally move forward a little, and after another hour I was only a little over 100 people from the front. A steward appeared intermittently and announced that there were no more tickets, but that notwithstanding small clusters of people were still being let in. All of those around me in the queue were evidently determined to wait anyway, and so was I. A number of people, perhaps looking for somewhere to channel their restlessness, started to badger the steward with questions.

'Why do you keep saying there are no more tickets and then letting people in?'

'Where did you get your lovely luminous vest?'

'Do you want to be a real policeman when you grow up?'

Then a voice from further back in the queue cut through the silliness with a serious demand.

'Can you tell me why you lot never do anything about the touts?'

Voices of consent were soon raised.

'Yeah, exactly. They ruin the cricket, and they try and price real fans out of the game. They're a disgrace and yet you don't do anything about it.'

I was extremely embarrassed by this talk. The argument from those around me was that touts set out to profit from any tickets going spare, and by offering large sums to those who had tickets to get rid of, were preventing there from being any tickets left over at cost price for the fans. I had never truly considered the logic of this before, and I felt ashamed about my earlier attempts to get past the queue by throwing a bit of money about. The people around me all claimed to hold the same moral stance, and declared that they refused to pay a penny more than a ticket's cost price, even if it meant not getting in to see a game.

'People that buy from touts are as bad as the touts themselves,' said one fan, and everyone murmured their agreement. I murmured my agreement too.

Sensibly, the steward had slipped away quietly during the debate, and as there was now no one to answer their questions, the queue's conversation turned back to the day ahead. Very few were optimistic about getting in the ground, but nobody was yet prepared to admit defeat. The man next to me introduced himself as Andrew and asked if he could borrow my mobile phone to call his wife.

'I entered a competition on the radio for tickets, you see. I don't have a phone but I said I'd ring to find out if I've won. There are two tickets, by the way, you can have the other one if I win.'

He hadn't won, of course. But what he did do was to squat down on the pavement and delve deep into a rucksack, before finally emerging with what he called his 'last, desperate act'. It was a cardboard rectangle on which he, or possibly a child, had written the words 'WANTED: 1 TICKET FOR GENUINE FAN'. There was a string attached to it, and the man hung it around his neck to advertise his plight.

As I was taking in this image of woe, a familiar figure hove into view.

'Here comes one of the scum,' said a man further back in the queue, and I looked up to see Meaty Man 1 heading along the line in my direction. Other members of the queue pointed at the man and jeered. I tried to hide from him by turning my back, but as I stood there, hoping that he would carry on past me, I felt a tap on my shoulder. I turned around, and there he was, looking both pleased with himself and threatening.

'All sorted, mate.'

'I'm sorry?'

Those around me were now looking at me with disgust, as if a group of vegans had just discovered that one of their own had invested in an abattoir. The ogre, oblivious to the horror, patted the breast pocket of his anorak and said, 'It's right here. Two fifty you said, didn't you?'

I blushed with shame. The others in the queue were right. This man and his ilk were scumbags, whereas I was a cricket fan. If other real fans didn't buy from touts, then neither would I.

'I don't know what you're talking about,' I said.

Meaty Man 1 scoffed. 'You tried to buy a ticket from me an hour ago.'

'No I didn't, you just tried to sell me one.'

'Well, it's there if you want it.'

Did I want it? Well yes, I was desperate for it. But did I want it from him? I looked around at my brethren. The answer was obvious. I could no more take a ticket off this man than I could carve beef with a flip-flop.

'I'd rather never see a game of cricket again in my life,' I told him, 'than line your filthy pockets with a single penny of my hard-earned cash. You and spider man are a pissing great disgrace, and you should be strung up.'

I did not actually say this, obviously, but it was the definite subtext of what I did say. Which was nothing. I merely flayed my arms around a bit as if I could no longer handle English as a first language.

Meaty Man 1 walked away looking confused, but most of the people either side of me seemed satisfied with the reply I had given him, and only a few continued to regard me with suspicion. I was pleased to have stood my ground against the man, and felt quite sure that I had made the correct moral decision. In so doing, though, I also thought that I may have turned down my best chance of getting to see this potentially historic game.

And then, from nowhere, a blessing suddenly arrived: two men who had recently pitched up from Guernsey and were now standing next to Andrew and me in the queue. One of them tapped Andrew on the shoulder, and leant forward to speak softly into his ear.

'Do you want to buy a ticket?' he said. Frankly, the sign around Andrew's neck must have been a bit of a give-away.

'Have you got a spare?' said Andrew, hardly daring to believe this offer might be genuine.

'We've got two spare. We want to sell one to you because we liked your sign. You can have it at the price we paid.'

Immediately there was a surge of interest from other members of the queue, all asking if they could buy the other one. 'I'll pay double what you paid for it,' said one man, immediately exposing himself as morally bankrupt in the eyes of the others.

But Andrew pointed at me, and said, 'This man is my friend. He should have the other one.'

'Okay, it's his.'

As the four of us strode off in the direction of the turnstiles, I felt almost dizzy at my good fortune. As we waited to pass through the turnstile I thanked Andrew profusely. Andrew asked the men how come they were in possession of the tickets.

'Oh, we bought them online in January. We're members of the club. They're a tenner each, by the way.'

*

The cricket was sublime. England started well, with Vaughan in particular taking the attack to the Australians. But then McGrath dismissed him and Ian Bell with successive deliveries and England were on the wobble at 67–3. Warne dropped Pietersen off a Lee delivery with the score on 93 and we staggered over the 100 mark. But Warne then dismissed Trescothick and Flintoff, and when the players left the field at lunch our score was a miserable-looking 126–5. If we didn't last long after the interval, Australia would easily have time to knock off the runs required for victory and retain the Ashes. There was not, what is more, a cloud in the sky.

But then in the afternoon Kevin Pietersen came out and went ballistic. While Paul Collingwood blocked at one end, Pietersen took on the bowling. Collingwood eventually contributed ten to a partnership of 60. Geraint Jones lasted only five overs before he too succumbed to Warne and we took tea on an altogether much safer 221–7. And Kevin Pietersen had scored his first Test century off just 124 balls.

After tea he and, amazingly, Ashley Giles were imperious. Their stand of 109 put the game well beyond Australia's reach. Pietersen, when he was finally dismissed for 158, rightly received one of the most amazing ovations I have ever seen on a cricket field. it had been an astonishing take-them-by-the-scruff-of-the-neck innings. Coming in under pressure he had batted for over three hours and scored 15 fours and seven sixes. I was sitting at fine leg when he was taking on the pacemen and several of those sixes sailed high over where I was sitting.

We made it to 335 all out, and then Australia only faced four balls before they came off for bad light. And so it was that at quarter past six in the evening, the umpires Billy Bowden and Rudi Koertzen came out to remove the bails and somehow, unbelievably, the Ashes were ours.

'Yeeeeeeeeeeeeeees!!'

It was the most staggering and heady feeling. I had spent more than half of my life watching England being rubbish, and endlessly taking flak from cricket sceptics about our national team's ineptitude at my favourite sport. And now here I was, in a packed crowd, arms aloft, leaping and shouting, and high-fiving with strangers. I will always remember the generosity of Andrew the sign-holder and Ashley and Darren from Guernsey who enabled me to witness history.

There is only so long, though, that you can jump up and down and holler in the company of strangers before you start to feel self-conscious. After all the initial excitement, I found myself sitting there in the crowd, basking in the afterglow of our long-awaited victory, and I looked around the ground. The crowd were singing 'Jerusalem', the players were doing laps of honour and Andrew Flintoff was about 1 per cent of his way through a most unfortunate alcoholic bender. There were beer glasses everywhere, and scraps of ticker tape. At one moment I looked up, and for the first time on that absorbing day I noticed the press box; a huge glass structure that overlooked one end of the ground. I could see that it was full of journalists sitting at rows and rows of desks. And when I saw these people my first thought was, 'You lucky bastards. You have been paid to watch every single ball of this series.' But my second thought was, 'My girlfriend is wrong. There is a job that would enable me to watch more cricket.' And it hit me as suddenly and as instantly as my love for cricket itself had 14 years previously. 'That's what I'm going to do,' I thought. 'I'm going to become a cricket journalist. That must be the best job in the world. I want to be up there. That's where I want to be. Not down here. I want to do what they're doing. Not what I'm doing. I mean, what am I doing with my life? I'm hardly doing any stand-up, I'm in a sketch show that's gone to shit. The only acting work I can get is prancing around in a pink kilt for the very slight amusement of children. This is why fortune brought me here today.

'I'm going to become a cricket journalist.'

Chapter Three

I left the ground that night feeling glorious about cricket, and thrilled by the decision that I had made. I was swept along Kennington Road by a sea of other England fans. They were strangers, and yet we had all been on a journey together. We had shared a moment in time. And in the headiness of that moment, I had decided to change my life, and embark on a completely new career path. My mind was made up, and life felt fantastic.

Before becoming a cricket journalist, I had to first fulfil the remaining commitments in my diary. Two days after England had secured the Ashes, *Balamory: Live!* opened in Birmingham at the National Indoor Arena. For the next two months we toured around Britain playing the sort of vast, ridiculous venues better suited to rock acts, recent *X Factor* rejects soaking up the last few rays of their moment in the sun or conferences for business types who wanted to learn the secrets of Neuro Linguistic Programming. After Birmingham we did three shows a day, four days a week in Manchester, Glasgow, Sheffield, and Edinburgh and then played the Hammersmith Apollo in London for two weeks. Just a few weeks previously during the Edinburgh Festival, I had been performing my stand-up act in a foul, dank basement, working my arse off for every titter and light smattering of applause from an audience of 50. Now, dressed in my Archie The Inventor costume, I could walk onstage, wave and then stand there while 3,000 people clapped and cheered for an age. It was like Nuremberg, only with more merchandising.

The hotels were pleasant enough, the catering was phenomenal, and, because we'd never finish later than half past six in the evening, we drank as if we'd been told the world was about to end and we would never see our loved ones again. It was, apart from the night in a hotel in Chesterfield when I decided to stand on top of a fruit machine and then promptly fell off it, the most spectacular fun. Yet – in my heart and in my head – I knew that it simply wasn't what I wanted to be doing. It must seem ungrateful, and I know there must be people out there whose souls would be nourished by simply prancing around in a pink kilt in a bid to entertain children. But I also imagine that some of these people are deeply, profoundly unwell.

To cap it all off, just as the England team were setting off for a punishing and ultimately unsuccessful tour of Pakistan, I took a train north to Aberdeen to play Simple Simon in *Jack and the Beanstalk*. I had taken this job months ago entirely on the basis of the fee that I had been offered, and fully expected that I'd spend the whole time sticking forks in my eyes. There was very little rehearsal time, the script had been cobbled together from various different pantomimes and the director had a habit of disappearing at lunchtime – to where I would not dare to hazard a guess. We had 900 people in the audience for the first night, and we had still not yet managed a full run-through or tested the beanstalk. We had to just fly by the seat of our collective pants. It turned out to be a brilliant job. I loved the camaraderie, the silliness, the pranks; I loved the boozing, the curries and the filthy jokes. And I continue to love the fact that I have stood on a stage in front of a thousand people between the '70s songstress Marti Webb and Cameron Stout, winner of *Big Brother 4*, looking into the wings to see the two constituent halves of a pantomime cow having a punch-up inside the costume because, as it turned out, the front end had called the back end 'a fucking slut'.

But when in early January I woke up the morning after the final night of the run, all I was left with was a hangover, some money in the bank and nothing whatsoever marked in my 2006 diary until 1 March, when England would commence the first of three Test matches against India. I would be there, I decided, and that would be when I would start my new career. It was simple. All I had to do was turn myself from an actor and comedian into a cricket journalist. There was also the small matter of convincing my girlfriend that this whole thing was a good idea.

'You're actually going to do this?' she asked one evening whilst we were sitting in a bar in Bruntsfield.

'Yes. Definitely.'

'Oh.' She looked genuinely surprised. 'I thought it was another of those things that you just talk about.'

'No. I'm serious about it. This is what I want to do.'

'Are you sure? I mean, what's wrong with what you're doing? It seems to be going well. You're making money.'

'But it's not what I want to do. You told me to get a job that would enable me to watch even more cricket.'

'Did I?'

'Yes. During the Ashes.'

'I suspect I was joking.'

'Well you've been an inspiration.'

'And when are you going to start your new career?'

'March.'

'March? But you can't start being a journalist just like that. You don't know what you're doing.'

Rachel, I concede, was making a very good point. I must stress at this point that despite feeling strongly that I would be well suited to the role of a cricket journalist, I really had virtually no experience whatsoever in the world of journalism. I had encountered various critics over the years, but not really engaged any of them in polite conversation. I once wrote a nice review of an amateur production of *When We Are Married* for the *Edinburgh Evening News*, but I think most people would agree that this would be unlikely to serve as a particularly helpful calling card.

I needed a plan. And its inspiration came, perhaps surprisingly, from Barry Norman. A friend of mine used to keep a copy of Norman's autobiography in his downstairs lavatory and, over the years, I became rather familiar with it. I was intrigued by a period of his life in which he had almost no work on whatsoever, and so decided that the best thing he could do was to dress smartly, go to El Vino on Fleet Street every morning and then spend the day there looking busy. If any journalists or editors he knew came over and asked him how he was, he would say 'busy'. After a while he found that people would come over and say, 'I know you're terribly busy, Barry, but could you possibly do a job for me?' By putting himself in a position where he looked like he had work to do and more than enough to be getting on with, he had actually managed to generate work.

By logical extension, I reckoned that I could take the Norman method even further. What if I started by pretending to be a journalist? If I could somehow blag my way into the press box claiming to be a journalist, and once safely inside pretend that I had all sorts of stuff to occupy me, then I too might be in a position to generate work. I realised, of course, that in order to get into the press box I would require some sort of accreditation: a press pass. But then it occurred to me that even though I had little journalistic experience, I did actually have some rather useful contacts. One was a lady called Mary Macfarlane, who was a sports producer for BBC Radio Scotland. The other was Charles Boase, a subeditor on the *Western Mail* in Cardiff and also my girlfriend's father. My elaborate plan was this: I would ring them both, and I would lie to them. I would tell them that I was going out to India to write a book, and that I had just noticed that my trip appeared to coincide with England's tour.

Would they, perchance, be at all interested in me doing some writing or broadcasting about the cricket for them?

Nervous of failure, but even more nervous of my girlfriend's father, I rang Mary first.

'Hello. Mary Macfarlane speaking?'

'Hello, Mary, it's Miles Jupp. I don't know if you remember me.'

I could hear what sounded suspiciously like a confused silence.

'We worked together on Children In Need last year.'

'Did we? Right. Well, in that case, hello.'

'How are you, Mary?'

'Fine.'

I could now hear her tapping her fingers impatiently on the desk in front of her.

'Is there something I can help you with, Miles?'

'Ah. Yes. The thing is, Mary, I'm going to India in a few weeks because I've been commissioned to write a book.'

'Oh, congratulations!'

'Thank you.'

'What's it about?'

'Er...it's about...it's about India,' I said.

'Good place to start.'

'Well, I thought so, but listen, the thing is, I've noticed that while I'm out there England are playing a series against India.'

'England?'

'That's right.'

'I see. What sport are we talking about?'

'Cricket.'

Come on, Mary. Keep up.

'Oh.'

She didn't sound thrilled by this prospect.

'And I was wondering, Mary, seeing as I'm going to be out

there…if I might offer my services, as a cricket correspondent?' I ventured.

'Mmmm,' she said. This didn't seem to be going very well.

'Is that something that could conceivably be of use to you?'

'Well, we don't give cricket a great deal of coverage on BBC Radio Scotland, to be honest.'

'No, I appreciate that. But I just thought that seeing as I will be there and on-hand, as it were, it might give you the option to include a bit of cricket coverage should you…should you…desire it.'

After this odd Shakespearean turn of phrase, there was then a rather long pause in the conversation during which I heard Mary eat four crisps, and then take a slurp on a drink that was obviously a little hotter than she was expecting. It was a hot chocolate, I think, because the next thing she said was: 'Oh this fucking hot chocolate. Jesus.'

'Mary? Are you all right?'

'I'm fine, yes. I was just thinking about what you were saying. God that was hot.'

'Right. Well, would you consider some broadcasts about cricket from me?'

'Listen, as you're going out there anyway, why don't you email me if there's anything very exciting happening and we can maybe take it from there? I can't promise anything, but the more you keep us informed as to what's going on, the more likely we are to use you.'

This, I realised, thinking on my feet, was as good an offer as I was likely to get from Mary.

'Well, that would be great, Mary. Thank you. Gosh – the thought suddenly occurs – if you were to ask me to make a broadcast about the cricket I'd probably need some sort of press pass, wouldn't I?'

'You would, Miles. Yes.'

'Right, well, in that case could you possibly write a letter on BBC Scotland headed notepaper for me saying, you know, "To whom it may concern", that sort of thing, "Miles Jupp is our cricket correspondent", and then send it to me?'

*

And to my amazement, she did.

As soon as the letter arrived, I rang up the England and Wales Cricket Board and said: 'Hi there, it's Miles Jupp, I'm the Chief Cricket Correspondent for BBC Scotland. Would it be possible to sort out my accreditation for the India tour?'

Yes. It would. They sent me some forms, I filled them in and sent them back with a copy of my proof of employment letter. A few days later I received an email containing an assurance that my press pass would be waiting for me when I arrived in Nagpur for the First Test.

I then rang my future father-in-law, and told the same lies to him. He asked me to leave the matter with him, and returned my call a few days later with some surprising news.

'Miles, I've just been speaking to the people on the sports desk. This is the deal: they would like you to write as many articles as you can about Simon Jones. Now, Miles, do you know who that is?'

Of course I knew who Simon Jones was. Simon Jones was the splendid Welsh fast bowler who had spent much of the previous summer bewildering the Australian batsmen with his deadly reverse swing. He had shown a remarkable knack of taking a wicket almost every time that Michael Vaughan had brought him on to bowl. Not only had he taken 18 wickets, he'd scored some vital runs in a last-wicket partnership with Andrew Flintoff that had contributed to England's famous victory in the Edgbaston Test. He'd had to sit out the final game of the Ashes series at the Oval, and then missed the whole of the tour to Pakistan whilst recuperating, but he was now fully recovered and would be returning to the England fold in time for the India tour.

'Charles, I know exactly who Simon Jones is.'

'Good. Because it is only Simon Jones that they are interested in. If you can send lots of articles about Simon Jones back from India telling us what he's up to and how he's getting along, then the sports desk will be very happy to print them.'

'Charles, this is fantastic. It's amazing. Thank you.'

'Well, don't get too excited just yet. I have to tell you that the money will not be all that good.'

It was paid!

'I'm sure I'll be very happy with what I'm given, Charles.'

'Right then. Well good luck, and try not to get ill.'

'I shall do my utmost, Charles, to return as healthy as I am now.'

'Perhaps you could come back thinner? I'm sure my daughter would appreciate it.'

I let his final comment pass and put the phone down in a state of total elation. Actual paid work! My contact at BBC Scotland had enabled me to acquire accreditation, but this completely unexpected news from the *Western Mail* meant that I would be able to arrive in India with the press corps and make the legitimate claim that I was a working cricket journalist.

Meanwhile I rang my dad's cousin, a former cricket administrator, and told him about my plans. He explained to me how being a member of the press corps worked and, crucially, told me who booked all the travel for the press. If I got in contact with them I would definitely be able to travel as a member of the press corps. Immediately, I made the call.

'Hello, Sunsport.'

'Hi there, it's Miles Jupp here. The journalist.'

'Okay.'

'I'm going to be covering the tour of India.'

'Right. And you need us to arrange your travel.'

'Yes, please.'

'Are you doing the whole tour? Tests and one-dayers?'

'Just the Tests.'

'No problem.'

This had all been remarkably straightforward.

'Who is it you work for, Mr Jupp?'

'BBC Scotland and the *Western Mail*,' I said proudly.

'Okay. And which of them shall I send the invoice to?'

This was a shock.

'Oh God. Neither,' I gabbled. 'Please don't send anyone anything.'

'No?'

'It's just a bit complicated actually. It's probably best to invoice me, and I'll claim it back from them.'

'Okay, we can do it that way.'

Another result! That was it. It was all definitely happening, and it hadn't even been so terribly hard. All I had had to do was tell a few little fibs to people. I was going to go to India! I was going to turn up, look like a journalist (wear linen trousers), act like a journalist (carry a laptop), do the work that I'd already been asked to do, and enthusiastically do any other bits of work that came my way. I knew that I was taking a gamble, and so to make it all seem a little less terrifying I set myself four reasonably modest objectives.

First, I definitely wanted to get an article printed in the newspaper. If I did that even once and received payment for it then I could make the legitimate claim that I had worked as a cricket journalist.

Secondly, I wanted to make a broadcast about cricket on the radio. If I managed to do that even once and received some payment then I could also make the legitimate claim that I had worked as a cricket broadcaster.

Thirdly, as a result of doing those things, I wanted to try and generate some other work.

And fourthly, at no point did I want to hear anybody use the phrase 'But aren't you the bloke from *Balamory*?'

*

My other preparations involved organising a visa, buying a course of anti-malaria tablets and panicking about the idea. Other than an afternoon spent filming a tiny part in a sitcom about the police, I mainly flailed about telling people that I was going to become a cricket journalist, and was shortly to be flying out to India to join the press corps. I rang the ECB a couple of times to check that my accreditation was in order and each time I was told that there would be no problems with it. I could collect it from the England team's press officer when he arrived. To my delight, two weeks before my departure I started receiving text messages from the press officer telling me important bits of information for the press, such as when practice sessions would be, and in which room in which hotel there might be a press conference that I could attend.

And Rachel had slowly warmed to the idea. She knew that my plan was a bit of a long shot, but she could also tell that I was passionate about making it work. The fact that there was paid work on offer certainly helped her to take the whole thing a little more seriously. She offered as much support and advice as she could, as well as watching over me while I packed in order to prevent me taking anything unnecessary. She also helped me choose suitable clothes and took me out shopping to buy new short-sleeved shirts. My brother Ed, who I shared my flat with, came home one night with a copy of *The Lonely Planet Guide to India* which he'd seen in the window of a charity shop.

*

In the last week before my departure I became restless to the point of despair. I paced up and down the hall corridor of our small flat in Tollcross, never sure if there was something more that I could do to prepare for my trip. I had begun my course of anti-malaria tablets and, on the advice of a friend, had started downing huge quantities of live yoghurt so that my stomach contained enough bacteria to do battle with any antagonistic food I might encounter during my trip. For a short spell my restlessness evolved into efficiency, and my brother Ed was surprised to encounter me vacuum-cleaning the carpets and mopping the lino. I performed lengthy washing-up ceremonies, and then did all the drying-up myself, even polishing the glasses. Once the floors were spotless, the skirting boards dust free and the videos and DVDs had been placed in alphabetical order, my nerve-induced efficiency was left with nowhere to go and so morphed into pointless displacement activities. One afternoon I packed and unpacked my suitcase eight times in a row. I attacked the videos and DVDs again, and tried arranging them first by genre, then by director and then by date of release. Finally I placed them back into alphabetical order again.

With three days to go I placed a final call to the ECB to check that my accreditation had definitely, definitely been processed. My persistence in this regard was rewarded with grumpiness, and the lady on the end of the phone instructed me to ring something called the BCCI at a number in Delhi from now on. I dialled the lengthy number she had given me, heard a loud crackling noise and then heard the voice of an Indian gentleman who told me that I was through to the offices of the Board Of Cricket Control In India and then asked how I might be assisted.

'I'm a journalist,' I told him, 'and I'm just checking that everything is in order with my accreditation. I need a press pass for the cricket, you see.'

'Have you applied for it in London with the ECB?'

'I have.'

'And what have they said?'

'They've said to ring you.'

'Right.'

'Right?'

'I think that everything will be okay.'

'Is there a way that I can definitely check that when I arrive in India I will be given a press pass? I don't really want to leave Britain without having that confirmed. It would be rather frustrating to arrive in India only to discover that I couldn't actually see any of the cricket.'

There was a lengthy pause during which I wondered if he might have been cut off, but finally the Indian gentleman spoke again. 'I think that you will find everything to be okay. You have asked for a press pass and so you shall be given one.'

'Marvellous,' I said, although part of me couldn't believe that it was really this simple.

'You are coming to India?' added the Indian gentleman, throwing me slightly.

'That's the idea.'

'I think that should be okay,' replied the Indian gentleman one last time, and then rang off.

*

I was leaving for India on Sunday, and so on the Saturday night Rachel had arranged a small farewell dinner party for some of our friends. The guests were not due until seven in the evening and Rachel had specifically requested no help in the kitchen. I had repacked my suitcase, which stood leaning against the radiator in the hall, and now had nothing to do except stomp about the flat in the way I usually did before auditions.

'Miles, why are you stomping?' called out Rachel from the kitchen.

'I'm preparing for my role as a journalist,' I yelled back. 'I'm trying to get into character.'

I heard no more questions from Rachel; only the sound of the kitchen door closing. But I was taking my preparations seriously. I had decided that if I was going to be accepted by the journalists as one of their own, I had to become one of them in the same manner in which I tried to become the characters if ever I got an acting job. Whenever I went up for an audition, my agent had always told me to try and appear like the character as soon as I arrived. One way of doing this was to try and dress as the character, perhaps even arming myself with a few subtle props. I was now trying to create the character of a journalist abroad, and so was decked out in boat shoes, linen trousers and a pink short-sleeved shirt and I had my laptop carry case draped over one shoulder. I then tried to make some casual gestures whilst rolling out a few phrases that I thought sounded suitably journalistic in the direction of the mirror.

'Excuse me, chaps, I've just got to nip back to the hotel to file a bit of late copy.'

'That press conference was a bit of a shambles, wasn't it? Still, I got the quotes I needed.'

I decided that a good hat might complete the look; a panama would be ideal, but I didn't have one. I remembered a straw hat that I had bought at the Glastonbury festival a few years ago that might do the business, but when I finally uncovered it on a high shelf in the wardrobe it appeared to have gone into some sort of organic meltdown. All I could find was a beige and floppy bushranger effort, and I decided that it would do well enough for now. I fixed it on my head, looked sardonically in the direction of the mirror and said, 'Anywhere you can get a drink in this airport?' I was pleased with the final look, and so went into the kitchen to show Rachel, who stood by the sink in a misty haze, draining some steaming water from a pan of something.

'Hi, there,' I said, introducing myself, 'Miles Jupp, cricket journalist.'

'Very good. Very realistic.'

'What about the hat?'

'Well, it's not especially attractive, but it might help prevent sunburn.'

'Safety first. You know me.'

I was trying to be jocular, but I returned to my room with serious anxieties about the month ahead. My first fear, I knew, was about fitting in with the other members of the press corps. My instincts told me that they might view me with suspicion rather than interest. My father had warned me that the first few nights away would probably be quite difficult, lonely even, rather like the first few nights away at university, or, in my case, boarding school. The other people in the party would be old hands, with experience, reputations and the proper credentials. I, on the other hand, was a chancer, a blagger, trying my luck without any real experience. And I didn't want to reveal myself as an actor, even if it might be a useful conversational gambit. People might not take me seriously.

'For the first few days you should play it by ear and keep your head down,' I told myself.

*

While I was in Edinburgh crashing noisily around my flat in preparation for my trip, the minds and bodies of various England squad members had been quietly coming apart at various venues around India. By the time that I was due to arrive in Nagpur – the venue for the opening Test – the England team would not have looked out of place in a field tent in the Crimean War.

Everything came to a head in that last week before I arrived. One of Michael Vaughan's ever dodgy knees had been giving him trouble for much of the winter, and before the final warm-up match in Vadodara, it went so wonky that not only did he have to miss that game, but it was now doubtful that he would even be able to play in the first Test. Kevin Pietersen suddenly developed such bad back pain whilst batting that he had to leave the field and play no further part in the game. Paul Colling-wood's back then started spasming and he had to miss large portions of the match. Liam Plunkett played, but was incapable of bowling because he had a bruised heel. At one point in the game all three of our spin bowlers – Ian Blackwell, Shaun Udal and Monty Panesar – as well as Simon Jones, were suffering from a stomach bug, which must have turned the dressing room into a most unsavoury environment. So many of our players were out of action that one of the coaching staff, Matthew Maynard, had to field for long stretches of the game. Then, when the game finished, there was a sudden and unexpected announcement that Marcus Trescothick was going to fly home for what was only described as 'personal reasons'. Whilst I was busy trying to look as much like a journalist as possible, the England team had started to resemble the Kennedy family.

*

The dinner was a muted affair, or at least I was mute for most of it. Everyone else talked freely whilst Rachel and I served the food and tried to keep wine glasses full. Everybody apart from me seemed to have something to say about travelling in India or being a journalist. A few of those present had been to India, usually on their gap years prior to university, and they had much advice to impart. One guest said that I should only drink bottled water and that I should avoid salad. The heat, another told me, would be unbearable. Somebody as fair as me would be sunburnt by the time he reached the airport terminal. Everybody told me that I would be ill – a lot. One of the guests told a story about losing seven kilograms in a single weekend spent lain prostrate on the floor of a youth hostel bathroom. Another guest, unaware that nobody else in the room had the same sort of familial connections as he did, spent nearly a quarter of an hour describ-ing how one should dress and behave when having dinner at a

British consulate. Most things that I was told that evening added to my sense of panic and fear about heading off into the unknown to attempt a job for which I was not remotely qualified. Few around the table had anything helpful to say about journalists. 'They're miserable all the time,' said one. 'If they're nice to you it's only because they're trying to steal your ideas,' said another. 'I always imagine that they're the most depraved people on God's earth,' said the most depraved person present. Only one guest had any journalistic experience at all, working on their student newspaper, and they had nothing to offer whatsoever apart from the advice that 'it's always worth carrying a notebook', which was generally scoffed at.

That night, before going to bed, I went through the contents of my packing one last time and felt suddenly and woefully unprepared. 'What on earth,' I wondered as I slipped a couple of notebooks into my suitcase, 'do I think I'm doing?'

Chapter Four

'The 22:00 Virgin flight to Delhi is soon to commence board-ing. Could all passengers please make their way to Gate 24.'

I had been at Heathrow for several hours before I finally heard this blessed announcement. I'd booked a stupidly early flight down from Edinburgh just to be on the safe side, and having finally managed to get to grips with Virgin's DIY check-in (a service that may just have been invented to benefit passen-gers who have an entire day to kill), I had spent my day leafing through other people's discarded tabloids, roaming around the duty-free shops and wondering what sort of traveller might possibly wait until they had the reached the departure lounge before it occurred to them that they needed to buy a set of matching suitcases.

I made my way apprehensively to the gate. It was only there that I thought I would get my first glimpses of people I could be sure were my fellow journalists. Sure enough, at the last minute before the gate was opened, a crowd of 20 or so men approached the waiting area, nearly all of them with a laptop carrier hanging from their shoulders. These must surely be them, I thought. This supposition was confirmed when moments later this group was joined by Nasser Hussain and Michael Atherton. My apprehen-sion turned instantly into feverish excitement. Here was my hero! I had been convinced that my plan would enable me to meet my heroes and here was the biggest of them all, walking amongst us. This was exactly what I thought my trip ought to be like; sharing planes with cricketing legends and the greats of sporting journalism. Now I could start thinking of them as colleagues, and soon they would think of me in the same way. I'd meet them all on the plane, and we would all share drinks, stories and laughs.

But my hero did not stop where I was waiting. Instead Atherton and Hussain carried on straight past me and were shown to a roped-off area nearer the gate. But of course. I realised that people like that would be travelling first class. It looked like even the BBC people (this being pre-austerity) were going business. The introductions, the drinking, the stories, the laughs: they would all have to wait.

*

Some time after the other journalists had boarded, I finally stepped onto the plane and showed my ticket to an air stewardess who flashed me quite a satisfied smile for a lady who had the word 'Virgin' emblazoned on her chest. She directed me towards the back of the plane and so I headed quickly through the sparse business-class area and down the aisle in preparation for the longest flight I had ever been on. Clearly, the first-class cabin was filled to the brim with cricketing legends of one shape or other – presumably all popping open bottles of champagne and looking forward to a long night of luxury and pillow fights. Back in economy there can't have been much more than a dozen of us, dotted about like people queuing at a doctor's surgery. I was just lowering myself into an aisle seat and arranging my legs when a broad, breathless man in a scruffy white suit came up the aisle with a battered laptop case slung over his shoulder. He looked, and I mean this as a compliment, like the sort of man who liked cricket. I wasn't alone, after all. This fellow must surely be one of my colleagues in the press corps.

'You here for the cricket too?' I asked, as he drew level.
'Sorry?'
'You here for the cricket? I'm Miles Jupp from BBC Scotland.'

'Right. I'm looking for seat 43A. Which I think is that one,' he said, pointing to the seat immediately next to me. 'Would you mind just...'

'No, no.' I got out of my seat and let him and his laptop case manoeuvre past me. A quick look around the cabin confirmed that no other passengers had been positioned next to one another. What a stroke of luck. This would give me the perfect opportunity to meet a fellow scribe, and try and learn about the ways of cricket journalism. I lowered myself into my seat once more, ready to resume our conversation, but he had now started fidgeting, attempting to pull his seat belt across both him and the laptop case.

'Would you like me to put that in the overhead locker for you?'

'Eh?'

'Your laptop case. Looks like it's getting in the way a bit.'

'Oh. No. No thank you. It would probably be better if I did it myself. The contents are rather delicate. Would you mind just...?'

'No, no...'

I got out of my seat again, and opened the overhead locker for him, while he slowly and breathily negotiated his way out of his seat and past mine, like the Fat Controller trying to clamber out of a desert tank that's been blown onto its side. Once he had climbed into the aisle and managed to force himself vertical he peered into the overhead locker and started sucking air through his teeth.

'Oh dear. Right. Yeah. Hmm.'

'Can I help?'

'Well...' he said eventually, having first run his tongue around all of his teeth as if he was convinced there was a bit of stray meat somewhere, 'the problem is...my locker's already quite full.'

The locker immediately above our row of seats contained just my own laptop case, and one small bag. The rest of it was empty, as were the two lockers either side. And the ones either side of them.

'I see,' I said, wondering if he was perhaps suffering from an extremely rare eye disease that causes people to see lots and lots of luggage at those moments when there is in fact hardly any. 'It looks like there's lots of other space?'

'Well, the thing is I do really prefer to have any of my hand luggage immediately above the seat I'm in. I really don't like it to be too far away from me.'

'Right. Well perhaps I could just move my...'

'Do you know who this stuff belongs to?' he said, pointing at my things – the things that were immediately above our seats and not remotely approximate to any of the other economy passengers.

'Yes. It's mine.'

'This is yours?' He looked most taken aback at this news.

'Yes. Perhaps I could move it along for you, so that there's space for yours just above your seat.'

'Because, I really would prefer to have my things immediately above where I'm sitting.'

'Really, it's no problem.'

'Is everything all right?' said an air hostess who had suddenly drawn alongside us.

'Yes,' I said.

'No,' said my fellow passenger.

'What is the problem?'

'Well...' began the man from 43A quite promisingly before gesturing in my direction and shrugging his shoulders.

'It's a luggage issue,' I said. 'There doesn't seem to be enough space for everybody's luggage.'

'I see,' said the hostess, scanning an almost entirely empty row of overhead lockers and then eyeing us both with some incredulity.

'My fellow passenger would like to put his bag immediately above our two seats here, but unfortunately my things are already there,' I said.

'I do really prefer my luggage to be as close to me as possible,' added the man.

The hostess looked at us both, then at the floor, and then took a long, deep breath.

'Perhaps you could move yours along a little, sir?' she suggested to me.

'Yes. Fine. That's really no problem. I was just about to, actually.'

I looked at my co-conspirator for confirmation that I had indeed already made this offer. But rather than acknowledge that this was the case he leant towards me and said quietly, 'Probably better just do what the lady says, son.'

I let out the tiniest of exasperated sighs and then slid my laptop case and little bag along the floor of the overhead locker, whereupon he immediately thrust his case into the space I'd made, closed the locker door and embarked upon the physical rigmarole required to return to his seat. I then turned to the hostess, whose features were now displaying an expression of both pity and sadness.

'Thank you,' she said. 'I hope you and your father have a pleasant flight.'

'He's not my father,' I whispered in what I hoped was a helpful manner, but judging from the slightly embarrassed look she gave me had clearly come across as conspiratorial. She performed a hurried bow, and then turned on her heels and marched in the direction of the first-class cabin.

I lowered myself into my seat for the third time, and turned once more to address the man in the next seat.

'She seemed nice,' he said. 'Very helpful.'

'Yes. Anyway, pleased to meet you. I'm Miles Jupp from BBC Scotland. I take it you're a cricket journalist too?'

'I thought you'd said "cricket". No, not at all. I'm on my way to a conference. Just outside Delhi. It's about water technology. I've not been to India before. Actually, between you and me, I'm quite a nervous flyer.'

He and I spoke little for the remainder of the journey, although just as we took off he closed his eyes and said 'Christ' rather loudly. Even when he wanted to be let out to go to the lavatory, he didn't really speak to me; he would just nudge me with his elbow and then point at his crotch apologetically.

He nodded off after we'd been in the air an hour or so, and I moved to the central row of seats to try and spread out a little. I attempted to sleep, but found it difficult because once I was slumped in the dark silence, I immediately began fretting about what the month ahead held in store for me. Not only was I literally airborne, but personally I was in a figurative state of limbo. In the last few months I had left my agent and also told the promoter of the *Balamory* tours that I absolutely did not wish to be involved in any future tours. I also knew that regardless of what happened in India, once I returned to the UK then the time had probably come to move from Edinburgh to London. But Rachel was still completing a master's at Edinburgh University, so I did not know just how much I would be able to see of her in the coming months. Halfway through the flight, I dragged my sleepless self off to the bathroom and stood staring into the mirror, having one of those moments when you feel as if you're the only person in the world who is awake – apart from the pilot, obviously. As if to underline what a transitional period I was in, close scrutiny of the early, scratchy stages of my beard revealed an occasional spot snuggling up next to the odd grey hair. Shouldn't there be a moment in your life when you have neither?

I returned to my seat determined to be positive. Was this really the best moment in my life to bugger off to India and pretend to be a journalist? Yes. It was the perfect moment. Was this whole thing really a good idea? Yes. It was a brilliant idea. Could I really pull it off? Undoubtedly. Well, possibly. Perhaps. Maybe. The absolute reality of the situation was if I was going to have any doubts about my mission then I should have had them in the last few minutes before I spoke to the tour operator, told them I wanted to go ahead with the trip and then reeled off the long number on my credit card. 'This will be fun,' I told myself. 'This will be an audacious and exciting adventure.' Already at the airport whilst waiting to board I had seen the likes of Michael Atherton and Nasser Hussain, and it had given me a massive, almost teenage, thrill. And now here I was, sitting on the same plane as them. How many other of my cricketing heroes would be up there with them? It probably wouldn't just be Hussain and Atherton. Perhaps David Gower was up there? Or maybe Ian Botham. Derek Pringle, perhaps?

As I pulled a blanket around my shoulders and put on my eye mask, the fact that I would now definitely be spending a month in the company of so many of my heroes began to really sink in. I would certainly get the chance to meet them. Then having achieved that, I might spend a few days on nodding terms with each of them. If I could make it past this phase, I could perhaps actually get to know one or two of them a little. Then I might even become a bit chummy with them. And then what? Perhaps they would want to start hanging out with me on a regular basis. How splendid would that be – to become chums with one's heroes?

One evening I'd be relaxing in the bar after a long hot day at a game, and I'd hear a voice say, 'Hey, Miles, do you want to get something to eat?' and I would turn around to see Nasser Hussain standing there. And I'd say, 'Something to eat, Nass? I love eating. Do it every day. Come on, let's do it.' Another time there'd be a pat on my shoulder and it would be Michael Atherton practically begging me to come to a casino with him. 'A casino, Athers? Not really my thing but, hey, if you need someone to string along with you then, yeah, I guess I don't mind keeping you company.'

Perhaps Angus Fraser would try and drag me along to a nightclub. 'A nightclub, Angus? I would love to. I haven't been to one for quite a while and I find myself increasingly unsettled by loud noises, but I'm more than happy to dust off a few of the old Jupp moves in aid of a bit of bonding.'

David Gower would almost certainly try to lure me onto a yacht for some party with the Gettys where there would be a tiger on-board. 'David, David, David, I'd love to but I haven't got anything suitable to wear, I dislike shaving and I can be prone to the most excruciating bouts of seasickness.'

'Please, Miles. I hate turning up to things on my own. You'd be doing me a favour.'

'Oh, David. You really must learn to become more socially at ease, to stand on your own two feet. But look, seeing as it's you...of course I'll come.'

I'd probably – just to keep on the right side of him – even allow myself to be cajoled into partnering Ian Botham for 18 holes of golf.

Bit by bit, like a red-faced and slightly squidgy version of Mr Ripley, I would inveigle my way into the lives of these men and become part of their circle, so that I became so socially indispensable that none of them would be able to contemplate the possibility of not inviting me to accompany them whenever they headed of for an afternoon of fly fishing, falconry or glass blowing. And if I always accompanied them with good grace, a cheery manner and an enthusiastic spring in my step, then I could gain the reputation of being a decent, stand-up sort of bloke.

This, in turn, would stand me in good stead when any opportunities to further my new professional career arose.

What if a member of the *Test Match Special* team was suddenly brought down by a mystery virus, and the producer was urgently looking around for a replacement?

'Who can possibly fill in at this notice? Any ideas, Aggers?'

'It's funny you should ask, Peter, because only last night a bunch of us had dinner together and at the end of the meal, as per, we each took it in turns to recite some poetry. And do you know who turns out to have a wonderful speaking voice? It's that Miles Jupp from BBC Radio Scotland. He gave us *The Wasteland* – the whole thing, from memory, and it was delightful. Made Richie Benaud's *Beowulf* sound frankly ridiculous.'

'Oh wonderful. He's got the job.'

Maybe one of the Sky team would be indisposed owing to visa difficulties and they needed an additional guest at short notice to indulge in a bit of harmless banter during the lunch interval.

'David, who do think we could possibly get as your lunchtime guest?'

'Well,' Mr Gower might say, 'this is in no way the disaster you imagine it to be, because only yesterday afternoon a select bunch of us took off in a hire car together to indulge our shared passion for brass rubbing, and do you know who turned out to be great fun on the journey? Miles Jupp – from the *Western Mail*. He's got absolutely heaps of chat, and knows the lyrics to loads of songs. He's got a pretty effective rubbing technique too. Knocked off some lovely stuff.'

'Well, David, if you can handle a live wire like that in the studio, let's get him on. I only hope he doesn't turn out to be too fun.'

Perhaps some sort of vile lurgy might tear through the England team itself and they would find themselves desperately short of a fielder. The coach Duncan Fletcher would ask his old lieutenant Nasser Hussain for a recommendation.

'Any ideas, Nasser?'

'Well, a couple of years ago I would have offered to do the job myself, of course I would, but I'm not getting any younger, Fletch. My eyes are going, and I've got fingers like old, dried twigs. This might be a bit left field, but I think there's only one man for the job. Earlier this week there was a rather ill-tempered press corps visit to one of India's premier abseiling centres. A new chap called Miles Jupp proved to have a calm head on his young shoulders. Very good with his hands, too.'

'Ooh, thanks for that, Nass. We might even ask him to wicket-keep.'

As I slowly drifted off to sleep there was a part of me – just a part of me, mind – that wondered if that was how things would work out.

*

I was woken by a lady's voice asking me to return to my original seat in time for landing. I removed my eye mask and looked straight into the face of the hostess who had had to contend with our luggage difficulties at the start of the flight. I then looked across the aisle at my original seat, which now contained the laptop case belonging to the man in 43A. He was still fast asleep, with one hand on the case. I pointed at the laptop and then gave an apologetic look to the hostess, who gently lifted his hand and put it on his lap before stowing the case in the overhead locker. She gave a little wink, and then gestured for me to take my rightful place, before leaning across to open the window screen.

As the seatbelt signs flashed on and then a grinding noise signalled that the wheels were being lowered, I felt a nervous shiver run through me and an uneasy feeling slowly crawl north up my guts. I knew that if I was to stand any chance of making a success out of this trip and hold my own amongst my heroes, then I simply must not allow myself to be overawed. I could not catastrophise or get flustered. I would have to relax, or at least appear to be relaxed, and for goodness' sake I would have to stop staring – something that I was simply unable to do as we approached Delhi airport and I caught my first sight of the huge shanty towns that sprawl towards the runway there.

We landed smoothly, and as the plane decelerated, and someone smooth welcomed us all to Delhi over the tannoy, I heard the sleeping form on my right begin to stir and clear a few airways before uttering the words 'Where the hell's my luggage?'

*

I once got off a plane at Ben Gurion airport in Tel Aviv in something approaching 70 per cent humidity, and instantly felt soaked. In Delhi, as I clambered down the steps of the plane I felt a very different sensation as I was struck by the sheer force of the dry heat. By the time I laid a foot on the tarmac I was reeling – all moisture evaporated from my eyes and they began to sting as if they had been peeled. The scent of hot petrol filled my nose and I could feel my cheeks begin to redden. I opened my mouth to let out a feeble grunt and instantly felt the back of my throat turn dry. As I walked towards the terminal building, I looked back over my shoulder at the shanty towns bordering the runway. All that stood between me and them was a dusty haze created by convection.

In the run-up to my trip I had devoted most of my thinking time to contemplating the cricket and the journalism. What I hadn't given nearly enough thought to, I now saw, was India itself. Delhi, Nagpur, Chandigarh, Mumbai: these were just names typed on the itinerary that I had been sent by the travel company. Visas, travel jabs, malaria tablets: these were just items on the to-do list that I had scrawled on the back of an envelope sitting at the desk in my Edinburgh tenement and gradually put ticks next to as my departure approached. Shanty towns, heat, petrol fumes and rising dust: this was all real.

In the terminal building I passed quickly through passport control, and then stood at the luggage carousel waiting for my case, looking around nonchalantly to see who was there that I recognised. There were many: Simon Hughes and Derek Pringle from the *Daily Telegraph*, Mike Selvey and Vic Marks from *Test Match Special*. There was a flurry of beeps as everyone turned on their mobile phones at the same time and received messages welcoming them to whatever Indian network they were now part of. Then a new wave of beeps swept through the baggage retrieval area, followed by resigned shrugs and the odd shaking head. I looked at my phone to see what the news was: a message from the press officer was telling us all that Michael Vaughan was returning to the UK. As I digested the news I felt someone staring at me and looked up to see my hero, Michael Atherton, eyeing me with gentle suspicion and immediately looking away. Because I had received the text message at the same time as everybody else that signalled that I was there travelling as part of the press corps, and as the new boy I was bound to attract a little bit of attention. A few other men who I did not recognise also looked over in my direction with puzzled expressions.

It wasn't long before Atherton himself started attracting attention. So too did a bleary-eyed Nasser Hussain. An excited murmur started buzzing around the baggage hall, and airport staff and a few soldiers started moving in their direction. It was inevitable in a country as mad about cricket as India that two former England captains could not go unnoticed for long. Suddenly they were surrounded by people eager to help them with their luggage and make sure that they knew where they were going. Neither of them was allowed so much as to pick up a bag; everything was loaded onto trolleys for them, and each was then flanked by two soldiers. Atherton and Hussain both looked slightly sheepish at this treatment, not least because the only other people about were other journalists and a small group of people heading to a water technology conference. A group of 20 or so of us followed the former England captains and their entourage out to the exit and into the heat, where fresh confusion reigned. We were due to fly on to Nagpur this evening, but for now there was a day to kill in Delhi. Waiting at the exit were a number of taxi drivers with signs requesting specific passengers. Some were unrecognisable, some were famous but misspelt. Others were well known but most definitely not here.

'Are you Miles?'

I turned around to see a man I did not recognise, but with a voice that I did: Simon Mann, one of the *Test Match Special* commentators.

'Yes.'

'I thought you might be. You're the only person whose face I don't know. You're travelling with me. I'm Simon Mann.'

We shook hands, and then I followed the 40-something Mann with his tidy hair out into the car park, where a people carrier was waiting with its doors open. An Indian gentleman said, 'You are Mr Miles, yes?'

'That's right.'

'Hello, I am with tour operator. Welcome to India.'

'Thank you.'

'I'm Kevin,' said a Yorkshire accent attached to a bald-headed man appearing from the other side of the vehicle. 'Kevin Howells, from BBC Sport.'

'How do you do? I'm Miles.'

By this time my suitcase and bags had already been whisked from me and slotted into the crammed boot, and so Kevin, Simon and I clambered into the back seat. The tour operator was sitting in the front passenger seat, and the driver climbed in, shut his door and started the engine.

'Been to India before?' asked the tour operator.

'Yes,' said Simon and Kevin.

'No,' I said.

'So then, Miles,' said Simon as we pulled out of the car park, 'who do you work for?'

'BBC Scotland. And the *Western Mail*.'

'Where's the *Western Mail* based?' asked Kevin.

'Cardiff.'

'Ah. Then have you come across Edward Bevan? He's the BBC Wales cricket correspondent.'

'Edward...Bevan. No, I don't think I have.'

'Thought you might have come across him, that's all. He's not here at the moment, but I hear he might be coming out.'

'You weren't in Pakistan, were you?' said Kevin.

'Pakistan?'

'The last tour, just before Christmas. I don't remember seeing you there.'

'No, no. This is my first tour.'

'Your first tour? Then welcome.'

'India for your first tour...' said Simon quietly just as his phone beeped with a text message. 'Oh. It's Agnew.'

'Is he already in Nagpur?' asked Kevin.

'He is. He says the hotel's shit and the beds are impossible to sleep on.'

'Where are we going now?' I asked the tour operator.

He twisted around in his seat. 'A hotel. Very nice hotel. You can stay there until flight.'

We swept up a drive and came to a halt outside a huge, immaculate white hotel called something like The Palms and designed to happily accommodate the business traveller. A porter in a maroon uniform sprang out of the hotel with a brass luggage cart, swiftly emptied everything from the boot onto it, and then disappeared back inside. The tour operator handed each of us a colourful folder with bundles of paperwork in it.

'These are for you. They are gift from tour company.'

'Thank you.'

'What happens now?' asked Simon.

'You go into hotel. There are rooms. You rest. I come back this evening.'

'Is everybody coming to this hotel?'

'No. Only you three.'

'Oh right. Why's that?'

A shrug, a smile.

'What time are you coming back?'

'Nineteen forty.'

'Twenty to eight?' Simon checked.

'No. Not twenty to eight. Nineteen forty.'

'Yeah, nineteen forty. That's twenty to eight.'

The tour operator shook his head, sadly.

'No. No.'

'Okay,' said Simon. 'We'll see you at nineteen forty.'

'Yes, exactly.' The tour operator breathed a sigh of relief, bid us a good day and disappeared.

I looked around the ludicrously vast lobby that contained only us, some potted palm trees and a porter with our luggage on a cart. There was also some sort of dot in the far distance.

Simon and Kevin did not seem completely impressed with this arrangement, probably wondering why they had been cut off from the rest of the group and forced to spend the afternoon with the new boy.

'Where would you like your luggage?' asked the porter.

'We don't know yet,' said Kevin. 'Does this hotel have a....?' He glanced around the lobby. 'Does this hotel have a reception?'

'It is just there,' he said, pointing in the direction of the dot in the far distance.

As we walked towards the dot it gradually grew bigger until eventually it was possible to make out a small man sitting behind a polished wooden counter. The porter followed us with the cart, one wheel squeaking as per the regulations, and echoing around the dazzling chamber.

'Good afternoon,' said the little man behind the desk, also dressed in a maroon uniform. He had a kindly face, and round wire-rim spectacles. 'Would you like to check in?'

'We're just here for the afternoon,' said Simon. 'But apparently something has been booked for us.'

'Just for the afternoon? What name, please?'

'Mann.'

'We have nothing for a Mann.'

'What about Howells?'

'Howells, let me see...no, there is nothing for a Howells.' What about, er...sorry, what's your surname, Miles?'

'It's Jupp.'

'Anything for a Jupp?'

The man behind the counter laughed gently.

'We have nothing for a Jupp either.'

Simon and Kevin both sighed, so I sighed too.

'What about BBC?' tried Kevin.

'BBC? Oh no. We certainly have no room booked for BBC.'

'Sunsport?' I suggested.

'No. I am afraid not. Did you book this room yourself?'

'No. It was our tour company,' said Simon, ominously.

Kevin looked at me and then said quietly, 'I'm not saying this is typical, but...'

'Well, we'll just have to book something for ourselves,' said Simon.

'Couldn't we just hang out in the lobby?' I offered.

Kevin and Simon looked at me as if I'd just suggested that the three of us pool our life savings and open a dog-grooming salon together. In Hull.

'We need a room, Miles. We need to have showers and things,' said Simon.

'And somewhere to sit down,' said Kevin.

The porter leant into our conversation. 'Where would you like me to take your luggage?'

'We don't know yet. Just leave it here, please,' I said.

'Here?'

'Yes, please.'

'Okay, sir. Please enjoy your stay.' And then he stayed exactly where he was. I looked at him.

'Thanks.'

'Thank you, sir.' Still he stayed. What was he doing? Why was he looking at me like that? Oh, of course – a tip! I needed to give him some money. I pulled out my wallet, which contained only the notes I hurriedly got from an ATM at the airport. I hadn't even counted them, or looked to see what they were. I pulled one out at random, folded it and handed it to him. As he took it a look of amazement briefly flashed across his features.

'Thank you, sir,' he beamed. And off he went with a spring in his step. He may even have been whistling.

'Did you just give him a tip?' asked Kevin.

'Oh yeah. Just a little one...you know.'

'How much?'

'Oh, nothing really. Just a note. A small one.'

I had no idea. No idea at all.

'Right, we'll just have to get a room ourselves,' said Simon, again.

'Absolutely,' I said and held up my wallet, anxious to display that I wasn't just some shower-dodging backpacker anxious to camp out in hotel lobbies.

'Don't worry, the BBC can pay. It's hardly an outrageous expense. Three of us to a room.'

'You would like rooms?' The little man behind the desk had clearly got wind of our big scheme.

'One room, please,' said Simon. 'Just until about half past seven.'

'Just one room?'

'That's right.'

'I am sorry. Is the room for yourselves?'

'Yes.'

'You want a room for three gentlemen?'

'Please.'

The man looked deeply troubled.

'I am not sure that we can give one room to three men. That is quite...it is a little...unusual.'

'We only need it for the afternoon,' said Simon.

'I am really not sure we have anything suitable. All of our rooms only have one bed.'

'I doubt any of us will be sleeping much. Even if we do, we'll probably be taking turns.'

The receptionist turned away, almost blushing as the full possibilities of the nature of our afternoon slowly dawned on him. Clearly the three of us were intent on using the hotel where he worked as the setting for a triangular homosexual tryst that was going to be conducted according to a rota system. On top of that, our ringleader seemed to be arrogantly behaving as if any form of sexual activity were automatically deemed to be more wholesome if conducted solely within the hours of daylight.

'We all work for the BBC,' explained Kevin, as if to confirm the receptionist's very worst suspicions.

The kindly man did a brief bit of soul searching, then finally said, 'Okay. Do any of you have a credit card?'

Simon handed one over, and as the little machine it was slid into clicked and whirred, the receptionist removed his glasses and rubbed his eyes, as if to despair about what had become of the British. Then he handed Simon's card back and informed us we could have a room on the twelfth floor. Obviously the environs of the twelfth floor would provide the most appropriate atmosphere for our vile carryings on, and we'd stand less chance of upsetting other guests or the hotel staff. A key was handed over, and some lifts were pointed out.

'Now then,' said Simon turning towards the lift, 'where's the porter gone?'

'Miles paid him off,' said Kevin.

And so it was that I, having paid goodness knows how much for the privilege, was given the job of conveying the luggage cart from the lobby to our room on the twelfth floor.

*

Simon's journey had begun in Wandsworth, Kevin's in Leeds, and so by dint of having travelled the furthest, I was nominated to make first use of the shower. That was certainly the reason that Kevin and Simon gave for me going first at any rate; they may just have been being polite and I was actually the smelliest. I had, after all, just travelled for over eight hours in economy class, whereas they had been enjoying the comparative luxury of business.

I rummaged around in my suitcase for a fresh shirt and undergarments, carried these with me into the bathroom, and locked the door behind me before selecting a large towel, leaning into the glass cubicle and turning on the giant, gleaming pressure shower. I then removed all of my clothes, took off my glasses, stepped under the spray and clamped my eyes shut as I felt the hot water powering into my face.

Suddenly there were cries from the bedroom.

'Miles! Miles!'

'What?'

'Shutters!'

'What?'

'Shutters!' Kevin was shouting. 'SHUTTERS!'

I turned in the direction of the cries and, to my surprise, was able to see both Kevin and Simon looking back at me, their faces frozen with horror. Only then did I notice that one wall of the bathroom consisted of a giant window, a window through which I could see two appalled – and real – journalists.

Simon was pointing to my left, and there I saw a wooden shutter, which I lunged at and slid slowly into place, finally establishing a screen between the other two and my shame. I then continued my shower, safe in the knowledge that I had begun my journalistic career by exposing my arse and then genitals to two men that I had only met half an hour previously. Mind you, this was probably quite mild behaviour compared to what the man at the reception desk would have imagined we were up to by now. When I finally emerged from the bathroom, clean and redressed, Simon and Kevin were sitting in two armchairs looking more serene. Both had largely recovered from the shock, and perhaps feelings of inadequacy, that I had subjected them to.

'I'm sorry about the whole naked thing, chaps.'

'It's okay,' said Simon. 'If anybody asks us what the new boy's like, we'll just say that he's got a very relaxed attitude to personal privacy.'

'And definitely has an arse and genitals,' added Kevin.

*

If this had been a family holiday, and one had this many hours spare in an unknown foreign city, then I'm sure there would have been a mad attempt to fill every minute by seeking out cathedrals, museums and postcard shops. As it was, this was a business trip and no one appeared to have the slightest intention of going anywhere.

Looking out of the window, I could see the sun beating down on a collection of completely abandoned loungers next to a deserted and ripple-free pool.

'Anybody want to go for a swim?' I asked.

'No thanks,' said Simon.

'Not really,' said Kevin.

'Sunbathe?' I offered.

'Sunbathe?' Kevin seemed disgusted by the idea.

'Fair enough. You probably feel as if you've seen enough of my body for one day.'

'Well, exactly.'

We passed the afternoon reading books and newspapers that we'd brought with us, occasionally chatting idly about cricket and our predictions for the coming Test series. Kevin also told us about the tour he had been on to Pakistan prior to Christmas, which didn't sound like it had been a particularly happy trip. Certainly not when he had drunk some water from an unsealed bottle and consequently spent two feverish days thrashing around in a hotel room thinking he was about to die.

Every now and then our mobile phones all bleeped simultaneously with messages saying things along the lines of 'Andrew Flintoff will give a press conference at 4 p.m. in the Exhale suite at the team hotel' or 'The Flintoff press conference will now be at 4.30 p.m. in the Exhale suite' or 'The Exhale suite is no longer available. The 4.30 p.m. conference will now take place in the Cayenne Room.' Then later: 'Andrew Flintoff is no longer available for the press conference. Andrew Strauss will instead attend press conference at 4.45 p.m. Venue to be confirmed.' Then finally, 'Apologies. There will be no press conference this afternoon. Team will be practising at the ground from 10 a.m. tomorrow, as planned.'

In the midst of all these updates, my phone emitted a solo beep and I picked it up to see that the screen contained three words that heralded all sorts of possibilities; the words 'New Message: Mum'. My mother is not a lady who has embraced many areas of modern life. She calls the radio 'the wireless', she calls the computer 'the word processor' and she thinks that 'the word processor' is a thing that 'the email' lives inside. She can just about cope with tea bags, as long as they're the square ones, and has a curious inability to match remote controls to the device that she is attempting to operate.

Each and every technological advancement of the last 30 years has only succeeded in making both of my parents far more paranoid. They have a totally irrational belief that all modern manufacturers would consider it a sensible idea to market machinery that had a button on it that would, if pressed, instantly render the thing unworkable. In fact, they sometimes appear to believe that these unmarked buttons are capable of causing damage on an almost cosmic scale whilst simultaneously letting it be known to the world at large that it was their fault. I think my mother fears that one day she will switch on the wireless to hear a report stating that 'large parts of the Brazilian rainforest were destroyed today as a result of Mrs Jupp using the pulse function on her Magimix blender for slightly too long. It's been a bad week for the Jupps, coming as this does just days after Mr Jupp inadvertently blew up seven visiting dignitaries whilst attempting to access his voicemail.'

And yet, despite all this, text messaging is an arena in which she really lets herself go. She used text abbreviations long before I ever knew what they were. At first I thought that she was abbreviating simply out of necessity as she was afraid of pushing too many buttons. She sends messages that read 'AOK? alm', as if she's using street patois. 'Where u now? how u do?' There is no news my mother thinks won't be given more gravitas by being sent via text message. That said, the vast majority of texts she sends still come about as a result of her forgetting to operate the key lock and then sitting on her phone.

So it was with a great deal of curiosity that I hit the 'Read now' function. The text simply said: 'U india? Jones injrd'.

This news instantly set me off in a panic. Surely this couldn't be happening? Jones was injrd? Which Jones, anyway? It could be the wicketkeeper Geraint Jones. Would she know the difference or even that there was a distinction to be made? Was she definitely referring to cricket? How would she even know at all?

'Guys, I've just had a text from my mother saying that Jones is injured. Could that be right? Could she have heard that?'

'Which Jones?' asked Simon.

'She didn't say.'

'Well, we've not heard anything, have we? We'd have had a text message from Walpole.'

'Or someone else would have phoned us,' added Kevin.

'That's a relief. It's just, you know, what with working for the *Western Mail*, that would have been pretty big news.'

'I don't think you need to worry,' said Simon. 'How would your mother know before we did?'

'Well exactly.'

I breathed a sigh of relief.

'Mind you,' said Kevin quietly, 'if a Jones had been injured, you'd probably bet on it being Simon.'

I considered Kevin's words, and also decided that the next time I was in the company of journalists and thought that I might be breaking some news, then I wouldn't open by saying, 'Guys, I've just had a text message from my mother.'

*

We were collected at the appointed time by the same driver and tour operator and taken back to the airport at Delhi. We checked in for the Nagpur flight, and then the three of us proceeded through security and sat in a lurid orange departure lounge. Before too long it started to fill with other members of the press corps, all drifting in looking experienced and travel-hardened.

'Oh, hello Simon, where did you get to all afternoon?'

'We were taken to a different hotel from everybody else.'

'Oh, that's a shame, we've had a lovely time; swimming, bit of sunbathing.'

Simon and Kevin introduced me to various other members of the press corps, including the wonderfully named Jo King, the scorer for *Test Match Special*. With her was Ted Corbett from the *Financial Times* and the *Glasgow Herald* who looked to me like a seasoned old campaigner. He was even wearing one of those sleeveless khaki numbers covered in pockets that are so beloved of a certain breed of war correspondent.

'Heard about Simon Jones?' he asked.

'What's happened?'

'We've only just heard. Injured. His knee's gone. He's just about to board a flight back to the UK.'

'Oh,' I said.

'Don't know who they'll be sending out as cover, but they'll need someone.'

Everybody else began discussing likely replacements, but I was quickly sinking into a glum stupor. I excused myself and headed off to the lavatory for a bit of a think.

Les mères, as the french say, *elles ont toujours raison*. Mothers are always right. Curses. Two things were troubling me. The first was that with Simon Jones suddenly being out of the equation, there was a very distinct possibility that the *Western Mail* would no longer be particularly interested in me sending them any writing. Charles had made it fairly plain that it really only was the goings-on in the life of Simon Jones that concerned them. Right now I was about to get on a plane, and so was not in a position to write and send them a quick article about his injury blow. Additionally, I was not going to be able to squeeze many words out of the little I had so far heard about the situation, which was simply 'Injured. Knee's gone.' That wording might be suitable for a telegram, but would probably not be worthy of space in a newspaper. And it was only an article about his injury that I would be able to write. Any further Simon Jones news would only concern his rehabilitation and I was in no place to find out about that.

The second thing that troubled me was how on earth my mother had heard this news so many hours ahead of people whose job it was to know exactly this sort of thing. I sent her a text message: 'I am in India. How did you hear about Jones?' She replied swiftly. She had heard about it on the *Today* programme.

*

Two hours later we touched down in Nagpur, and were collected and driven in people carriers to a red brick hotel not far from the airport. I had heard and read little about Nagpur, mainly because not much is written or said about it – other than that it was an odd place to hold a Test match. It would be a little inept to describe a city as nondescript. All that I can say about it at first glance is that it was like an Indian version of Peterborough or Crewe – somewhere that you would only really visit deliberately if you were hoping to experience the sensation of changing trains.

A long queue formed at the reception desk, and by the time I had completed the necessary form filling and carried my luggage upstairs I felt a little panicked. Now that there was no one to tell me what to do, I felt a little alone. It would be up to me to fend for myself.

'There's a few people having a drink upstairs,' said Kevin, passing me as I fiddled with the lock on the door of my room.

'I think I might just unpack,' I said – not through any real desire to go to bed but out of a sudden sense of social unease. Going up to the roof bar would mean having to introduce myself to people, do more posing as a journalist. There might be any number of legends up there all backslapping and greeting each other like old chums. I would rather tread my way in carefully, not try and do too much too soon.

'I'll wait for you if you like,' said Kevin. 'I could introduce you to a few people.'

'Er, okay. Yeah, why not?' I said, not revealing how grateful I was for this offer.

Upstairs was a bar and restaurant largely open to the elements and lit by hanging lanterns. At a long table were sat a variety of journalists and broadcasters, many of them with faces well known to me. It was largely a *Test Match Special* gathering: Mike Selvey, Victor Marks, Peter Baxter, Christopher Martin-Jenkins and Jonathan Agnew. Also there, looking relaxed and genial, was the great David Gower. As Kevin and I sat down at one end of the table, he and Agnew were just coming to the end of a shared anecdote about what sounded like an astonishing piss-up in Jamshedpur. As it finished, a waiter came over to hand Gower a drink and nervously asked if he was England captain.

'A long time ago, I was,' he replied.

'Ah,' said the waiter.

'But a victorious one,' added Gower.

'Only Douglas Jardine won here before you,' said a knowledgeable voice from further down the table.

'And Tony Greig,' added Gower, who was coming across as both modest and passionate about the game.

The party, to which I contributed precisely nothing, broke up after just one more drink. Just as everyone was leaving Kevin introduced me to Gower.

'Hi, there. What are you here for?'

'Oh, just a spot of gentle journalism,' I replied, trying to sound as languid as he does.

He laughed. 'Nothing's gentle here.'

Chapter Five

I found it hard to sleep that first night. The beds were precisely as uncomfortable as Jonathan Agnew had warned that they would be – with mattresses as thin as pizza bases laid on a rock-hard frame, so that it felt like sleeping on a yoga mat. On top of that I was hot, restless and excited. Up on the roof I had been thrilled, but also in awe and a little out of my depth. These were people with heaps of experience and splendid track records who were very much in their natural habitat. I had just sat there silently, trying to look calm and collected, but under the surface I was kicking away furiously like a duck, amazed at the company I was in.

I did eventually get off to sleep for what must have been a couple of hours, but then my phone began to ring. Despite being mid-dream, with almost Pavlovian reflexes, I stuck an arm out, answered it and held it to my ear without even checking who it was. A stranger who had, quite reasonably, no idea that I was in India, was yapping on, rather less reasonably, about a survey being conducted into mobile phone providers. Someone in a call centre was reeling off a script at me, and it was a while before there was a break in their rant long enough for me to inform them that I was in India. This was clearly not one of the responses that they were briefed to handle and so they just ploughed on, completely failing to acknowledge that the UK and India are not in even vaguely adjacent time zones. On and on they went about price plans and insurance options whilst I repeated the phrase, 'I'm in India' until in my sleep-deprived state it finally occurred to me that I could just press a button and make them stop. The cessation of their prattling was not enough to allow me to return to sleep, so I just lay there, flat on my back and wide-eyed, waiting for the morning.

Seven o'clock, the time that I had set my alarm for, could not come soon enough. In fact, it seemed like it wasn't coming at all and so at half past six, I gave up waiting and decided to start the day. It's not easy to spring out of a bed that has never itself been sprung, but I made a valiant attempt at it by performing one very slow sit-up. Bleary-eyed and with aching joints, I lurched to the window to open the curtains and let in what little of the morning light they hadn't already allowed to pour through. I parted the curtains and leant against the window to take in a remarkable view that I was absolutely not expecting.

If you have ever had the chance to examine a brochure for the Nagpur Hotel Quality, you might have seen some delightful photographs of its splendid, outdoor swimming pool. Shaped like a kidney bean, with striking white tiles around its edge, its welcoming contents reflect the clear blue of the sky. Around it are arranged tables and chairs, at which sit eager business travellers and the odd family group. A uniformed waiter holds a tray on which stands a tall glass containing an iced drink. He will soon be placing that drink down on a table in front of a pretty young lady – just as soon as she has finished giggling at the antics of her lover, who is about to leap into the deep end.

It would be hard to work out when exactly that poolside scene had been photographed, but if any of its subjects saw the condition that the pool was now in, they would have felt a bit like Jane Torvill and Christopher Dean will have done when they saw images of the Sarajevo Olympic Stadium where they had won Gold in 1984 after it had been destroyed by Serb shelling in the 1990s. The pristine white edges of the pool were now grey and cracked. It was still shaped like a kidney bean, but no longer contained water. Instead, perhaps in the interests of diversification, the pool now served as a landfill site and was filled with tyres, rubble and construction waste. If the handsome young man from the photo leapt into the deep end now, he would not have hit water but collided painfully with one of several old toilets.

I showered and dressed and slipped out into the silent corridor to see what else the Hotel Quality had to offer. What little I had seen of the restaurant up on the roof had looked splendid, but the sight of the swimming pool had been a bit of a let-down. I'd sent a travel company a handsome sum not just to see lots of cricket, but also in the hope of a little pampering, and in advance of my trip had been looking online and in guidebooks to see what our various billets would be like. The website for this hotel had promised wireless Internet access, a swimming pool and a health club. The view from my window told me what state the swimming pool was in, my laptop had told me that there was no wireless signal to be found anywhere in the vicinity, and so I hoped that the Health Club might make up for the other failings.

There were no other journalist types up and about yet, only hotel staff who all smiled and bid me a good morning as I shuffled past them. There was a sign at the end of my corridor pointing me in the direction of the Health Club, and so I followed it, but all I found was a window affording me another view of the swimming pool. I asked a cleaner where I might find it, but was only given a smile and a shrug. After 15 minutes of wandering about, asking for directions and being shrugged at, I was forced to come to the conclusion that the Health Club at the Nagpur Hotel Quality simply didn't exist in any tangible form.

Having got over these petty disappointments, I started getting ready to go down to the dining room for breakfast and as I did so began to feel nervous – that same feeling of butterflies in the stomach that you might experience on your first day at a new school. The other journalists would be up now, and would also be in the dining room. Would there be anyone I had yet met that I could sit down with? Would breakfast be a good place to start making introductions?

Before I left the room, I picked up a novel as a kind of social shield. If I was forced to sit on my own, then I could just bury my head in my book and would hopefully not look too out of place. When I walked into the dining room, any fears about who to sit with instantly evaporated as the room was devoid of other guests. There were, however, three mustard-keen waiting staff anxious to dole out the contents of the various steaming cauldrons that were lined up in front of them along a row of tables. I was not entirely relaxed about eating whatever was served up to me. The regrettable truth is that anyone from Great Britain who travels to India is told that at some point they will get the shits. Having this knowledge so close to the surface of your brain makes you a little guarded when faced with all manner of exotic-looking goodies. It was probably paranoia, but I was desperate not to suddenly come down with something on the first day that made my guts even slightly wet and explosive. This would be, I felt, a bad impression and one that might take considerably longer to shift than anything that was in my bowels. This chain of thought was doing little for my normally uncontrollable appetite, and as the staff cheerily explained to me what was in every bubbling cauldron, and talked me patiently through all the different treats crowded onto the hot plates, I became less and less hungry, and eventually opted for a pathetically safe choice of a small bowl of porridge and a couple of pastries.

Having disappointed the waiting staff with my stereotypically bland British tastes, I sat down on my own at a table at one end of the dining room and waited to see what would happen. What happened was that when everybody else arrived, they all sat down at the other end of the room and completely ignored me.

I tried to lower my head nonchalantly into my novel as the other end of the room slowly filled with cricketing and journalistic legends. Atherton, Agnew, Baxter, Gower and Hussain all filed in at intervals, as did another 15 or so journalists. It appeared from watching the goings-on at their end, that if I wanted to look more like a proper journalist, then what I would need to do would be to enter the breakfast room looking tired and then make a sarcastic comment about the hotel to no one in particular, which is probably equivalent to actors wandering into a rehearsal room and saying 'Morning, luvs' in an accentuated theatrical accent. I was well prepared for this, I realised, as I had already spent much of the morning making sarcastic remarks about the hotel, but having no one to voice them to, other than hotel staff – which would have been rude – I had just been making them under my breath, like a mad man. They all appeared to be having a jolly-enough time down that end of the room, but I didn't really feel I could go over and join any of them. Simon Mann had come in but had sat himself down at an otherwise full table. No one was looking in my direction anyway, so I didn't feel overly self-conscious about being on my own. They probably all just thought I was here for a water technologies conference.

What I heard a lot of people saying, though, was that they would be heading down to the ground as soon as breakfast was over. Then I would do the same. One of the text messages we had all received the day before told us that press passes could be collected from Andrew Walpole, the England team's press officer, at the ground. I quickly headed upstairs to go and do my teeth and then be ready and just happening to be hanging out in the lobby when people were leaving so that I could cadge a lift with them. Luckily, when I came downstairs again Kevin Howells had taken up occupancy of one of the leather sofas in the lobby.

'Oh, hello, Kevin. Sleep well?'

'No,' he replied in the same slow and mannered tone I imagine he uses whether he's ordering a slice of cake or hiring a hit man. 'Did you?'

'Not really, not really. Are you going to the ground by any chance?'

'Yes.'

'Could I come with you, by any chance?'

'I'd have thought so. I'm going to be sharing a car with Peter Baxter and Jonathan Agnew.'

'Oh, splendid.'

Inside I felt a sudden surge of excitement. Last night I'd been amazed to see the pair of them at the far end of a table that I was sitting at. Now I was definitely going to meet them. These were two men who I admired enormously. Since 1973, Baxter had been the producer of the great *Test Match Special* and Agnew was the BBC's chief cricket correspondent. Ever since I became a fan of cricket I had been listening to them commentating on the radio, and was as familiar with their voices as I was with many members of my own family. And now here they were, striding into the lobby to meet Kevin and carrying an assortment of flight cases.

'Morning, Kevin!' said Baxter.

'Hello.'

'Any sign of the car?'

'Yes, it's outside. I said we could give a lift to this gentleman.'

'Oh yes?' Baxter turned towards me, and then put down whatever heavy object he was carrying.

'Hello there, Peter Baxter. BBC Radio,' he said as he stuck his hand out to shake mine.

'And I'm Jonathan Agnew, also BBC Radio,' said Agnew, also putting something down and then proffering his hand.

'I'm Miles Jupp,' I said as I shook each hand in turn. 'BBC Radio Scotland.'

One of Peter Baxter's eyebrows rose ever so slightly on hearing this news, and then we all stepped outside into the fierce morning sun and loaded all of the broadcasting equipment onto a waiting people carrier.

I clambered into the back seat and said nothing for the duration of the journey, but laughed regularly as I listened to the three of them exchange stories about rotten hotels they had stayed in and violent bouts of diarrhoea that they had succumbed to.

*

The Test ground in Nagpur is officially known as the Vidarbha Cricket Association Ground. The journey from the Hotel Quality to the ground involved going over and under a series of rather daunting fly-overs for 25 minutes, and didn't feel all that different from travelling in heavy traffic through the Hammersmith area on an exceedingly hot day. The driver parked up on the kerb, and we all unloaded the vehicle and walked straight through the nearest set of unattended gates into the ground. Kevin was here to set up his broadcast post to send regular updates to BBC 5 Live. Baxter had arrived intent on setting up the *Test Match Special* studio, and Agnew was anxious to make his way straight out onto the pitch, and with Baxter's help, set up their satellite phone and then make a live broadcast to BBC Radio 4 to trail the next day's coverage. Other than get my hands on the press pass that I'd been promised a month or so earlier, I didn't really have anything to do other than look reasonably busy, so I decided to try and hang with this little gang for as long as I could. Besides, I liked walking around carrying an equipment case marked with the letters 'BBC' on the side. It made me feel important. Getting a lift with the big boys, walking straight into the ground; so far it all seemed too easy. And indeed that proved to be the case, as within minutes we ran into difficulties. The route out to the pitch that Agnew and Baxter wanted to take involved going through another gate, but this time it was attended by a pair of keen young security guards with machine guns slung over their shoulders. They took exception to Baxter just trying to open the gate and walk through.

'Excuse me, sir, where are you going?'

'We need to get out onto the pitch.'

'What is your business there?'

'We need to make a radio broadcast.'

'All of you?' The guards looked at us all.

'Just us two,' said Agnew, indicating himself and Baxter.

'You need special passes,' they were told.

A lengthy argument ensued between the two journalists and the enthusiastic security pair. Agnew and Baxter's bargaining point centred around the fact that the middle of the pitch was the best place for them to do a live trail from as it would provide the listeners at home with the best atmosphere. The crux of the security guards' argument seemed to be that they were the ones with the guns – presumably a debating tactic left behind by the British 50 years previously. Baxter and Agnew repeatedly tried to plead their case but with little success. Kevin wasn't overly keen to get involved, and I stood well back from the debate, guarding the rest of their broadcasting kit and starting to panic about my own accreditation status. The text message telling me that passes could be collected at the ground had been a circular one, and not one specifically addressed to me. If the likes of Agnew and Co. could be so thwarted in their attempts to get where they needed to be, then how easily would a fraud like me find it to get into places that I merely wanted to be?

The upshot of the debate was that the broadcast was abandoned, and we were all directed to a building specifically set aside as a place where people could go to argue with officials. Peter Baxter went into an office expecting to be on the giving or receiving end of a haranguing, whilst Kevin, 'Aggers' and I sat down on sofas in an anteroom. An exasperated quiet slowly turned first into a relaxed hush, and then finally permutated into an awkward silence which hung over the three of us, and which I, for no good reason, felt duty bound to relieve. I decided to start the conversational ball rolling by reminding Aggers of the time when we had both appeared on a BBC Radio Scotland show a few years previously. He did not appear to have any recollection of this, and so I told him about the show in rather more detail and at some length, describing to him the show's host, former Scotland rugby international John Beattie. That got little response and so on and on I went, reminding him of a few of the areas that our conversation had covered – the Ashes, county cricket and a brief bit of chat about which former players were now the best regarded speakers on the after-dinner circuit. By now Kevin was looking at me as if I was either a maniac or a bad choice of guest at a dinner party he was hosting. Agnew was silently staring at the floor with a furrowed brow.

'Hmm. I think I might vaguely remember that, actually,' he said eventually, but politely.

I cursed myself inwardly as I realised that I had crossed some sort of invisible line. What on earth did I think I was doing? 'Rein it in, Jupp,' I told myself. 'Don't try so hard.' This wasn't the manner in which a fellow journalist would behave. This was more like the sort of thing a fan would put in a letter to Eminem. Quite why I imagined he might have remembered our chat over the airways, I have absolutely no idea. The man is the BBC's chief cricket correspondent and consequently appears on all of the BBC's different radio stations hundreds, possibly thousands of times a year. It was, of course, extremely unlikely that he would even remember the incident, let alone have anything to say about it. This sort of nervy, excited chatter was bound to mark me out as a total amateur, babbling on and on like an insane, obsessive punter, trying to make some small event sound like it was of great significance. It was as if I was someone who had once been in the crowd when the Queen had opened a civic centre somewhere, and years later, on happening to be briefly introduced to her again, had attempted to remind her of the fact: 'Well, of course, ma'am, this isn't the first time we've met is it? You must remember. Let me prod your memory. Peterborough? The Andy Bell (from Erasure) Civic Centre opening? I was one of the people outside. Yes. You pulled up in a car and walked past us all waving, and we all waved back, do you remember? A lady handed you a bunch of flowers and you said "thank you". Well, I was standing two along to her left. Yellow pullover.'

'Hmm,' the Queen would eventually say. 'I think I might vaguely remember that, actually.'

A silence descended once again, and it wasn't long before it occurred to both Kevin and Aggers that there were better things they could be doing with their time than watching me blush and fidget, and so off they went to do them. It was Baxter's responsibility to get press passes to all of the BBC's commentators and reporters and so they didn't need to worry about anything. By contrast, I didn't have anything better to do, and so I waited for Peter, who soon emerged still having failed to secure passes for any of the BBC people. This seemed more than a little ominous. It transpired that in the days running up to the tour, a rather convoluted agreement had arisen between various television and radio rights' holders. This had now apparently been resolved, but one upshot was that much of the accreditation paperwork had been caught up in a backlog and that a small number of media passes had yet to be processed or materialise. Another upshot was that without any passes, all of the broadcasting kit required to set up the *Test Match Special* studio at the opposite end of the stadium would now all have to be carried around the outside of the ground to the media entrance as Peter could not yet gain access to any short cuts. Peter stood surveying this little mountain of kit and shaking his head at it.

'I could help,' I said.

'Oh, that's very kind. You sure you don't mind?'

'No, no.'

'Well, thank you.'

Would I mind carrying the *Test Match Special* kit to its studio? Would I mind playing a small part in bringing *Test Match Special* to air? Of course I wouldn't. I would love to. To a devotee like me, that was the equivalent of someone begging me to help them jump-start the A-Team van. Or someone ringing up my mother and asking if it would be all right for an episode of *The Archers* to be recorded in her kitchen.

Between us we picked up the various trunks and cases and staggered out onto and then along the street that ran around the outside of the ground. As we made our way slowly along the crowded pavements with our heavy load, Peter told me about how tricky touring around India can sometimes be, occasionally breaking off to swear at anyone or anything that got in our way. 'Just so many obstacles,' he said, as we picked our way through a whole row of parked bicycles that had keeled over, and now littered the pavement like a spilled cargo washed up on a beach.

We reached the media entrance, and though it was more heavily guarded than the other entrance that we had tried, we were waved through as soon as anyone saw the letters 'BBC' emblazoned on our load. As long as I could stick with this lot things might just be all right. That, of course, depended on whether they minded a cocky young interloper sticking with them. The press stand itself was a relatively spartan three-storey affair that had been whitewashed, although not terribly recently. All of the radio commentary boxes were up on the top level, we were told, and so we carried all the kit up the narrow staircase and onto the top level, of which the studio set aside for the use of *Test Match Special* was the only bit with a roof and was almost totally empty, other than a few wires and dried leaves. Peter was due to spend the rest of the day unpacking the cases and assembling their contents into a studio. There was clearly little else I could offer by way of help and so I headed off to see where else I could go.

As we had climbed the stairs we had passed a doorway marked with the words 'Press Box' and so I nipped back down one flight determined to have a peep around. There was an incredibly smart soldier standing next to the entrance. 'Good morning,' I said, and walked past him. An arm shot out, and a hand was held up in front of my chest.

'Where are you going, please?'

'I just want to have a look at the press box.'

'Why is this, please?'

'Oh. I'm a journalist. This is where I'll be working tomorrow.'

'Do you have a pass?'

'Well, not yet. But that's why I've come to the ground. To collect my press pass.'

'I'm sorry but you need a press pass to go in this room.'

'Well, how about this?'

From my back pocket I pulled the folded letter on BBC Scotland headed notepaper, and passed it to him. 'This proves that I am a journalist.'

He unfolded the letter and read it slowly, before folding it again and passing it back to me. 'Okay, you may go in.'

'Thanks.'

As I walked through the doorway, he called to me over his shoulder. 'Tomorrow, you will need to have a proper pass.'

'Absolutely. Thanks.'

I was in! I had looked up at those men in the press box at the Oval and dreamt about gaining acccess to one myself, and now five and a half months later and 4,000 miles away, I had done it.

I felt a real sense of elation as I walked through the doorway into a place that held an almost mythical status in my imagination; this was my Atlantis, my Camelot. What treasure untold lay beyond these doors?

It was a simple, high-ceilinged room filled with seven or eight steeply raked rows of desks and chairs, perhaps providing enough space for 80 or so eager journalists. It was open-fronted and perfectly positioned directly opposite the pavilion at the other end of the ground. It was not high up like the media centres at a lot of English grounds are, but only just above the level of the sightscreen. There was a rail running along the front of the box, and if you leant out over it you were practically hanging over the edge of the pitch. The view from here would be incredible once the game was under way. At present, out on the field were just a few ground staff giving various bits of the pitch a bit of a trim, and nailing down bits of matting with sponsors' logos on them. Also set up in the corner of the ground to the right of where I stood was a set of practice nets, and waiting keenly in the seats nearest them were a crowd of about 400 Indian fans.

There was only one other man in the box, who looked about my age, and introduced himself as the cricket correspondent from 'the *Sport*'. (Did he mean the *Daily Sport*? Could that be right? I thought they dealt exclusively with gentle pornography and stories about sightings of Elvis.) I told him I was 'the BBC Scotland guy'.

'First tour?' he asked. 'I don't remember you being out in Pakistan.'

'No, I wasn't. This is my first one.'

I walked slowly about the room along the various rows and climbed up to the back of the box where I sat down to take it all in. It was there I realised that the desks already had the names of journalists scrawled on them in pencil or biro. People had been coming along and reserving the places well in advance. I started working my way back along the desks down to the front of the box, again looking for a spare place that had not yet been claimed. As I did so, a few other journalists shuffled into the box below me, and instantly wrote their names on some of the desks near the front. They all had big shiny press passes on, suspended from their necks by chunky lanyards. Amongst them were Angus Fraser and Derek Pringle, both of whom I used to watch on television when I was at school. In fact, Angus Fraser once signed his autograph for me in Uxbridge, where I'd gone to watch a crucial top of the table county championship clash between Middlesex and Northamptonshire. After the Agnew disaster I didn't think that this would be an especially good conversational starting point so I just walked over and introduced myself as if I were a fellow journalist.

'Hi there, I'm Miles. I'm from BBC Scotland.'

'Gus. Hi there.' He looked even more exhausted now than he used to as a player when walking back to his mark during yet another Brian Lara hundred.

I introduced myself to the others too; Derek Pringle from the *Daily Telegraph*, Stephen Brenkley from the *Independent On Sunday* and David Lloyd from the *Evening Standard*.

'Who did you say you worked for again?' asked Brenkley.

'BBC Scotland. And the *Western Mail*.'

He and Lloyd seemed most amused by the idea of a Scottish cricket correspondent.

'You're just out here on a jolly, aren't you?' said Brenkley.

'Well, we have to see how things turn out, won't we?' I said weakly.

These men all had a confidence about them, a slight proprietorial swagger as they leant against various bits of furniture and surveyed the ground. I was still looking for an unreserved place, as this bunch of experienced hacks seemed to have taken all that were left. And then I finally found the one place in the box that had not yet been claimed, and I couldn't believe my luck; it was bang in the middle of the front row! 'What a fantastic seat that would be,' I thought. And so I took out a pen and wrote across the desk: 'MILES JUPP, BBC SCOTLAND'. Instantly I felt a little bit professional.

At that moment there came an almighty cheer from the crowd of fans away to our right, and I looked out across the pitch to see the reason; emerging from the pavilion at that moment were the Indian team striding in the direction of the nets for their morning practice. The first batsmen were quickly padded up and were warmly applauded just for taking up their positions in the nets. I leant on the rail and watched the action from my vantage point. If this was the way a small crowd behaved when watching a net practice then the atmosphere during the games would be incredible. They clapped and roared at every stroke the batsmen played and let out a giant 'Ooooooooh' in unison at every good ball or play and miss. The response Sachin Tendulkar received for merely entering his net was phenomenal but would be nothing, I reckoned, compared to the response that would greet every run he scored against us once the match was under way. Tendulkar's average at Nagpur was very close to a hundred, which worried me a little. I love to watch him bat, but not against us. I wanted to see him dismissed as cheaply as possibly, and ideally by a Welshman with strong Scottish connections.

At the opposite corner of the ground another set of nets had been erected for England's use, and now one or two of our players emerged from the pavilion and headed in that direction in their distinctive red and blue practice kit. This aroused the interest of the other journalists in the box.

'Come on, let's go and have a look,' said one.

'Does anybody know where I'll find Andrew Walpole?' I asked. 'I've still got to collect my pass.'

'Yes, he'll be over by the pavilion. That's where we're going now.'

And so we walked downstairs, past various uniformed types with guns, and when we got to the bottom, rather than turning right as I expected us to, back the way I had come along the outside of the ground, everyone turned left and just walked out onto the pitch. I followed them and instantly felt in the thick of things. Our party walked around the boundary perimeter just next to where the next couple of Indian batsmen were padding up for the nets. We then passed just feet away from where Sachin Tendulkar was practising, a remarkable and compact-looking player who has been playing international cricket for more than half of his life. In the adjacent net was the long-haired MS Dhoni who was hell-bent on spanking all of the bowlers back over their heads. The Indian crowd briefly broke off from applauding Dhoni's showboating to wave at us all and make excitable noises. Gus Fraser and Derek Pringle were walking just ahead of me and would presumably be recognisable to any serious cricket fan. Hands were shoved through the protective wire fence to be shaken or even just touched and we were all pointed and giggled at. I have no idea if they were being affectionate or if they were just mocking us and our silly pasty faces, but either response would have been totally acceptable. Then Pringle peeled away from our group.

'I'm just going to have a word with Athers,' he said before walking right out into the middle where, it turned out, my hero was indeed standing and inspecting the pitch and talking to a couple of our players.

Outside the front of the pavilion things were beginning to look busy. More and more of England's players were emerging from inside, and various members of the coaching and security staff were buzzing about. Journalists stood about the place chatting in twos and threes, occasionally breaking away from their discussions to speak to any players with whom they were on good terms. Someone pointed out Andrew Walpole to me, a bald, wiry man dressed in England's practice strip, although not, I imagined, about to be pressed into any playing capacity. He was deep in conversation with Andrew Flintoff, although every now and then someone would walk up to him and he'd rummage around in a sack he was holding and then pull out a press pass and hand it to them. I felt a little shy of interrupting while he was talking to the stand-in England captain and so waited until their conversation was over before I introduced myself in the hope of being handed the big blue laminated and lanyarded beauty that would get me all the access I would need for the next month.

'Hello there, it's Andrew, isn't it? I'm Miles Jupp from BBC Radio Scotland and the *Western Mail*.'

'Hi there.'

'I believe that you have a press pass for me.'

He looked confused. 'Sorry, what did you say your name was?'

'Miles Jupp. BBC Scotland. I was told that you would have my pass.'

'Miles...Jupp? Actually, I don't think I do.'

'You don't have a pass for me?'

'No, I'm afraid not. I'm pretty sure I'd remember if there was one with your name on it.'

Shit. This must be a mistake. There had to be a pass with my name on it. I'd filled in the forms. I'd sent them in. I'd had an email.

'Are you, er...are you...sure?'

'I'm pretty sure. Let's have a look, shall we?'

And with that he turned the sack upside down and emptied its contents onto the outfield. There were loads of the things, and so I got down on all fours and rummaged through them, desperate to find evidence that Walpole was mistaken. I must have been through the whole lot about four times before I was forced to come to the completely maddening conclusion that he was not in error, and not a single one of these utterly beautiful passes had my name and photo on.

This was a disaster.

Getting one of these passes was the reason I had come to India in the first place. I had to have one. If I didn't have a press pass then that meant that I couldn't automatically get into every Test venue that we played at. It meant I couldn't gain access to the press boxes with their views and facilities. It meant that I would be unable to attend any of the press conferences. It meant that I would be extremely unlikely to meet any players. It meant that I had very little chance of turning my slim, tenuous contacts into genuine journalistic opportunities. It meant I could not easily start my new life as a cricket writer. It meant I was fucked.

When the last of these realisations had passed through my head I stood up again and let out a sigh.

'Who organised your press pass for you?' asked Walpole. 'Was it your work?'

'Well...well...' I stammered. 'I did, I suppose. On their behalf.'

'But your pass would have said "BBC Scotland" on it?'

'It should have done, yes.'

'I think,' he then said very deliberately, 'that it's probably been destroyed.'

'What? Why would anyone destroy it?'

He patiently explained to me about some more of the fallout from the disagreements over the rights issues. At one point during the negotiations it seemed highly likely that the BBC were going to be given no chance of covering the games, and at that moment the Board for Cricket Control in India – who had never seemed particularly laid-back about life in general and business in particular – ordered a member of their staff to pulp every single press pass that had already been assembled which included the letters 'BBC'. When negotiations had then continued and an agreement reached that the BBC could have rights to broadcast coverage of the series, someone at the BBC was asked to reapply for all of the passes again. That someone, it turned out, had been Peter Baxter. And there was no way that he would have reapplied for my pass because he would have not known that I was meant to have one on account of me not actually being a real journalist. As it was, I now knew that even the BBC people who were meant to have passes had not yet been given one, and thus I was in an especially bad position.

'It's really Peter you need to talk to, then,' said Andrew. 'He should be able to locate your pass for you.'

'Right.'

'Let me know if there's anything else I can do for you.'

'I will. Thanks.'

And off he went to talk to someone else, and hand out press passes to real journalists. I tried to take this development on-board stoically, but inside me a panic was growing. I took a deep breath and looked around the ground, taking in the scene. And as I did so, I began to feel a quiet sense of optimism rise within me. Yes, I had travelled a long way in the belief that I would be given a press pass, and yes, I was now 4,000 miles from home and had discovered that the pass I had been promised did not exist. But despite that setback I had got into the ground, and I was – pass or no pass – now standing on the pitch just 30 yards from where the England team were practising. It hadn't been too difficult to get in that position. It was just a matter of following other people's lead, and latching myself onto other more confident and entitled groups at important moments. I could also take some confidence from the fact that the reason that my pass had not materialised was more to do with some rights wrangling and associated administrative errors than with the fact that I was not a real journalist. This being the case I felt that I could share my woes with a few members of the press corps and try and get some advice about what to do next. Ted Corbett from the *Herald* and the *Financial Times* offered some support and sympathy, but also suggested that it may well not even matter. As long as I talked firmly to people and told them that I needed to be in a particular place with the requisite confidence then I could probably get myself anywhere I wanted.

Another journalist expressed a similar sentiment in a rather more old-fashioned way.

'Look, the fact of the matter is you've got a white face. You tell people where you want to go, they'll probably let you.'

'Right.'

'I'm not being racist,' he added without then qualifying his remark in any way.

I chatted with a few others, but then spotted Baxter making his way around the boundary rope positioning effects microphones.

'Peter,' I asked. 'I don't suppose that you have a pass with my name on, do you?'

'No. In fact, I don't have any passes yet. But when I do get them there won't be one with your name on, because I didn't apply for one with your name on.'

'Yes, you see I spoke to Andrew Walpole. And he told me all this pulping business. Sounds like my pass must have got caught up with that lot.'

'I would have happily reapplied for a pass for you, only for some reason no one at BBC Scotland got in touch with me to say that they were sending anyone.'

'Did they not?' I said, feigning surprise. 'That is irritating. But, strictly *entre nous*, not untypical of them.'

'I tell you what, though,' added Baxter, 'they have always been absolute suckers here for a bit of BBC headed notepaper. I've got reams of the stuff if you need it. Try the office that I was dealing with earlier. They might be prepared to give you a temporary pass.'

That sounded like a fine idea, and so calculating from where we'd been before that I could reach the office by walking through the pavilion and turning right, I walked towards the doorway that I'd seen all the players emerging from. Kevin Pietersen was coming the other way as I reached the entrance, all padded up for a session in the nets and performing a vigorous series of stretches and warm-ups as he went.

A soldier blocked my way. 'Where are you going, sir?'

'I'm going through here,' I said, attempting the Ted Corbett method.

'No problem,' said the soldier, acquiescing to my confidence, I hope, and not my skin colour.

I walked through the rather slight pavilion, and then turned right through the anteroom we had been sitting in earlier and climbed up a flight of stairs and knocked on a door marked 'Offices of The Vidarbha Cricket Association'.

'Come in.'

It was a lime green, L-shaped room, with tiled portraits of Indian cricketers of the past displayed on the walls. From the ceiling hung a wicker propeller fan, which hung at a slightly lower height than would normally be considered practical, and which was slowly rotating in a clunking fashion that meant it made far more noise than it generated cool air. Three gentlemen were sitting behind wooden desks piled high with paperwork, and five other staff members scurried around with yet more bits of paper, depositing them in pigeonholes and filing cabinets.

'Can I help?' said the man sitting behind the furthest desk from the door.

'Yes, I've come about a press pass. I'm the cricket correspondent for BBC Scotland.'

He put his hands up in protest. 'I have spoken to the man from the BBC. We are doing everything we can. People will get their passes as soon as possible.'

'Yes, the thing is, I don't think I'm getting one of those passes.'

'Why not?'

'Because I think my name fell off the list somehow.'

'You're not on the list?'

'I don't think so.'

'I have the list here. What is your name, please?'

He rummaged around in his desk drawer, and then triumphantly pulled out a piece of paper with the BBC logo on it, and a number of handwritten names.

'Miles Jupp.'

'Miles…Jupp…No. No, you are not on this list.'

'Yes, I didn't think I would be. There's been some sort of mess up.'

'Why are you not on this list if you work for the BBC?'

'Well, because these people all work for the BBC in London. I work for the BBC in Scotland. They're different organisations really. They work…independently of each other a lot of the time.'

'I see.'

'I think I had a pass ready, but then it got destroyed because it had the letters "BBC" on it. Then the BBC people in London reapplied for the passes again. But they didn't apply for one for me because they didn't know that I'd be coming.'

The man looked a little embarrassed. 'Yes, I think there were some…destructions.'

'So I was wondering if you might be able to issue me with a new pass?'

He sat and pondered this for a while, giving me time to try and read some of the paperwork spread out on his desk upside down. In front of me was a sheet of paper with a list of which hotel room each member of England's touring party was in during their stay in Nagpur. The names Andrew Flintoff and Steve Harmison were bracketed together next to the words 'Adjoining rooms'. Quite why the man I was dealing with needed this sort of information was beyond me. Perhaps he needed to get hold of our players at night and discuss administrative matters with them.

'Can you prove to me that you work for the BBC?'

'Yes. No problem.'

I handed him my sheet of paper, and he read it carefully.

'Yes, this seems okay. Thank you.'

And then, to my horror, he placed my vital bit of BBC Scotland headed notepaper in a file, and put it in his desk drawer.

'Sorry, would it be all right if I kept that?' I said.

'You need this paper?'

'Yes. It's the only proof I have at the moment.'

'Well, I need it for my records.'

'Well, I need it for my work,' I replied. 'Could you not maybe photocopy it?'

He nodded in the direction of a large photocopier in the corner, at which a small queue was formed waiting behind one young man working his way through a small mountain of bundled documents.

'We could photocopy it,' said the man behind the desk. 'But in this case you would have to wait.'

'Then I'll wait, if that's okay.'

I needed that letter. I might have to go through this performance at every ground.

'Please bring me the photocopy when you have it,' he said.

And with that he got up from his desk and disappeared into a back room.

I joined the queue at the photocopier and waited. For half an hour. At this point, the young lad photocopying the bundles of documents looked at me and saw that I was holding just one sheet of paper.

'You are just waiting for to copy one sheet?'

'Yes.'

'This is silly. Pass it to me, please.'

I passed it to him, and he instantly copied it and handed me back the two sheets. I then returned to the furthest desk, to which the fellow I had been dealing with had not yet returned.

'Can I help?' said the man behind the next desk.

'Yes, this man was helping me sort out a press pass. Do you know where he is?'

'What is that paper?'

'It proves that I am a journalist.'

'Could I have it, please?'

I handed him the copy and he too disappeared into the back room. Fifteen minutes later one of them returned with a blank form for me to fill in. He stood and waited for me to fill it in, took it from me and then just as he was turning towards the back room again said, 'And we need a photograph, please. You have a photograph of yourself?'

'No. No, I'm afraid I don't.'

He sighed, and then continued on his way. I had no idea what was happening. Was I being given a pass or not? Should I be celebrating or despairing?

I sat down on a chair and was just stretching my legs out when a third man appeared with a camera.

'You need a photo? Up against the wall.'

He seemed like an efficient sort of man. I looked down the lens, he clicked the button, said, 'Okay, you may sit down again,' and then he too disappeared into the back room. I obeyed and then waited for something, anything else to happen. When nothing did, I took the bold step of knocking on the closed door of the back office.

'Come in.'

It was an almost identical room, with an almost identical scene. There was even someone photocopying a huge bundle of documents.

'Yes?' said the first man I had dealt with, who was kneeling down next to an open filing cabinet drawer.

'Sorry,' I started nervously. 'I just wondered about this pass business. Are you going to give me a pass, or do I…?'

'Yes, yes,' he cut me off. 'Of course. Everything is fine. You must just come back in three hours.'

'Fantastic!' I beamed at him. 'Thank you! Thank you very much,' and practically skipped through the offices and back down the stairs.

*

I did not dare leave the ground for the next three hours, paranoid in case, having been promised a pass, my headed notepaper would suddenly be insufficient for me to regain access. I did not want to risk losing it. I returned to the side of the pitch to find that England's practice session was now finished, and just a few journalists were loitering by the boundary swapping notes and discussing tomorrow's game.

'I heard you had a problem with your pass, Miles,' said one.

'It's all sorted,' I said. 'Just an admin thing.'

'It's not an accreditation problem, then?' he laughed.

'No, of course not,' I laughed nervously. 'Oh no. Everything's completely above board.'

The sun was now so high in the sky that I was finding it hard to cope in the open, and so I retreated into one of the stands, pulled my sun hat down over my eyes and within minutes had fallen fast asleep in the way that members of the MCC tend to do during particularly exciting passages of play. I woke with further time to kill, and strolling around the ground I bumped into a man I recognised from the plane journey. We hailed one another in a rather vague way, but then fell into conversation about the game, and England's team situation. I asked if he too was a journalist.

'No, not really. I do a lot of broadcasting though. Back in England.'

'What sort?'

'Fighter planes.'

'Were you a pilot?'

'No, no. But I'm a bit of an expert in them. The noises really.'

'The noises?'

'Yes, I am an authority on the various noises that different types of fighter planes make. And, as you'd expect, I get asked to give quite a few interviews on the subject.'

'I see.'

Oh dear. I had never considered the matter before, but before he had been speaking very long I had discovered that fighter planes and their associated noises is a subject that I am almost pathologically desperate to avoid hearing about. I would far sooner have been queuing to use a photocopier again.

'I think it surprises a lot of people when they realise just how differently two engines are capable of sounding just owing to a different fuel capacity or alloy type.'

'Mmm,' I said, thinking they were probably more surprised to realise that anybody finds the subject even remotely interesting.

But no sooner had he started giving me a few fascinating titbits about the sheer range of noises to be heard, he then started bitterly bemoaning his treatment at the hands of various broadcast networks who had approached him for interviews.

'I mean these people, they're deranged. You talk to them and they just cut what you say to pieces. I did one recently and I must have given them about twenty-five minutes of absolutely blinding material, and when I listened to the programme they had only used thirty seconds of it. Thirty seconds!'

'Well, yes that does seem a bit…hmmm. You couldn't scratch the surface of the subject in thirty seconds, could you?'

'Personally, on a subject like that, I don't think you could scratch the surface in an hour and a half.'

Oh God. For a brief moment I panicked that he was about to demonstrate this to me, but thankfully at that moment a number of camera crews rounded the corner and started buzzing about asking English people to speak to them. A man with a microphone approached us.

'Are you Barmy Army?'

'I'm not, no,' I said.

'Could we ask you a few questions about them anyway?'

'Well, I don't know really,' I said. 'I don't know all that much about them. They do a lot of charity work I think.'

'I can tell you all about the Barmy Army,' boomed airplane noises man gleefully.

'Ah then, perhaps we could interview you both,' said the man with the microphone.

The camera was turned on and pointed in our direction, and a microphone thrust towards me.

'Tell me, please, what do you think of the Barmy Army?'

'Well, I rather like them,' I said. 'They've been going since the mid-nineties I think…'

At this point Mr Airplane Noises leant into shot and into the microphone.

'And they've been making a bloody racket ever since.'

'You do not like them?' asked the interviewer.

'No, I do not. They are just one of many problems with the world today. I mean look at President Bush. The man's a monster. And yet you're allowing him to visit your country this week. Aren't you? Aren't you?'

'He is coming, I think,' said the man with the microphone. 'But we are making a piece about the Barmy Army. Can you please tell me...'

But our new friend had nothing further to say about the Barmy Army, and burst straight into a long, possibly even rehearsed, rant about the axis of evil. The interviewer nodded politely throughout this and made several hearty attempts at steering the conversation back to the Barmy Army but Mr Blah Blah was by now in the middle of a rather complicated analogy involving suicide bombers and wasn't about to be interrupted. I glanced at my watch and saw that it was the appointed time, excused myself and headed back to the Vidarbha Cricket Association office where the temporary press pass that I had been promised was finally handed to me. I thanked the staff there, and then once outside the office I pumped the air in a brief celebration. A few hours ago, I was on all fours on the edge of the pitch in a state of despair, now I knew that I could definitely go everywhere I wanted to for the duration of the first Test.

But even though I had what I needed for now, I wasn't entirely happy with the situation. The pass I now held in my hand was just a flimsy pink thing with a safety pin sellotaped to the back of it. I had seen the other passes. They were big and beautiful and blue and laminated and had lanyards. With my funny little pink affair, I would stand out from the others. I wanted to get my hands on a proper pass like the one that everybody else had. I wanted to be part of the group, not like the weird boy who turns up at a new school two months after everyone else, has his uniform made out of a different material and has to take all his meals in a hyperbaric chamber.

I returned to the hotel by rickshaw, which I absolutely loved for the first 20 minutes of the journey, until the fumes from the traffic slowly filled up the cabin and I began to cough with regularity. Breathing difficulties aside though, it was not the terrifying experience that I had been led to expect. Instead I found it rather calming. There is something rather relaxing about having absolutely no control whatsoever in the midst of a sea of such hectic and seemingly rule-free traffic. I just sat back and went with the crazed flow.

Chapter Six

Some hours before the first Test match of the series was due to begin I was lying on my unyielding hotel bed with the covers thrown back suffering from both jet lag and a hangover and harbouring a combination of nervous excitement and confusion. The nerves were caused by the task that lay ahead of me. Today I was starting not just a new job, but a new career – one in which I had no experience, for which I was not remotely qualified and on which I was embarking by lying to nearly everyone I met.

The excitement I felt was for purely cricketing reasons. So much had gone wrong for the England party in the few short weeks that they had been on this tour that the team was already verging on the threadbare. From the perspective of a watcher of the game, I always find this sort of position really engrossing. Yes, one always hopes to see your team playing at full strength, but at the same time there is a great sense of fun to be had from watching something a little more cobbled together being flung into the cauldron and then seeing if they can flourish in a death or glory situation. In a play, if someone goes off sick and an understudy has to take over their part, it always forces the remainder of the cast to focus just a little bit more than they might usually just in case anything goes wrong. This had happened during the Christmas pantomime in which I had just been giving my Simple Simon in Aberdeen. I had not been in a 'proper' pantomime before and I was staggered – and some of my colleagues were appalled – at how utterly impossible I found it to concentrate during scenes of any length. Fun as it all was, once the show was up and running and we'd performed it to big houses a couple of times without mishap, I found it harder and harder to give it my full attention. This did not make me an especially helpful or reliable colleague. I would be standing on stage busily compiling a shopping list in my head or thinking about going for a curry after the show, when I would become aware of a strange silence descending on the auditorium, and snap out of my reverie in time to hear Alan McHugh, who played the Dame, saying, 'Simon? Simon? Are we keeping you up? Oh look at this poor, wee laddie, boys and girls. He's in a world of his own.' The audience would laugh, I would slowly get my bearings and then we'd somehow finish the scene before exiting into the wings where Alan would shake his head and call me a 'useless ballbag'.

The night, however, that an understudy was on, and the fairy was played not by Marti Webb, but by a 19-year-old who was still at drama school, and who had only a vague inkling of her lines and was so nervous that I genuinely thought she might pass out, I found that I was fully focused throughout. It was great. In order to be as helpful and supportive to her as possible we all needed to be on our best behaviour, and that meant doing the show as we had rehearsed it and not just dicking about. I hoped that a similar spirit might prevail in our heavily changed England team. Our '70s musical sensation Michael Vaughan was taking time out, and Alastair Cook was leaving the ranks of the dancers to open the batting.

The confusion I felt was caused by the fact that I had just noticed that all of the clothes that I unpacked the day before and then just left piled on the armchair in the corner of the room had been taken away, laundered and were now neatly folded on that very same chair in tidy piles. This was very kind of someone. This had clearly been done with care, attention and expertise. What was confusing me though was that I hadn't asked for anyone to do this. It simply didn't need doing. I had washed everything that I was going to take with me to India before I packed it. Perhaps I hadn't pressed it all, or folded it with any great care, but it was all clean. And I was doubtless going to be charged for it, and goodness only knows how much. For a man whose only certain paid employment had slipped from his grasp the day before with the injury of Simon Jones, this was not just shocking overindulgence, but wildly profligate behaviour – the equivalent of drinking champagne in the queue at the Jobcentre.

On top of all of these emotions, though, I did have some things to be cheery about. Firstly, I had a pass for the game; secondly, I had sent messages to my potential employers detailing that there was no shortage of exciting stuff to write about; and thirdly, breakfast would now be being served downstairs and today I was in no mood to nervily fork a few pastries. I was going to attack the whole buffet with vigour.

But after I had showered, dried and started to dress it became apparent that the unsolicited job on the laundry might not just have been dangerous to my wallet, but also to my health. I pulled on a pair of socks – I always start with the socks, call it a habit or call it exhibitionism – and I was just about to reach for a T-shirt when I felt a burning, searing pain start to spread quickly across the tops of my feet.

Within a few agonising seconds they both felt as if they were on fire. I started peeling the socks off again to take a look at whatever was happening to my feet. Now I do not have, it must be said, particularly attractive feet. They might have very high arches, which is apparently pleasing to the eye from a distance, but up close they appear like a photograph on a poster distributed to warn against the dangers of serving meat that has been stored at the wrong temperature. A friend of mine, the Glaswegian comic Frankie Boyle, once described them, when we were sharing a dressing room, as looking like they belonged to a corpse that had just been dragged from a reservoir by police divers after a three-month search.

The damage to my feet was immediately visible. I had certainly hoped to get a bit of colour when I came to India, but had not intended to start with these particular bodyparts. In the few seconds that they had been in contact with my freshly but weirdly laundered socks the tops of both of my feet had gone dark red and raw. Would every part of my body react in the same way to whatever laundry powder they had used? Had my clothes turned into a time bomb?

I pulled the T-shirt on over my head and it started to have a similar effect, but nowhere near as severe – a manageable itch. I then braved some pants and experienced not so much as a tingle. My feet slowly stopped hurting and returned to their more normal dragged-corpse hue, and so I tried on another pair of socks. The same painful sensations as before returned but this time were even more intense; much hotter, much itchier. I removed that pair of socks again, and once more waited for the pain and redness to subside. What on earth was happening? I was clearly having some sort of strange allergic reaction to the washing powder that the hotel laundry used. But why was it only the tops of my feet? I had pants and a T-shirt on, why didn't my back hurt or my balls? Did they use different detergent for different parts of the body? Or could there be a substance that only my feet were allergic to? Hoping that whatever it was had only contaminated those two pairs of socks, I selected a third pair and, bracing myself, slipped them on.

Oh. My. God. It was as if someone had bought a pair of larval socks from an extremist joke shop and then tucked them into my suitcase. My feet, from toe to ankle, were aflame. Not only was the burning and itching at its most severe yet, but they had been joined by a crawling sensation, the like of which I had never experienced. The whole effect was completely overpowering. Before I could even hope to remove the socks, my whole body was gripped by a spasm of such awesome brutality that I careened into the bed, the chair and the wardrobe in rapid succession as if I was suffering from St Vitus's dance. I had lost all control of my person, and was nothing more than a slave to the pain. Trying to take a handle on the situation I was effectively forced, amidst the twitching and stomping, to chase after my own feet. After twice hitting my head against knee-high objects, I managed with a huge and final effort to catch up with myself, and bring myself down by grabbing hold of my own ankles so that I overbalanced and hit the floor. Having thus effectively completed a rugby tackle of which I was both the perpetrator and the victim, I pinned myself to the ground and, lying hunched on my side, I was able to reach behind me, remove the socks and then gulp down lungfuls of oxygen so that I could breathe some huge sighs of relief.

I rolled over and lay on my back, quite exhausted by this early battle, as if I had just vanquished an invisible intruder. As I caught my breath back, and the pain slowly ebbed from various parts of my body, I wondered if this sort of thing would perhaps be of more interest to Radio Scotland than anything about the cricket? It was certainly worth an email.

Once I felt I could use my feet again, I stood up, hobbled to the bathroom and took a cold foot shower. Then I put on yesterday's dirty socks and felt no discomfort at all other than acute hunger.

Down in the lobby I met a trio of journalists.

'Hey, I have weird question,' I proffered. 'Has anyone else had any trouble with their socks. Mine have been a nightmare.'

The three of them looked at me blankly, until one of them eventually said, 'What?'

I looked down, and saw that they were all wearing flip-flops. 'Nothing,' I said. 'Is breakfast still on?'

'It is, but you haven't got time. The buses are about to leave.'

Flaming Nora. I hurtled back upstairs to my room, which looked like it had just been the scene of a forced kidnapping, grabbed my laptop bag, and then fled downstairs again. The journalists I had just spoken to had disappeared and so I ran out of the lobby and at the bottom of the hotel's drive I could see an elderly and rather small minibus crammed full of disgruntled journalists. Next to its open back door stood a member of the hotel staff who was holding a clipboard.

As I jogged towards the bus I could hear someone shouting from inside. 'Come on. We need to go.'

'Sir, we are waiting for one more gentlemen.'

'No we're not. We're all here.'

'There is one more name on the list,' said the gentleman scanning the clipboard. 'Here we are. We are waiting for Mr Jupp.'

'Who?'

'Mr Jupp, sir.'

'Who the fuck's that?' asked another voice.

'Hi there,' I said. 'I'm Mr Jupp.'

The man with the clipboard put a tick next to my name and I clambered aboard the back of the minibus. Typically the only spare seat was at the front, and the aisle of the bus was already packed with laptop cases, bags of camera equipment and the bare legs of middle-aged men. Everybody sat silently as I picked my way slowly and delicately through them, tripping over things, and squeezing through gaps. A few of them did that particularly British thing of tutting at someone who they could just as easily be helping, giving me that unhelpful 'late for the theatre' look –

'Oh hark at this idiot. Getting caught up in a bomb scare while the rest of us are all trying to enjoy *Hamlet*.'

I reached the empty seat and squeezed into it. Well, perhaps squeezed onto it would be a more accurate description – it turned out to be only half empty. I gently folded myself into a perching position, and then pulled my bulky laptop case onto the half of my lap that was sitting and broke into an instant sweat. I felt incredibly hungry.

The traffic was heavy, the going was slow and the atmosphere was generally hushed. At one point, after we had not moved for nearly a quarter of an hour, Jonathan Agnew looked at his watch despairingly and sighed. 'Forty-five minutes until "Hello, and it really is a glorious morning in Nagpur."'

Across the aisle from me, Simon Hughes was quizzing Mike Selvey.

'Do you always bring a guitar with you on tour?'

'Yes.'

'Do you like Coldplay?'

'I don't.'

Otherwise there was only talk of one thing: everybody agreed that given the weather, and the state of the pitch they had all seen yesterday, then England should definitely bat first if they won the toss. The road around the ground was closed to traffic, and so the closest to the media entrance that we could be dropped was at the other end of the ground behind the pavilion. We unfolded ourselves from the bus, dusted ourselves down, and did a few stretches. The 15 of us looked around for a moment, and then we slung the tools of our trade over our shoulders and began to walk. Men. With our tools. On our way to work. It was like a remake of *Reservoir Dogs* in which everyone wore crumpled linen, suffered from the heat and a spot of dyspepsia was doing the rounds. It felt great though. The first morning of a

Test match. Always a buzz. And me with some sort of press pass attached to my shirt pocket with a safety pin.

Some sort of press pass, indeed. 'What sort of pass is that?' was the question I was asked by the guard at the media entrance.

'It's the one issued by the ground.'

'Why have you not got one like the others?'

I tried to remember that thing about just being firm and saying what you needed.

'Ah,' I said. 'The fact that I am only in possession of this type of pass, is owing entirely to a mix-up.'

'Sorry?'

'A mix-up.'

The guard continued to examine it as if it was the first of its type that he had ever seen. 'I think you must wait until the others have gone in.'

I stood to one side as the other journalists all filed past, vaguely waving their lanyards in the direction of the guards, and flashing me looks as if to say 'Can't you manage to do anything in a straightforward manner?'

I was so envious of them as they all nonchalantly filed through. And I was hungry. Once the last of the real journalists had entered, a group of guards huddled around me and I was inquisitioned about the pass again.

'You got this here? When?'

'Yesterday. From the office.'

'Who gave it to you?'

'I don't know. A man in the office. I'm meant to be here.'

'Okay. You may go in, but you really need a pass like the others.'

I know, I know. I want one. I am hungry.

Finally they let me through and I sprinted up the steps to the press box, anxious in case the seat that I had reserved the day before had been snaffled by anyone else. But it hadn't. There was one empty seat in the whole box, and it was my one – bang in the middle of the front row.

I sat down, and introduced myself to the next chap along, who was about my age.

'Hi there. Miles Jupp. BBC Scotland, *Western Mail*. First Tour.'

'Hi. Paul Coupar. Cricinfo.'

'Have I missed anything?' I asked.

'I don't know,' he said. 'I've just sat down.'

Another older English journalist was standing just in front of us, leaning against the rail that ran along the front of the box, looking out over the pitch. Paul asked him if we had missed anything.

'Just the toss,' he said.

Oh. I recognised that voice. It was that charming Mr Who The Fuck's That? from the minibus.

'Who won?' said Paul.

'England.'

'Oh good,' I said. 'Are we batting?'

'What?' The man looked suddenly incredulous.

'Are we batting?'

'Are we batting?'

'Um, yes.'

He turned towards me crossly, but with one arm pointed out in the direction of the wicket. 'Are we batting? Can you see anything about that pitch out there that would make you want to do anything other than bat first on this wicket?'

'Um...'

'Of course we're fucking batting.' He leant towards me, put his face close to mine and then shook his head vigorously. 'Fucking hell,' he said, disdainfully, before stomping off up to his own seat.

What a delightful man. Writes excellent tabloid copy apparently. I should have given it a minute and then called back to him, 'Sorry, what did you say we were doing again? Was it batting?' I didn't though. I sat there, feeling embarrassed and unwelcome. Everyone around me had a laptop open in front of them and a notebook and pen ready, so I took mine out and waited for play to start, hungrily. I connected my computer to the pressbox's Wi-Fi and checked my email. There was nothing from BBC Scotland, and nothing from the *Western Mail*. A few minutes later, England's opening batsmen came out of the pavilion, and I started to clap enthusiastically. Then I looked around, and realised that I was applauding alone. Apparently one does not clap in the press box.

*

Regardless of the antics of Mr Who The Fuck's That? and my own display of inexperience I was still able to enjoy the morning session. The view from where I was sitting was amazing, England didn't disgrace themselves and the other people sitting near me were friendly. On the stroke of one o'clock as the players were leaving the field, trays of lunch appeared and were handed out by cheerful and enthusiastic attendants. I ate the lot at double speed, and then checked my email again. Still nothing. I would just have to keep trying and to keep waiting.

By three in the afternoon, however, I had become incredibly uncomfortable. I was finding the heat more and more unbearable, and the sun was now at such a point in the sky that it was beaming down onto the pitch, reflecting off it and then coming up at me from underneath like a solar bouncer. If the sun had just been coming from directly above I would probably have been fine with my sun hat. But the sun's glare was attacking me from an angle that would have been very hard to defend oneself from without being dressed in a ruff, which was hardly the sort of inconspicuous look that I was aiming for.

It was at this point that I realised why this was the only seat in the box that hadn't been reserved. Because due to some strange architectural quirk in the buildings at the other end of the ground, and as a result of the shape and positioning of the roof above my head, only the occupant of my seat suffered in this way. Everybody sitting behind me or immediately either side of me was happily in the shade, whereas I, and I alone, was being bruléed. I spent the rest of the day's play with my face practically in my laptop, just my eyes peeping over the top of the screen like a squinting ninja, or at least a strange, pink man with profound difficulties.

*

England had laboured to 246–7 when the day's play finished at around six o'clock, and everyone flooded from the press box and dashed around the outside of the ground to a function room in the pavilion where the press conference was to take place. A table with some microphones on it had been set up in front of a large hoarding emblazoned with the names of various sponsors. The room was packed with journalists of all persuasions. Some people were perched on chairs, others were kneeling on the floor in front of the table. I had just joined the huddle at the back near the door, when Andrew Walpole came in, leading Alastair Cook who had made his debut that day and scored a very creditable 60. As soon as he sat down at the table behind the row of microphones, many of the people kneeling leant forward holding out Dictaphones at arm's length, leaving our young debutant as the nervous figure at the centre of a modern-day Adoration of the Magi.

Even from my vantage point at the back of the room I felt close to the action. This was the sort of access I had been desperate for. What I now was desperate for was summoning up the courage to ask a question in this situation. People fired all sorts of queries at him. How does it feel? Was this a baptism of fire? Is this what you dreamt of as a child? This last sort of question has always seemed disingenuous. Playing your favourite sport for your country is the sort of thing you daydream about, not dream. I would have liked to hear someone answering this sort of enquiry with genuine honesty: 'No. I didn't dream about playing for England when I was a child. I was usually being chased around a weird version of my school by an evil BA Baracus.' These days that is almost exactly how Graeme Swann answers questions of that type.

But after ten minutes of exactly the sort of thing you would expect, a fresh line of questioning led to Alastair Cook suddenly revealing a piece of information that excited me greatly. It turned out that his mother is from quite near Swansea. This was music to my ears: he had provided me with an all-new Welsh angle. Fantastic. Never mind Simon Jones, I could tell the readers of the *Western Mail*, there's a brand-new Welshman to look out for. Or someone who might be a quarter Welsh. Or something.

As soon as the conference was over I hurried back to the press box and laboured over a report of the day's play with as much of a Welsh angle as I could manage. I should have probably made it sound even more Welsh – 'Bore dar from Nagpur, isn't it? England have been saved, not for the first time, by a Welshman. Alastair Cook, WHOSE MOTHER IS FROM SWANSEA, played out of his skin at short notice and was generally utterly marvellous. If I was a druid, this would definitely put me in a choral mood for a bit of close harmony work…bloody Margaret Thatcher etc.' – but that sort of thing, I felt, would be less likely to be published.

I read through the real report several times, and then sent it to the sports desk at the *Western Mail* before firing off an email

to my contact at BBC Scotland asking if they'd be at all interested in a broadcast about how an injury-hit England were
faring. I also sent a message to the Board for Cricket Control in
India detailing the confusion regarding my application for a press
pass and asking if, given everything had been resolved with the
BBC, perhaps they would like to send me a new one.

By the time I had finished my first day's work as a cricket
journalist, the press box was nearly empty, but I shared a ride
home with Simon 'The Analyst' Hughes. He was a nice fellow,
although a bit more serious than I had expected him to be from
his books. That said, in his books he claims to have just been
a journeyman cricketer, whereas in reality he was very highly
regarded indeed. He has an excellent talent for explaining cricket
and making it accessible. He told me about previous tours to
India that he had been on, both as a player and journalist, and
said that cricket was losing its popularity in India. To illustrate
his point he mentioned a game that he'd played in for a Christ-
ians in Sport XI in the '80s. It was an inconsequential fixture but
40,000 people turned up to watch. That was at least four times
as many as had turned up to watch the opening day of this Test.
Oddly, whilst many of us had squeezed into something the size
of a camper van that morning, Hughes and I had a whole coach
to ourselves. Logic did not seem to be a consideration.

*

At dinner that evening I was in a buoyant mood, feeling confident that my Welsh angle would guarantee publication and that
BBC Scotland would find England's current situation interesting
enough to warrant a little report. Jonathan Agnew and Peter
Baxter joined Kevin and me and they all told more stories about
players suffering from stomach troubles. Baxter told a delightful
one about an accident that befell Bruce French just as he was
squatting down to keep wicket. Agnew then told a story about

Alf Gover realising he was about to explode just as he was running in to bowl that made me laugh so hard that beer came out of my nose. Apparently as he was approaching his delivery stride, he became horribly aware of how desperately he needed the loo and so just carried on sprinting in the direction of the pavilion. 'Where are you going?' someone shouted. 'I've got to go to the loo,' he shouted back. 'But you've still got the ball,' they wailed. 'I just can't stop!' he yelled and disappeared for a lengthy and presumably uncomfortable spell, before finally coming back to resume his over.

Chapter Seven

When I arrived at the press box the next day I immediately checked my inbox to see if there was any response from the *Western Mail* about the report I had sent them. There was nothing from them, and nor indeed was there anything from BBC Radio Scotland. I looked around the website of the *Western Mail* for any mention of cricket but without success. This in itself was not necessarily a disaster. It was quite possible that not everything that went into the paper went up on the website. And it was also quite possible that my report had been printed in the paper, but that the email I had sent it attached to had gone unacknowledged. The sports desk in the hours prior to publication was probably a busy enough place already without emails having to be sent to all contributing journalists telling them just how super they were, as if they were actors.

It would still be very early in the morning in Britain, and so I would wait until four in the afternoon by which time their offices would be up and running and it might be easier to get in touch with them. Meanwhile I would continue making notes and send another report, perhaps giving it even more of a Welsh emphasis.

I had applied generous portions of suncream before I left the hotel, and also packed some sunglasses so that I could stand up to the afternoon's sun without sustaining lasting retinal damage. I put my laptop away to avoid the temptation of checking for news every five minutes, and instead opened my notebook and prepared to watch another day's cricket.

The previous day had ended rather limply for England, but that morning they fought back brilliantly, to the surprise of many of the press box's incumbents. There had been a lot of grumbling about the ways that so many of England's players had got out the day before. Special disdain had been reserved for the debutant Ian Blackwell, whose dismissal was particularly soft. There had been only 15 minutes of play left the night before when he had flung his bat at a wide ball without moving his feet and dragged the ball back onto his stumps. 'The thing about Ian Blackwell,' I had heard Mike Dickson of the *Daily Mail* proclaim in the minibus that morning, 'is that the stairs don't seem to go all the way up to the loft.'

This was a different story though. Our not-out pair were Paul Collingwood and Matthew Hoggard, and whilst you would have to be deranged to the point of no return to describe either of them as possessing flair, they set about their task with great diligence. The stodginess of their batting was greeted with sighs from some quarters, but to me it looked like Collingwood seemed to be playing with quiet intent. Given the state of our innings, I'd rather that they spent serious time accumulating the runs we needed rather than just stood there trying to spank everything, like a pair of hung-over Ian Blackwells taking swipes at an imaginary bee. When Hoggard eventually nibbled at a leg cutter from Sreesanth and was caught behind, their partnership of 20 had taken 70 almost totally excitement-free balls. But then Steve Harmison strode in looking uncharacteristically sparky and set about the Indian bowling attack with the nonchalance of a man playing an arcade game.

He cover drove Sreesanth for four, top edged a hook for a single and then proceeded to sweep Kumble to the boundary as well. Then he struck Sreesanth for boundaries through cover and gully. He brought up England's 300 with another four from a front-foot pull. When Harbhajan Singh was brought on to calm things down, Harmison responded by attempting to reverse sweep his first ball. Meanwhile Collingwood had eased his score into the seventies and then danced down the pitch to loft Singh for six and bring up a 50 partnership from just 58 balls. Harmison had contributed 31 of them. Two overs later Harmison danced down the track to Singh and lofted him for four over mid-on. He attempted it a second time and was stumped by a mile. His 39 runs had been full of attacking strokes and he had struck seven boundaries. More importantly he had helped take the score from 267–8 to a much stronger 327–9.

His wicket brought about the entrance of a man whom the Indian public were absolutely desperate to see. From the moment that Monty Panesar had been named in England's touring party, his fame had spread quickly throughout India. The left-arm spinner from Luton was the first Sikh ever to be selected to play for England and in so doing had achieved immediate popularity with the Indian public. As he took his first steps onto the field as a Test player, he received a booming and affectionate reception from the crowd. And the Indian crowd weren't just excited to see Monty arrive at the crease because of his heritage, but also because of his far-reaching reputation as a batsman of almost unparalleled woefulness.

Over the years, cricket crowds have come to realise that watching Monty Panesar walk out to bat is a lot like seeing a chat-show host introduce Johnny Rotten or Crispin Glover; whatever followed would almost certainly not be good, but it wouldn't be boring either.

And yet the gods were with Monty that morning. What he was doing out there certainly wasn't attractive, but it was working. He eventually stayed at Collingwood's side for over an hour. Collingwood, for his own part, farmed the strike cleverly. He had taken his score to 93 when Panesar survived two enormously close appeals from Kumble and these provided Collingwood with the impetus he needed. In the next over he hit Singh for a huge six over mid-off to take him to 99, and then brought up his century by chipping over mid-on for three. As he removed his helmet, and raised his bat heavenward, applause broke out behind me in the press box. I looked back and saw that it was only the Indian press who were clapping. England took lunch on a respectable 360–9.

During the lunch interval, more cardboard trays of food were handed out to us by some local volunteers, and most members of the press corps took the opportunity to stretch their legs and hurl a bit of banter about. I chatted to a chap called Rod Gilmour who had introduced himself earlier. He was in India working on behalf of a cricket website for whom his job mainly consisted of interviewing a series of cricketing legends (largely composed of the Sky commentary team). It was good to chat to someone of a comparable age, and about whom I also perceived a slight sense of feeling aloof from the main body of the press corps. Still, at least he had stuff to do; our conversation ended because he had to 'go and do an interview with Athers'. As he delivered this information he rolled his eyes slightly, as if this was a hassle he could well have done without. I nodded sympathetically as if constantly having to do that sort of shit was beginning to get on my tits too. After he had gone, I switched my laptop on to steal a glance at my email. There was still no word from either of my potential employers.

After lunch Collingwood lofted Pathan's first ball for six. The 50 partnership for the last wicket came off 82 balls of which Monty's contribution was a weighty 5. But with our total just seven short of 400, Monty was finally trapped LBW by a yorker from fellow debutant Sreesanth. The last-wicket partnership had been worth 66, and Collingwood had shown some incredible strength in his knock of 134 not out which included 17 boundaries.

In the third over of India's reply, Hoggard had Sehwag caught by Pietersen at short cover. I performed a solitary loud clap before remembering my place and changing my expression back to one of utter blankness.

Dravid came in and demonstrated the legendary defensive technique that has earned him the nickname 'the wall' and tea was taken at 41–1, after which things began to drift, largely in India's direction. By close of play India had made 136–1 with Jaffer 73 not out and Dravid unbeaten on 40.

The start of the final session had coincided with the time that, by my reckoning, the *Western Mail* and BBC Scotland should have opened for business. England may well have been slaving in the field for little reward, but my own frustration was starting to spiral out of control. I had still failed to receive responses from either of my potential employers. What I really wanted was some sort of response to yesterday's report before I commenced one for today. With about half an hour of play remaining in the day, the noise of fingers tapping on keyboards began to fill the press box as journalists shook themselves awake to start typing up their copy for the day. Not wishing to look like a man with nothing to do, I too began work on a piece.

Cricket: Report of Day 2,
First Test England v India,
from Miles Jupp in Nagpur

England fought back hard in the morning and afternoon of the second day's play at Nagpur to give themselves a good chance in the match. The star of the morning was Paul Collingwood who scored his first century in his sixth Test, continuing the run of good form that he showed in Pakistan and doing a great deal to demonstrate that he is more than just a handy one-day player. Today he showed the discipline that some of the more established batsmen had lacked slightly in yesterday's slightly below par performance.

Starting the day on 246–7, Collingwood and Hoggard batted with quite considerable care and attention – the sort of brilliant resistance that you might more readily associate with the Welsh...

I somehow managed to fit three more references to the Welsh in another 700 words, and then closed my laptop to let the article fallow while I was at the press conference. Hopefully I might come back with some juicy titbits to Welsh-up an otherwise all too English sort of a day.

*

Everybody had only just squeezed into the sterile function room for the press conference when the Indian team's press officer came in to announce that no Indian players were available to speak to the journalists. This prompted an immediate and angry rumbling from certain sections of the Indian press corps. 'Every bloody time,' one shouted. The press officer instantly looked rather embattled and appealed for calm.

'I understand you are not happy,' he said. 'I will try and find someone who wants to talk to you.'

The Indian journalists continued to grumble about the man's various inadequacies for several minutes until he returned a few minutes later in the company of an Indian player who I did not recognise. The pair then went and sat behind the row of microphones and scattered Dictaphones looking a little uneasy. Clearly the press officer had gone into the Indian dressing room and just grabbed the first man he could get hold of, regardless of whether or not they might have anything to say. In fact, whoever this person was, now that he was actually here the Indian press had very little to ask him.

'Does anyone have any questions, please?' pleaded the press officer on the player's behalf.

The English journalist Stephen Brenkley put his hand up and began to ask a rather earnest and specific question involving the man's playing career, and at that instant most of the other English journalists burst out laughing. I looked around the room confused as to the cause of this jollity. It was that hysterical, mocking, relieved, braying laugh that British men often let out that means: 'At this moment in time I am just so very glad not to be you.' It was the laugh that follows someone else's painful embarrassment: the fat man who slips on the ice; the lad who drops his glass in a pub; the guy on the stag weekend who gets a paintball in the arse. People were falling about and clapping their hands together in this instantly tribal atmosphere. Someone went 'That's not who he is.' Others were calling 'Keep up!' Clearly what poor Brenkley had done, was fail to correctly identify who this Indian player was. I, for one, fully empathised with him, as I was completely unaware who he was either. In fact, despite observing the behaviour of the rest of the room, I still couldn't quite figure out what was going on. Some people were shaking their heads and muttering 'Laxman!' others were giggling and saying 'Jaffer!' Instead of asking someone what the joke was, I cowardly stuck a big, shit-eating grin on my face and let out what I hoped would sound like a chummy and understanding laugh of my own and joined in the mirth.

And I was still standing hand on hips and chortling along a few moments later, when I heard a gentle voice in my ear.

'Hey, Miles, what's just happened?'

I turned around and saw to my horror that Andrew Walpole had entered at the back of the room and was now standing next to me alongside Paul Collingwood, our batting hero of the day.

'Hi, Andrew,' I said brightly, but ignoring the question.

'What's just happened?'

'Sorry, what?'

'Why is everybody laughing?' said Collingwood, slowly as if acting as an interpreter.

'W-w-well,' I stammered, and then pointed out Brenkley and the player, 'He doesn't know who that is.' And then I chuckled dismissively, as if everybody knew.

Collingwood absorbed this information coolly. But Walpole simply said, 'Who is it?'

'It's...well it's...it's...I don't know, Andrew. Is it...Laxman, maybe?'

Collingwood looked at me. 'It's Jaffer,' he said.

'Right,' I said. And then added a meek little 'well batted', which only added to the confusion.

Collingwood then took either Laxman or Jaffer's place at the table and said nothing that would interest the people of Scotland or Wales, and so I returned to the abandoned press box to send the piece that I had written earlier. Where everybody else had disappeared to, I had no idea. But as I was reading my report through for the second time, the rain clouds which had been threatening the ground for much of the day began to break, and by the time I had finished and packed up, the rain was coming down hard. I headed out onto the streets to look for any other journalists who might offer a way back to the hotel. There was no sign of any journalists, nor of the bus laid on by our hotel, neither the tiny van we had crammed into on the first morning, nor the one more akin to a train carriage from *The Titfield Thunderbolt* which Simon Hughes and I had shared the day before. It was just me, dressed in linen trousers and a sleeveless shirt, with my laptop case slung over my shoulder, standing in a rainy street whilst the odd bicycle skidded by in either direction. A security guard popped his head through the gate by which I had exited the ground, looked up and down and then started to lock the gate.

'Taxi?' I said to him, and he laughed and shrugged his shoulders. 'It is raining,' he added helpfully, with a cheery smile.

I stood in the rain for a few minutes not knowing what to do. I didn't even know the address of the hotel, just its name and the fact that it was quite near the airport. I began to walk, whether towards or away from the hotel I did not know, for ten minutes, maybe more. I had a pair of light, absorbent shoes on and no socks. A lone motorised rickshaw materialised in the gloom ahead of me without any lights on, but I leapt into the road and waved my hands around frantically. The driver stopped and turned on a light.

'Please,' he said. 'My pleasure.'

I climbed into the back and gave him the name of the hotel. He performed a U-turn and then sped off in the opposite direction. It was now quite dark, and as we weaved our way into the denser traffic away from the ground, the rain became heavier. The driver turned round to check the name of the hotel again. 'Airport?' he asked, as if I'd rather go there.

The laws of traffic in India seem to favour whoever honks loudest, whether you are at what would normally be a level-crossing or a busy set of crossroads complete with sets of entirely arbitrary traffic lights. This enables vehicles of all manners and sizes to compete, both undertaking and overtaking, in one huge and terrifying fury. It was into just such a storm of traffic that my driver headed at great speed as the rain continued to lash down.

After a short distance he stopped very suddenly without warning and got out, leaving me feeling a little vulnerable in the right-hand lane. Then he reappeared on the other side of the windscreen, mopping it and waving at me. He jumped back, checked the name of the hotel once more and screeched off with just the faintest hint of a skid. Something then started flashing and he rounded a corner and stopped to queue for petrol at a reasonable 50 rupees a litre. By now it was pouring very heavily and he honked the horn loudly at someone about two metres from us who may or may not have been thinking about queue-jumping. The attendant pumped in the petrol and we roared off again as the driver turned back to shout something at me. It sounded like 'airport'.

The further we drove, the heavier the rain became. I started to get splashed by more and more passing cars and motorbikes, and then steadily dripped on by the rain which was now beginning to trickle through the roof of the rickshaw and onto my shoulders. I pulled my sun hat as firmly onto my head as I could and clung to my laptop. All I could see now was water and blurred lights as we dodged more collisions and sped across fly-overs. There are many signs up by the sides of roads advising of the dangers of speedy driving: 'Life is more valuable than speed' reads one. They'd have to place an unbelievably high value on life if that is true.

It occurred to me that it might be worth taking some pictures with my digital camera to see if anything good came out in the incredible conditions. I hung on to my laptop with one arm and snapped away. We were forced to make a stop at one point and a motorbike pulled alongside, driven by a soaking man with an equally drenched lady clinging on behind. They grinned at me in my rickshaw so I asked if I could take a photo. They smiled beautifully for me, and I took it with the flash. As they revved off, I checked the picture on the camera. It was a beautiful shot of two Indians with delightful smiles on a motorbike in a downpour, snuggling up to my thumb.

I had to put the camera away shortly after that as I needed an extra hand to cling on for dear life. Rainwater was now liberally splashing down on the driver and me and the traffic was becoming more panicked. The driver pulled over and leapt into the back with me, not for his own comfort but for mine: he was pulling down the rolled-up plastic drapes that help to keep the rain out. We both struggled with them in the soaking wet but our efforts finally paid off and we got them fixed down. As we set off I realised that I was now still getting just as wet, but I could no longer see anything. I was terrified; I just didn't know of what.

I peeped out to see where we were only to find that we were riding between some flimsy railings on a bridge on one side and a bus on the other. I couldn't look any more, so I just had to sit back. Then there was a cacophony of horns and screeching and we swerved violently before ploughing on. The driver looked back, not to check the name of the hotel this time, but to see if I was actually still there. I gave him the thumbs up to show that I was all right. 'It is raining,' he shouted back.

I still wasn't exactly sure whether or not the driver knew precisely where I wanted to go. He knew, I could sense, that it was somewhere near the airport, but I still felt it was my responsibility to handle the nitty-gritty. I started to keep a look-out for any memorable features in the vicinity of the hotel, but as I was struggling for a decent view from the back with the rain flaps tied down, I leant forward into the driver's cabin for a better one.

He was surprised by this. 'Are we there?' he asked, as if he were the passenger.

'I'm just looking out for the hotel,' I replied.

'We are not near it yet,' he said. Just at that moment I glanced up and saw the Hotel Quality whizzing past on the other side of the road.

'That was it!' I shouted.

He stopped and pointed at my hotel. 'Here?' He seemed disappointed by my choice of accommodation, but with the requisite honking and bravery he executed the necessary U-turn and then turned up the hotel's drive and braked hard outside the front door before helping me out.

'How much is this by the way?'

'A thousand,' he replied.

'A thousand?' I asked. This was easily twice more than I was told anyone had paid previously.

'Five hundred?' he offered. I agreed.

But rather than accept the deal as over, he wrong-footed me by coming in with an even lower price.

'One hundred?' he said. It was his final offer. I handed him a note, and then squelched into the lobby. I checked the contents of my wallet before pocketing it, and saw that despite my rigorous haggling I had handed him a note for one thousand anyway. My wallet, in common with everything that I was stood up in, was soaked through. Before heading upstairs to change into dry clothes I put my face up against the window of the dining room and bar across the lobby. Inside an incredibly clean and dry-looking Sky commentary team were sharing a bottle of wine.

*

I showered and changed, and then thought about my dinner. I started to make my way to the rooftop restaurant on the fourth floor, but by the time I got to the landing of the third floor, I could see water streaming down the stairs. I continued on the off chance, but was met at the door of the restaurant by two damp and disappointed-looking waiters. The roof of the restaurant was, it turned out, permeable.

'So we are closed,' said one of the waiters, sadly.

'It rain,' said the other. They were both right.

I returned to the bar downstairs where the Sky legends had now moved on to dinner, and I chose a table on my own and settled down with my novel. Kevin then appeared and plonked himself down.

'How are you getting on with the *Western Mail*?' he asked.

'It's going okay.' I said. 'Quite slow, I suppose.'

'BBC Scotland?'

'They don't appear to be all that interested at the moment. It'll pick up though, I'm sure.'

'Course it will.'

I concealed the complete extent of my work frustration, trying to suggest that it was merely a little bit annoying at times. Yet the reality was that I was starting to get extremely nervy about the utter lack of feedback. My response to my problems was to keep ordering bottles of cold beer and knocking them back as fast as I could. On top of the depression and all the beer, there was a live band playing from a somewhat eclectic set-list at a volume that might just have been acceptable in a room seven times the size of the one in which we were attempting to eat. The meal itself was disastrous, with no two dishes arriving at the same time and several items having to be ordered twice over the din of the band.

'Could I have this but with lamb, please?' I asked.

'Sorry, sir?'

'With lamb, please.'

'You want it with lamb, sir?'

'Yes, please.'

'There is no lamb, sir.'

'Oh, then what is there?'

'Mutton, sir.'

'Mutton would be lovely.'

'Sorry, sir?'

'Mutton would be lovely,' I said.

'Lovely, sir?'

'MUTTON!' I shouted, struggling to make myself heard above a synthesised version of 'Smoke On The Water'. 'I WOULD LOVE SOME MUTTON.'

The food, the shouting and too much beer being poured into a dehydrated system quickly began to take its toll, as did a seven-minute version of 'Happy Birthday'. I suddenly felt crazed. 'I think I'm about to be extremely ill,' I said to Kevin, and then flung a few notes in his direction and bolted upstairs to the obscurity and privacy of my bathroom where I rid myself of all that I had just consumed in one clinical sitting. I rang Rachel and managed to get through to her just as she had reached the counter of the university shop in Edinburgh, a million miles away back in my own world. We arranged to speak the next day before hanging up, whereupon I instantaneously broke into a gentle sob.

*

The atmosphere in the bar and restaurant was considerably calmer when I returned there the next morning for breakfast. The boozy smell that had hung in the air the night before had disappeared and so too, thankfully, had Nagpur's loudest synthesised covers band, even if one or two of their more striking interpretations still echoed around my skull. I took a bowl of porridge and a plate with a few sausages on it to a corner of the room, and also picked up copies of several local newspapers that had been laid out for our delectation.

Each of the papers carried a version of one particular story which served as a useful reminder that when English people go abroad – just as our teachers would tell us before school trips – we are all ambassadors. Yet one English cricket fan had failed to remember this key advice and succeeded in besmirching our reputation. It transpired that the fellow in question had visited one of Nagpur's restaurants for dinner one evening, and in addition to sampling the local cuisine he had also poured enough wine and beer down his neck to sedate all of the members of the Happy Mondays. He had somehow managed to return to his hotel, and once there he realised that he was no longer sure of the whereabouts of the camera that he was certain he had brought with him to the restaurant earlier in the evening. Instead, however, of then chalking it up as a casualty of drinking and then sensibly passing out in a pool of his own piss and effluent, he returned to the restaurant and accused two waiters of stealing his camera. Then he called the police to report them, before returning once more to his hotel.

So far, so undignified. But then two mornings later the man had been going through his luggage and happened upon his missing camera in, as the paper told me, 'the pocket of his Bermuda'. To his credit, our English friend immediately got in touch with the police to inform them of his error, but the Indian legal system had already leapt into action with surprising alacrity in response to his inebriated finger wagging; the waiters had been arrested, and were appearing in court that very morning. Thus the accuser had to turn into a saviour, and made it to the courthouse just in time to sign an affidavit stating that the two hapless waiters were not responsible for the imagined theft. They were granted bail, and the English cricket fan who had brought the camera to the court with him to prove that it had not in fact been stolen, then had his camera confiscated by the police. In the circumstances it might have been more reasonable for the judge to call for the words 'hopeless ballbag' to be written onto his forehead in henna ink, and thus remain there for the duration of his stay.

The porridge that morning was a delight, but the sausages turned out to have been a rather cocky choice for a man whose dinner had passed almost straight through him just hours earlier, and for the second meal in succession I found myself sprinting from the table in an ungainly fashion for a hastily scheduled meeting with my bathroom toilet.

Much as I relished the opportunity to refamiliarise myself with the spartan surroundings of my en-suite lavatory, the quality time that we shared together cost me the opportunity of taking my place on the journalists' bus to the ground. Instead I shared a cab to the ground with a brace of cricket fans. Peter and Angela were a charming couple from Preston who told me that their entire life was organised around being able to go abroad to watch England play as often as they could. These sort of fans make a huge difference to England's fortunes overseas, and I hope it means a lot to the team that even when they travel to play in the warm-up games or Tests that have been staged in remote indus- trial cities which don't cater at all for holiday makers, they can still rely on an army of loyal supporters to be there willing them on.

After we had paid for the cab and bid each other goodbye, I watched them walking off in the same direction as other groups of supporters dressed in replica England shirts and it dawned on me that I envied them. I was going to trudge off to spend a day in the businesslike and sober environs of the press box whilst they were going to be surrounded by other cheering fans who did crazy things like clapping.

*

That morning's cricket was certainly worthy of wild applause. In the third over of the day Hoggard trapped Dravid leg before with a ball that came back a long way and in so doing brought Tendulkar to the crease at 140–2. The response he gets from a home crowd for simply entering the arena is phenomenal, and a complete contrast to even the most devoted of England fans at our more raucous venues. Even Billy Connolly wouldn't receive that sort of response taking to the stage in his native Glasgow. And yet when Tendulkar got off the mark by flicking Hoggard through midwicket the crowd managed to go up a gear, errupt- ing into the sort of roar that a messianic Bob Geldof might expect when taking a bow at Live 8.

Hoggard then got one to swing away from Jaffer who was caught in the slips by Flintoff for 81. VVS Laxman, who may or may not have been the star of the previous day's press conference, made less impact out in the middle; he was adjudged LBW first ball to a full-length in-swinger from Hoggard that struck him on the pad before he had even moved. India had slipped from an overnight score of 136–1 to 149–4, and the England players were looking fired up.

By the drinks break India had made just 15 runs in an hour. It had been a hugely encouraging start to the day for England, but less of one for me, as still nothing in my inbox suggested I might be any closer to doing some actual journalism.

Soon afterwards Panesar took his first Test wicket, and what a wicket it was: Sachin Tendulkar got half forward to a ball that went straight on and became the third LBW victim of the day. In his excitement Monty sprinted so far that the team ended up forming their celebratory huddle somewhere near third man. That brought the big-hitting Dhoni to the crease, but he was soon caught behind attempting to slog Flintoff over mid-on. At lunch India were 190–6, and the morning had belonged to England.

Whilst I was delighted by Panesar's first scalp, I was just as thrilled for Matthew Hoggard who had looked at his absolute best and torn through a talented Indian middle order in spectacular fashion. Despite being capable of such feats he has always appeared to possess a completely unfussy attitude towards his cricket. It is said that he dislikes cities and that his favourite pastime is walking his dogs on the Yorkshire moors, his hair doubtless flapping in the breeze in strict rhythm with that of his dogs' ears. He is not a man to complain, rather he quietly gets on and does his best to do whatever is asked of him. That morning he had run in hard and, possibly benefiting from the overnight rain, had swung the ball into and away from the batsman.

*

At the start of the afternoon session Hoggard had Pathan caught at slip by Flintoff stretching a long way to his right. It was Hoggard's fifth wicket of the innings and meant that thus far his figures for the day were 8–6–6–4. We then endured a hugely frustrating partnership between Anil Kumble and Kaif. It was Kumble who saved the follow-on by edging Hoggard though gully for four and was then very nearly caught at cover after failing to pick the slower ball.

After the players had taken drinks Harmison got Kumble to edge one behind only for Geraint Jones to somehow drop it. It was impressive in a way, as it was the sort of chance that looked like it would have been much harder to put down than to cling on to. Perhaps this is a genuine problem for the skilful. In much the same way as people said that Les Dawson could only play the piano that badly because he was capable of playing so well, maybe more skill and attention went into Geraint Jones's frequent spills than we ever knew. Whatever the reasons, it would prove costly. Just prior to tea, Bell was brought on for a single over during which Kaif secured his and Kumble's 50 partnership and then, next ball, brought up his own half-century.

Throughout their partnership the heat had grown steadily more stifling and the roars from the crowd ever more deafening, leaving me with a thumping headache and a pronounced sense of discomfort. The middle seat in the front row offered, I knew, no protection from the sun's heat or glare. But on this occasion it was hotter and brighter than before and I could feel my face and the backs of my retinas being scorched. During the tea interval I climbed to the top of the stand and rang Rachel. I was standing in a rare shaded spot behind the *Test Match Special* box and from there I could see the commentators chatting away breezily, while back in Edinburgh she was listening to them on her radio. Somehow, despite being continents apart, this brought us closer together. After I had rung off she sent me a text saying that she had been waiting for my call all morning, which lifted my spirits further. It is very important to be missed by the people you're missing.

After tea Ian Blackwell, Monty and Flintoff received some fairly harsh treatment, and Kumble made it to 50, which the Indian crowd hailed with considerable glee. Finally Harmison struck as Kumble reached for one outside his off stump and offered a straightforward chance to Cook at slip, who accepted it gratefully. It had been a highly impressive innings of 58 by Kumble. He had scored just nine when Jones had put him down, and the pair had added 128. Moments later, in his forty-second over of the innings, Panesar bowled Kaif for 91 with a fantastic delivery which dipped, gripped, turned sharply and clipped the off stump. It was the sort of delivery that gets people talking and it certainly caused a frisson of excitement to spread through the press box, which showed just how special a ball it was. Frustrating as the partnership had been, India's score of 322–9 at the close of play still represented a good effort by England.

*

Matthew Hoggard had been put forward to take journalists' questions at the press conference, and I found his performance thoroughly entertaining. He just laughed at any questions he thought a bit ridiculous and made it politely clear that he didn't really enjoy this sort of fuss. Someone congratulated him on achieving his best bowling figures on the subcontinent, and he looked genuinely surprised to discover that this was the case, although appeared pleased by the news. He was also asked how he thought Panesar had got on, and he lavished praise on him. 'In fact,' he said, 'he played so well that it really should have been him sitting here talking to you instead of me.' This made Andrew Walpole, who was sitting alongside him in a chaperoning capacity, laugh a great deal.

But while Hoggard may have been entertaining he had failed to disclose anything that might be of interest to a newspaper only really prepared to carry stories with a Welsh flavour. Although I had taken notes diligently thus far, and noted down all sorts of quotations at the press conference, I didn't relish the thought of sitting down in the press box again and tapping out an 800-word report packed with a succession of tortuous Welsh crowbars – especially as I had received no clear indication that anyone was actually bothering to read them.

Instead, I went and stood behind the pavilion and rang Rachel's father at their family home in Wales.

'Hello?'

'Miles, is that you? Hello! How are you? Is India treating you well?'

'Well, the people of India have been delightful, yes.'

'And how is your book?'

Why did he want to know what I was reading?

'My book?' I asked.

'The book you went to India to write?'

'Oh yes, my book,' I said, my brain clicking quickly into the right gear. 'Heaps of material, very happy. Now, erm, it's actually the people of Wales I'm worried about.'

'Oh?'

'Yes, the thing is I've been sending bits and pieces to the sports desk at the *Western Mail* and I don't really seem to be getting much of a response. I don't suppose you might give them a gentle prod and ask if any of my stuff has been heading in the right direction?'

'Right. I'll speak to them. Call me back in ten minutes.'

Whilst Charles went off to speak to the sports desk, I paced nervily up and down behind the pavilion, while the minutes slowly passed. As I stomped about and chewed my nails, a succession of Indian soldiers exited the pavilion and started requesting that the large crowd of fans who had gathered there begin to move back a little. I too was asked to move away, and thus found myself at the front of the crowd who had gathered, it turned out, to get a glimpse of the teams leaving the pavilion and clambering aboard their team buses. The England players filed out first, and looked surprisingly glum after what had been quite a successful day in the field. As the first few members of the squad emerged the crowd surged forward, but instantly the soldiers formed a strong cordon and raised their batons.

Every time a fresh player emerged there would be another surge and again the cordon would form, the batons would go up and the soldiers would chant: 'Keep back! Keep back!'

Once the bus was full, the soldiers marched forward to part the crowd and allow the bus to pass through. Try as they might to force everyone back, people were still able to jump up and bang on the windows and try to attract the attention of the players within who all sat wordlessly, mostly with headphones on. They looked tense, anxious to be away from the mob and the ground, anxious to breathe again.

My ten minutes were up, and so I followed the team bus out through the gate and once I was away from the crowd rang Charles again on the home number. He picked up at once.

'Hello?'

'Charles.'

'There's a problem,' he said.

I thought there would be.

'Oh right,' I said, trying to sound unconcerned. 'What is it?'

'Well, I've just spoken to the guys on the sports desk and I'm afraid it turns out that since Simon Jones got injured, they are simply not concerned with the India tour anymore.'

'I see.' Gulp.

'It really was just Simon Jones they were interested in. I mean, without him it's just...it's just England. They only wanted Simon Jones stuff.'

'Right.'

This was awful news.

'Well, is there anything they would be interested in me writing for them?' I countered, trying not to sound too crushed by the news he was giving me. 'It's just that I'm actually at the ground today. As it happens.'

'Look, Miles, I asked them that and the only thing they say that they'd be prepared to pay you for would be if you could do an interview with Andrew Flintoff in which he specifically states how desperately England miss Simon Jones.'

'Right. Well I could try. That might be a little tricky, though. Nothing else at all?'

'That's the only Welsh angle. That's what you'd need to get.'

'What about Geraint Jones? He's Welsh, isn't he?' I tried.

'He's been done to death. Everything about him. He worked in a pharmacy in Aberystwyth. That's it.'

'Everybody knows that already do they?'

'Everybody.'

'Right.'

'I'd love to be able to help you more, Miles, but I'm afraid the trail's gone cold.'

'Don't worry, Charles. It will all be fine, I'm sure.'

As I hung up the phone there was a sudden cheering and frantic hullabaloo from behind me inside the ground that could only have been caused by the Indian team's own departure. I could hear the crowd surging again, and the voices of soldiers shouting once more: 'Keep back! Keep back!'

The crowd's elation was in stark contrast to the feeling of gloomy frustration that hung over me as I returned to the hotel by rickshaw and considered my situation which was, given my ambitions, bleak: I had no writing work, no broadcasting work and a press pass that would expire in two days.

*

The rickshaw driver charged me something quite reasonable, but then didn't have any change for the note I had on me, and so wanted me to wait outside the hotel with the rickshaw whilst he went in to find some.

'Please wait here, sir. I will return with the money.'

'It's okay. Really, just keep it.'

'I cannot, sir. Is too much.'

'Please. Just have it.'

He looked at me as if I must have been deeply troubled, but I shook his hand and told him to hold onto it. As I headed into the hotel I looked back over my shoulder and he was still standing there, holding the note in his left hand and looking as if I had burdened him. What I had tipped him, I realised, was roughly equivalent to four British pounds, which a London taxi driver would do well to get out of me. It wasn't largesse on my part, just impatience; a desire to march into the hotel bar and drink my frustrations away.

As I crossed the lobby to the hotel bar, I steeled myself to join a journalistic throng, perhaps a boisterous one even. But as I opened the door and peered into the room, I saw that it was in fact nearly completely deserted. A member of staff stood behind the bar, dressed in a maroon waistcoat, and was polishing glasses, and laying out bowls of nuts. There was just one lone drinker standing at the bar that I was walking towards, his back to me. But even with his back to me I knew exactly who it was: it was David Gower.

Now, to some people, David Gower would just represent a former team captain on the BBC panel show *They Think It's All*

Over. But if that's all you think he is, then you would be doing the man a raging disservice. For David Ivon Gower, born 1 April 1957, is so much more than that. He is quite simply one of the finest, classiest, and apparently languid batsmen that the English game has ever seen. For a brief time in the early '90s he was England's highest ever run scorer. He was the man I had got my detention for missing maths for.

My instinctive reaction to realising that the only other punter in the bar was the great man was to stop dead in my tracks. I was overawed. Scared. The night that I had arrived I had spoken to him briefly up on the roof, but there were other people there. There had been someone to introduce us. Now it would be just me and him. I couldn't go up to the bar and buy a drink without speaking to him. But what could I possibly say to a man who I held in the esteem that I held David Gower? Nothing, probably, other than a few delighted gurgles. The thought of this was too much to handle, and so I started to back slowly and quietly out of the room. But Gower must have heard the door open behind him and spun round in time to see me standing there in the doorway, staring at him as if I might drool or cry or both.

'Hello!' he said cheerfully. 'You look like you could do with a drink. What can I get you?'

I cannot begin to tell you just what a charming man David Gower is. I stood for a moment, panicking. I could hardly form any words, my mouth fixed in an 'O' shape. He still looked at me, eyebrows raised expectantly.

'I'llhaveabeerplease,' I managed.

'Sorry?'

'I will have a beer, please.'

'A beer? Certainly. Any particular sort?'

'Oh you choose,' I said breathily, like a cheerleader being offered a cocktail by the college quarterback.

You choose, David Gower!

'We met up on the roof the other night, didn't we? What's your name again?'

'It's Miles.'

'Miles, that's it. I'm David.'

I know!

'Hello, David.'

'So where are you from, Miles? Where do you live?'

'Oh, I'm from London, but I live in Edinburgh.'

'Edinburgh. Beautiful city.'

And that was it. Away we went. Just chatting away as if we were two perfectly ordinary people, and not one perfectly ordinary person and David Gower. This, I felt, was exactly the sort of thing I'd come out here for: to break into the inner sanctum, to hang out with legends, to become pally with them. But how had it been this easy? Why was it only us two here? Of course. It was a Friday. All of the real journalists had double the amount of work to do for the weekend editions, and must all have still been beavering away somewhere. I had nothing to do as normal, and Gower had spent all day presenting Sky's coverage and his work was done.

We told each other stories, and cracked jokes. Have you ever made David Gower laugh? It feels amazing. At one point, I think because of a discussion about how complicated the broadcasting rights are in India, he suddenly broke into the Judean People's Front sketch from Monty Python's *Life Of Brian*. He did nearly the whole thing. Word for word. All the different voices. And it was beautifully done, he absolutely nailed every punchline and I was utterly transfixed. David Gower was performing a Monty Python sketch for my benefit! But I just couldn't laugh, because all I could hear was a voice in my head screaming 'David Gower is doing the Judean Peoples' Front sketch from *The Life Of*

Brian! What on earth is going to happen next? Is Kevin Pietersen suddenly going to dance in singing "Nobody Loves A Fairy When She's Forty"?'

No. In fact the door opened, and who should wander into the room and over to the bar but Nasser Hussain, born 28 March 1968, one of our finest post-war captains. A man who turned England from a team of underachievers into a team who won four Test series in a row for the first time in nearly 20 years. And he made one of the most dignified exits from Test cricket ever; scored a century to win us a game, and retired there and then, with 96 Tests to his credit, for a younger man to take his place.

And as he walked in I heard myself say, 'Hey, do you want a beer?'

Nasser Hussain looked a little startled by this, but then Gower said, 'Nass, this is Miles,' which suddenly made everything okay.

He accepted my offer of a beer, then pulled up a stool to sit down on, and we all just carried on.

'So what are you here for, Miles?' he asked me. 'Are you on holiday?'

'Oh no. I'm a journalist. I work for BBC Scotland and the *Western Mail*.'

'That sounds like hard work.'

'It can be, yeah.'

He struck me instantly as a very honest man and seemed in an open sort of mood. He was born in India, and is aware that the people of India are incredibly proud of the fact that someone India-born went on to captain England. It sets him apart from all the South Africans that have done the job. Clearly, though, Hussain was affected by the pressure of their pride and expectations.

'They're just so nice to me here, Miles. All the time. They make a real fuss. I mean at the airport when we arrived I got an armed escort, they wouldn't let me carry my luggage. People want to have photos, to shake my hand. And the thing is, I feel like a fraud.'

You and me both, Nass. You and me both.

'This morning I went nuts at the guy servicing my room. Just because he'd sent all my clothes to the hotel laundry. I didn't want them to go to the hotel laundry, I hadn't asked anyone to send my clothes to the hotel laundry.'

'Had you just left them on your chair?'

'Yes.'

'Same thing happened to me. Were your socks all right?'

'Sorry?'

'Nothing. Do continue.'

'Well, I just went nuts. I'm not fussy about much but I'm fussy about my clothes, and I just went nuts. It's pathetic of me. That was awful, that was wrong. I mean, do you know what my batting average in India is?'

'Er, I don't know, no.'

He leant towards me like a man about to confide that he had been selling our secrets to the Russians for years.

'It's rubbish.'

'Oh God,' I thought. 'Is Nasser Hussain going to collapse tearfully into my arms?' If I was a real journalist, then I might have thought, 'Splendid. A scoop. Former England captain Nasser Hussain turns out to be mentally brittle.' But I wasn't a real journalist. I thought, 'Please be okay. I don't want to see a former England captain crying.' That would probably set me off.

'Oh well,' he said, sitting up straight again. 'Another beer?'

And on we all chatted like mortals about this and about that. These two Sky commentators' relationship clearly centred around gently mocking each other and taking the piss, and so the natural way to get on with them was to do just that, and so I joined in making silly jokes, taking the piss.

All the other journalists must still have been in their rooms furiously writing copy for we still had the place to ourselves. And then the door opened again. And who should walk in, but Ian Terence Botham, born 24 November 1955. A talismanic, mercurial *Boy's Own* hero. The first Test that I had ever taken interest in was when Botham had been recalled, and in a fairy tale ending to the 'Leg over Test', he had scored the winning runs. A *bona fide* legend.

He sauntered over to the bar, and plonked himself down on the free stool. 'All right guys?' Then he leant over and put out one of his huge paws to shake mine. 'Beef.'

'Miles.'

It transpired that guys like these are, in the flesh, easy-going and happy to talk. They've proved themselves at the highest level time and time again. They're convivial and jolly and happy to welcome a new face because it brightens up the tour, it's a little bit of variety. They know their place, and are assured of it because they are totally unthreatened. If you've played 118 Tests for England and anchor Sky's coverage, then a random young guy who turns up one day isn't likely to pose much of a threat to your position.

And so it was, just four days into my trip, I found myself drinking, chatting and telling stories with three men whose biographies I had read. Three men who between them had captained England 89 times, played 315 times, scored 19,195 runs, taken 384 wickets, held 261 catches. And they were decent and friendly and welcoming to little old me; no England appearances, very few runs in any form of the game – just 253 episodes of *Balamory* and five weeks as Simple Simon in *Jack and the Beanstalk*, His Majesty's Aberdeen, Christmas 2005.

The bar suddenly started to fill up with journalists and commentators. Clearly they had all finished whatever it was they were all doing at the same time. Sure enough, a new crowd of people gathered around Gower, Hussain and Botham and my time drinking with these legends was over.

Peter Baxter wandered over and looked at me as if I was Banquo's ghost.

'Are you all right?'

'Hello, Peter. Yes, I'm fine. Why?'

'Kevin said that you were horribly ill last night and had disappeared. He didn't think he'd seen you at the ground today.'

'I was,' I said. 'I feel absolutely fine.'

In fact I felt great. I had just spent an hour and a half in the company of legends and heroes and had already knocked back a large amount of beer.

'How's work going?' asked Peter. 'How are your BBC Scotland broadcasts going?'

'Um, not brilliantly.'

'I'm sorry to hear that. How are you actually making the broadcasts?'

Oh dear. He thought that they must be going badly from some sort of technical point of view, not badly in the sense that they were non-existent. But how would I be making broadcasts if they were real?

'I, er, I…I do them by phone,' I said. 'I use my mobile.'

'Your mobile? Oh, no wonder you're having problems. Well, don't worry. You can use all of our kit. We've got a satellite phone. In fact, we're going to be setting it up again in a couple of hours. What are you going to be doing in an hour and a half? We'll be up on the roof with all the gear set up. Aggers and I can operate it for you. It would be no problem. Why don't you ring your editor and tell them you'll be sending a report that way?'

'Oh Peter,' I stammered. 'That's very kind. Very kind. The thing is I've actually already done my broadcast for today. I haven't any other news to give them. Thanks though.'

'No problem. You know where to find us if you want to use it.'

'Marvellous.'

How kind. How excruciating.

It had already been an extraordinary evening by the standards of any cricket fan. I rounded off the night by having dinner with most of the *Test Match Special* team. I was very drunk, though, by the time that we sat down and the meal was something of a blur.

Chapter Eight

I awoke with only the vaguest recollections of the previous night's dinner, but was quite convinced that I was the only diner at our table who had been at all drunk. Odd snippets of the meal gradually popped into my head as I lay stretched out and groaning. I could remember that I had chatted at length with Mike Selvey about Twenty20 cricket, and I could also recall Christopher Martin-Jenkins repeatedly asking me who it was that I worked for, presumably because I kept failing to answer the question satisfactorily.

Once I had got up I sat on the end of the bed with my head in hands to take stock. Last night had been, drunkenness notwithstanding, a success. But my professional situation was a worry. There did not seem to be much that I could do about that for the moment, but I still had two days of this game in which to try and secure a press pass for the next game in Chandigarh. I had sent a few emails to the BCCI explaining that I appeared to have fallen foul of their negotiations with the BBC, and asking if they might reissue me with a fresh pass but, as yet, had heard nothing back from them. That would be my focus for the day; whatever was happening in the cricket would have to take a backseat to my attempt to do battle with Indian bureaucracy. The Chandigarh Test was just a few days away. I wanted to be even more 'embedded' by then. I was going to be travelling with all the other journalists, our accommodation was all booked together. But to stay a part of it all, I needed to be in the press box for the next game. I wanted the access, I wanted to get into print, I wanted to broadcast. I just wanted to be part of the blue lanyard gang. Without one to call my own I felt weird. Everyone else wandered about wearing one completely unselfconsciously, but not having one to wear made me stick out like a ninja in a high visibility jacket. Or the only member of a 4x100 relay team wearing slippers, and carrying shopping.

My head-in-hands deliberations had left me no time for breakfast, and I eventually trotted out of the front of the hotel just in time to squeeze myself onto the last remaining seat in the press bus. Everyone else was grumbling about travel agents and tour operators, but I had too much of a headache to contend with joining in. Just as we were about to leave a member of the hotel staff came to the window I was sat next to and started explaining something important about our journey back that evening.

'When you want to come back, call the number.'

'Sorry?' I said.

'The number. Call the number we will come.'

'What number?'

'The same number.'

'But what is the number?'

I was in no state to engage with these riddles, and before the man could give me an answer, the bus pulled out into the traffic. Somebody else would have to take responsibility for us getting home. Simon Mann was sitting in front of me.

'How are you feeling today?' he asked, in a loaded way. Clearly my level of inebriation had not gone unnoticed.

'I feel like shit,' I said.

'I thought you might.'

There was a coffee shop behind the press box to which a handful of the press corps were heading when we arrived at the ground. I followed them in search of sustenance. As I was the last to place my order, and the actual making and pouring of the coffees looked like it might take a while, it was hastily agreed by consensus that I should be left in the café with everyone's cash, wait for the coffees and then bring them and everyone's change up into the stand. Which I really wouldn't have minded at all if it hadn't taken 30 minutes to make five coffees, if the man behind the counter had given me enough change, and if when I finally got to the box with the coffees they were the same as the ones that people had ordered and that the other journalists hadn't all blamed me for getting the order wrong. If those things hadn't happened then I wouldn't have minded at all.

As it was I sat down at my desk in the box in a bad mood and with a hangover that was not yet ready to abate. I switched on my laptop and saw that I had two emails in my inbox. There was one from Charles Boase with the heading 'Hello' and one from the BCCI that said 'your press pass'. I opened up the one from the BCCI hoping that it would contain good news. It did not.

It said that they understood that there had indeed been a mix-up following on from the rights negotiations but that had now been resolved, and the BBC had resubmitted a list of everyone who needed a pass and my name was not on it. Thus, it did not appear that I was actually employed by the BBC, and therefore, I was not entitled to a press pass.

This was annoying, not least because it was true. But I fired back an instant plea to them. It was true, I said, that I was not employed by the BBC. At least, not by the BBC department who had sent them the list of approved staff. I was a freelancer, I explained, working on behalf of BBC Scotland, an almost completely different entity. It had been their responsibility to notify the BCCI of my presence, and they were, I was afraid to say, a little new to the whole cricket correspondent thing. In fact we both were. It is my first time covering a tour, I told them. I'm not very experienced. I need you to show me what to do, to hold me, to be gentle, to guide me in and not to show your disappointment if it's all over quickly.

Almost as an afterthought I opened the message from Charles. It turned out that Charles had had the idea of pitching to the *Western Mail*'s website people the possibility of me writing a daily blog for them. At this point in 2006, online diaries had only recently and, inexplicably, become a rather popular trend. But the *Western Mail* had never published one before, and were keen to pilot the idea. It would be unpaid, but that didn't sound like a problem. This arrangement meant that I could now claim to be writing for, and thus affiliated to, an actual newspaper. Charles had even forwarded me an email from one of the website's editors saying that they would love me to write for them. I sent Charles an immediate reply that I would love to be their blog guinea pig. I also added that it would be great if someone from the *Western Mail*'s editorial team could send an email to the BCCI confirming that I was now writing for them.

Charles, who was working the night shift, came almost immediately back to me saying that he would pass my acceptance of the offer on to the relevant people, and meanwhile would go and get one of the night editors to send the message to the BCCI.

By now some cricket was being played out in the middle of the stadium, but I wasn't really paying particularly close attention to it. I was more intent on following my fresh lead to get a proper press pass like all the big boys had. There was an early cheer from England caused by Hoggard removing Sreesanth, but I didn't look up in time to see what had happened, only our players celebrating and then walking off.

I wrote a fresh email to the BCCI and said to them, as you will by now have heard, I have been offered a job writing for the *Western Mail*. On this basis, could I please be issued with an official pass for the remainder of the series. They too responded promptly. My case had been passed on to an official called Rajun Nair for special consideration as had the new message from the *Western Mail*. If I came to the offices of the Vidarbha Cricket Association some time this afternoon, he would be able to help me. This news caused a surge of optimism to rush through me; I had taken great leaps towards finally securing not just a press pass but also something akin to some journalism to do. To celebrate I went to fetch a bottle of cold mineral water from the fridge at the back of the box so that I could go to work on my hangover whilst watching England bat.

India had managed a total of 323, and by lunch England, in reply, had ground their way to 90-something without loss.

*

After I had wolfed down my tray of lunch, I took a stroll around the ground. In English Test venues, moving around during the lunch break is almost impossible. There are tens of burger vans and pasty stands, merchandising stalls and people selling books and prints by renowned cricket water-colourists. Every stretch of open space is crammed, and some strange instinct forces the majority of the crowd to only move in one direction. Attempting to move in the other direction, one feels like a struggling salmon, and all around one can see people slowly becoming flustered and unable to cope with the cajoling. A similar level of congestion in India causes no upset whatsoever. People are entirely untroubled by chaos, and do not panic amidst a sea of people with different plans all heading in different directions like smoke particles. No stress seems to be caused by such scenes. Instead most things that would cause people in England to sigh and redden are viewed with an almost amused detachment. The atmosphere as I walked around the ground was thus frantic yet happy. Gangs of men and women stood about laughing and joshing, and English and Indian fans mixed freely and easily. It made me feel upbeat.

As the afternoon session started I knocked on the door of the Vidarbha Cricket Association office to see if there was any sign of this Rajun Nair character, and if I could persuade him to decide in my favour with regards to the awarding of my pass.

'Come in.'

I walked into the room which had been abuzz with activity the day before the Test, to find just one man behind the many desks. The other desks were piled high with paperwork, some of which spilled over onto the chairs and the floors. Many of the drawers of the filing cabinets were open, and folders were sticking out of them as if in suspended animation. The ceiling fan was still whirring around, but seemed to have slowed down a little since my last visit, and now tilted at a more precarious angle. It looked as if everyone had charged out of the room in the middle of something in a *Marie Celeste* moment. Apart, of course, from the one man sitting behind a desk reading a newspaper.

'Are you all alone?' I asked.

The man looked around as if to confirm that this was the case.

'Yes. Everybody is watching the cricket.'

Of course. Why wouldn't they be? In fact, why wasn't this man watching the cricket? Perhaps he didn't like it. Perhaps he was the one person who had applied for a job at the Vidarbha Cricket Association because of his love for admin work, rather than his love of the sport. Or his love of reading the newspaper and stroking his moustache with no one about to supervise him.

'Are you Rajun Nair?'

'No. Ha. No, I am not Rajun Nair.' Then he chuckled to himself and shook his head as if to say 'Me? Rajun Nair? The very idea.' And then he returned to reading his paper and stroking his moustache.

'Do you know when would be a good time to see Rajun Nair?' I asked.

The man lowered his paper again.

'To see Rajun Nair?'

'Yes. To have a meeting with him. I need to talk with him about a press pass. I've applied for a pass and he is making the decision. My case has been passed on to him.'

The man looked in the direction of the messiest and most weighed-down desk in the room, indicating that it was Mr Nair's, and then adopted a sympathetic expression. 'Well, good luck with that...' he would have said knowingly if he was the sarcastic flatmate in an American sitcom.

'Is he at the ground?'

'Rajun Nair? Oh yes.'

'Then do you think I could arrange a meeting with him?'

'No.'

'No?'

'Is not possible. A meeting with him is not possible and is not necessary.'

'Do you mean you can give me a press pass?' I tried.

'No. No.' Another chuckle, another sorry look. 'You do not need to arrange a meeting with Rajun Nair because he is all around. You just have to find him.'

I blinked, and looked at the man again. I was no longer sure if Rajun Nair was a cricket administrator or a spiritual concept. Feeling a little fazed, I turned back towards the door.

'However,' called the man after me, 'if you really need to meet with him, he is always at the press conference at the end of play.'

'Perfect,' I said. 'I'll see him then.'

*

There was nothing I could do for the moment but wait. I was optimistic, though, that once I could find Rajun Nair, my newly confirmed association with the *Western Mail* would mean that he should be inclined to award me the pass. It also meant that when I returned to the press box, I actually had some writing to do. I turned on my laptop and started tapping out a piece for the blog based on something Nasser Hussain had told me the night before about how difficult it was, ironically, to get hold of Indian tonic water here. It felt good to be doing something that I knew was going to be read by someone – anyone – and that it had something to do, no matter how vaguely, with the cricket. As I wrote I occasionally looked up and glanced around to check that people could see that I was busy and had things to be getting on with. Then I sat back to watch the cricket that up to now I had ignored so much of. We had lost two quick wickets, Strauss and Bell, while I had been away from the box after the lunch interval, but the debutant Cook and Kevin Pietersen looked to be taking control and started to grind out a healthy-looking partnership.

Later in the afternoon Andrew Walpole, the press officer, appeared and sat down on the step beside me.

'How's it going?' he asked.

'Not too bad,' I said. 'I've started writing more for the *Western Mail*.'

'That's good.'

'It is, but it means I need to find some Welsh angles.'

'Right.'

'I mean, do you know if Kevin Pietersen has any Welsh relatives, for example?'

Andrew smiled.

'He's hardly got any English ones,' muttered a gruff voice behind us, and Andrew laughed.

'Seriously though, Andrew,' I said. 'Is there any possibility that I might be able to do an interview with Andrew Flintoff?'

'Well...he is pretty busy at the moment. What with the captaincy and everything.'

He had a point. I ploughed on, though.

'The thing is, you see, the *Western Mail* are really keen to have a few quotes from him about how much he and the team are missing Simon Jones.'

'Right.' I could feel Andrew slipping into a slightly more professional mode. 'To be honest, he's not really got time to do interviews about who he's missing. And it's not fair on everyone who is here and playing for the team if he's going around saying he wishes Simon was still out here. From a morale point of view. I mean, people are doing a good job.'

'Yeah. Yeah. I understand.'

Balls. What about any other Welsh angles?

'What about Matthew Maynard, the batting coach? Could I interview him? He's from Wales, he played for Glamorgan.'

'He doesn't do interviews. Plus I don't know if you realise this, but he's actually from Chester.'

Chester. Well that's quite near Wales. That might be of some interest to the *Western Mail*. In fact, didn't Chester used to be part of Wales once upon a time? Perhaps Maynard and I could have a chat about boundaries? I tried to take the conversation in another direction, looking for some colour to write about in the blog.

'What does everyone get up to in the evenings, Andrew? Is there fun to be had?'

'Oh, all sorts really, you've got to keep occupied; few social drinks, bit of darts. Actually, last night we had a quiz.'

'A quiz? Great. Who won?'

'Nobody Welsh,' he said. 'Nobody Welsh.'

*

Out in the middle, the not-quite-Welsh-enough Alastair Cook was making history. After spending nearly six hours at the crease and facing 236 balls, he became not only the sixteenth England player to score a century on debut, but also the youngest. It was an extraordinary performance from a man who was called up so late as injury cover that he was still fighting jet lag when the game had begun. Kevin Pietersen had also swatted the ball around for a much quicker 87, and had indeed been lucky to be given not out when, with only 36 to his name, he had driven a delivery from Kumble straight back at the bowler who took a very low, but ultimately clean catch. Most of the talk, though, was about Alastair Cook.

I was standing by the door for the press conference when Alastair Cook walked in. I smiled at him and he flashed back a big grin. 'Well played,' I said, and he looked chuffed. In fact he already looked chuffed before I had spoken to him, but if nothing else, I didn't appear to have dampened his spirits. This was his second appearance behind the microphones, and he sat there saying modest things in a fairly collected way, but all the while grinning from ear to ear.

As everyone filed out after the press conference, I spotted a splendid-looking silver-haired and moustachioed Indian gentleman wearing a BCCI blazer. This, I instinctively knew, must be Rajun Nair.

'Excuse me,' I said as I approached him. 'Are you Rajun Nair?'

He turned and flashed me a delightful smile.

'Yes…I ..am,' he said slowly, opening his long arms wide, as if most people who approached him after press conferences were only after a big cuddle.

'I'm Miles Jupp. You've been asked to make a decision about my press pass, I think.'

'Yes. Yes I have. Everything is fine. There will be a press pass waiting for you at the ground in Chandigarh.'

Fantastic! I felt delight and excitement rise within me. I was just thrilled. I was going to have a blue, laminated, lanyarded press pass. Suddenly that hug felt like a good idea. In fact, I would have happily kissed him.

*

Back at the hotel the lift doors were just closing, but Jonathan Agnew squeezed through them dartily.

'Hello, Aggers.'

'You,' he said, 'have caught the sun a little.'

I checked in the mirror in my bathroom and found that the BBC's chief cricket correspondent had been a little generous in his appraisal of my dermatological state. My face was as red and ridiculous as it could possibly have been. 'But so what?' I thought. 'I've got some writing to do, a paper that I can claim to work for and a press pass guaranteed for the next two games.' I was in a mood to celebrate. I showered and put on a fresh shirt, first a pink one before realising that it clashed too horribly with my face and arms, and then replaced it with a blue. Then I trotted downstairs to the bar in the hope that another night of easy-flowing banter and beers with some of my legendary mates lay ahead of me.

As I entered the bar, I saw that it was certainly busier already than it had been the night before. Many of the legends were already there in a little crowd at the far end of the bar and deep in conversation. Another huddle of journalists were standing around next to them, and I didn't feel that as the new boy it would make sense to walk past them and straight over to the legends. Instead I ventured over and stood on the edge of their group. Then I ordered myself a drink and as I did so, looked around to see if anyone else wanted one. No one met my eye.

These were journalists that I had barely spoken to, and yet we had now all been sitting in the same press box for four days, and so I imagined that I might be on at least nodding terms with them. I didn't feel confident of introducing myself to the whole group at once, but felt that if I stood there long enough then one of them might look up and say something to me, perhaps introduce himself and then the others.

And so I stood there, lingering and hoping someone might say something I could latch on to, but nothing came. I sipped gingerly at my beer, like a loser at a disco. Then more journalists swept into the bar and all hailed one of the others. It was, it turned out, the birthday of one of them, and so tonight everybody was there for a celebration. As more and more journalists swept in, I became hopeful that one of the ones I had got to know well might appear and I'd have someone to talk to. They were, however, nowhere to be seen. And then something began to happen that made a knot start tightening in my stomach.

The configuration of the bar was that all the legends were at one end, then there was the cluster of others and then there was me, on my own sipping my beer and nervously fingering the novel that I had brought down with me just in case this very thing ever happened. But every time fresh meat in the form of more journalists and photographers arrived, they would slowly but deliberately squeeze in between that group and me, and thus with each new arrival I was nudged further along the bar. Every minute or so I was silently made to budge up along the bar again, and forced further and further into my own sudden loneliness.

And it was at that moment, as I stood there, feeling all dry-mouthed and excluded, that it dawned on me just how socially impaired I can sometimes be. The sort of trick that I was trying to pull off required someone gregarious and confident; someone used to easy conversation and banter. I am not that person. I can pretend to be that person for short bursts, but in reality I am someone that can slip, without warning, into silences that seem

to last for days. In that situation, surrounded by the other journalists – the real journalists – all talking away, I no longer felt like
an adult, but like a shy child surrounded by grown-ups with
better things to do than indulge me. And then I started to feel
more like a teenage schoolboy, completely consumed by that
burning desire to be part of a group; any group, even one that,
if you were completely honest with yourself, contained some
people that you didn't even like.

I stood at the bar, feeling quite stunned by the suddenness
with which all the excitement about the news of my press pass
had disappeared and been replaced by a gnawing sense of unease.
Why was everybody ignoring me? Even people who had behaved
in a friendly enough manner up until now just seemed to look
straight through me. Perhaps everybody had discovered that I
was a fraud?

Standing where I was, isolated but still on the edge of the
group, I could not help but overhear some of the conversation
going on around me. One journalist remarked that he hoped
England would start losing against New Zealand because that
way the hotel prices there would turn out much cheaper for his
family when they came out to stay with him.

Another cluster were discussing George Bush, who was in
India at the time, and religion. Holding court at that moment
was Mr Who The Fuck's That?, kindly sharing his wisdom on the
matter for the benefit of all who could hear. 'Let's face it,' he
said, and then rubbed his hands together as he prepared to
deliver his thesis. He had the misplaced confidence and manner
of a man who has done very nicely for himself and spends his
evenings being insufferable at a golf club. 'Every war in the
history of mankind,' he said slowly, 'has been caused by religion.'
He paused a little, to allow the group time to digest this stun-
ningly original line of thinking. 'I mean, look at Hitler,' he

added, not perhaps the best example to back up his theory, but, I imagined, probably the closest to him politically. 'His whole thing was about hating the Jews wasn't it?' There. Arms folded. QED. Take that, thinkers of the world.

And then, suddenly, to my right, I heard a voice. A friend? A saviour of some kind? No, only a hero. Michael Atherton was standing next to me, a mobile phone clamped to his ear, and he was pointing to the biro lying on my novel.

'Can I borrow that pen?' he whispered.

I passed it to him obediently like a child handing something over in exchange for a reward.

'Cheers.'

Well this was something – a start, an in. I had lent my hero a biro. So now he owed me. Admittedly it would have been better if he owed me because I had dragged him from a burning building, or even helped him change a car tyre. But still, he owed me. He owed me, at the very least, my biro back. And maybe when he came back with it, I could chat to him. Yes, I was going to take this opportunity to start a conversation with my hero. It was not as if I had anyone else to talk to.

In a minute or two he was back. He looked quizzically at me.

'Hi there,' I said.

'I just borrowed a pen from someone,' he said. 'Was it you?'

How, with the sunburn that I was sporting, he could have found my face unmemorable I have no idea.

'Yes,' I said. 'It was me.' And took it from him, and then shook the still outstretched hand. 'I'm Miles.'

'Oh hi. Mike.'

'I'm on this tour too. I'm a journalist.'

'Oh right.' He was able to digest this information very speedily. So speedily that he didn't even have time to alter his facial expression.

I nodded at him, gesturing with my eyebrows that perhaps he might like to say something else. He exhaled slowly and thoughtfully, frowning slightly. And then a thought struck him and he perked up a little. He'd thought of something to say. Good old Athers. I knew he would.

He said, 'Are you with us for the duration?'

'Just the Tests,' I said. And then threw in a few more nods.

'Well,' he said, 'thanks for the pen.' And off he went leaving me all alone, and no longer owing me a biro.

Thanks for the pen. That's not what you want to hear from your hero.

My friend David MacLennan was once walking in the Highlands with his son, and they came across a film crew apparently making an advert. And there, amidst this flurry of people, was Peter O'Toole. David said to his son, who was only 11 at the time, 'Shane, that's Peter O'Toole. You've got to meet him.'

'But why, Daddy?'

'Because...because he's Peter O'Toole. You'll be glad of it one day.'

'Okay.'

'No one will mind. Just go up and introduce yourself.'

'But what shall I say to him, Daddy?'

'Why don't you tell him that your mum's an actress?'

'Okay.'

And so, during a break in filming, Shane walked over to Peter O'Toole and shook his hand.

'Hello,' said Peter O'Toole. 'What's your name?'

'My name's Shane.'

'Pleased to meet you, Shane.'

'My mum's an actress.'

'Is she?' purred O'Toole. 'Is she indeed? Well then you tell your mother I'd very much like to meet her.'

So much better than 'Well, thanks for the pen.'

This encounter with my hero had done little to lift my mood or turn around my social awkwardness. If anything, as my hero retreated into the distance, I felt even lower. But still, try as I might, I just could not make any sort of social break. So I sat on a stool, with my nearly full glass of beer, and started to read my novel. Then a voice next to me said, 'Can you move your stool up as well so that I can stand here?' No other acknowledgement. No 'thank you'. I was simply in the way.

I once had a job doing red-carpet interviews before the premiere of a film. I was not good at it. But I got there early, and with nothing else to do and no crew to chat with I just wandered about a bit. It was a film called *Gumball 3000*, and instead of a red carpet they had had a special one made that had been inlaid with the logo of the film. It might have been vaguely interesting to someone very interested in carpets. Or inlay. And as I plodded about and walked past the bank of photographers setting up in time for any celebrity arrivals, one of them said, 'Excuse me.'

I looked up to see a paparazzo standing with a big fancy camera.

'Hello?' I said.

'Can you get out of the way so that I can take a photo of the carpet?'

This was how I was beginning to feel now. Alone, isolated and also slightly paranoid. I began to think that people weren't just ignoring me but also watching me being ignored by others. Although I was on my own, I imagined that all eyes were on me. It was like standing in the school dining hall with a full tray of food and looking around to see no one that I knew to sit with. I could feel a cold sweat rising within me. I would have to go. I would knock back a respectable amount of my beer, place the glass down and leave. And so I gulped down as much as I could, placed the glass down on the bar, got up from my seat and turned to walk out and head somewhere – anywhere – alone.

And as I turned, something happened. There was a voice calling from the other end of the bar.

'All right, Miles?'

I turned around to see who had finally spoken to me. And saw, to my amazement, that it was Ian Botham.

'Oh, hey Beef!' I said.

'How are you?' he called. 'All right?'

'I'm good, yeah. You?'

'Yeah, not bad. Nice to see you again.' And then he raised his drink in my direction.

And with this, immediately the mood around me changed. It was as if England's greatest all-rounder had marched over and whipped off the invisibility cloak that I had been shrouded in. People were suddenly looking in my direction.

Hey, who's this guy?

I don't know. But Ian Botham knows who he is.

Then, half a minute later, I heard the voice of David Gower, chatting with a group behind me, say the words, 'I was having this exact conversation with Miles the other night.' As he said my name, I turned and he smiled at me. This changed everything. Some people suddenly turned round and introduced themselves.

'Hi there. Miles? It's Ian Splunk from the *Daily Whatsit*. How do you do?'

'Miles. Hubert Tepenyaki Bladder. *Sunday Growl*.'

'Hello. Terry Buttocks. *Church Times. Enchanté.*'

And suddenly I was talking to people. Telling them about all the work I did for the *Western Mail* and BBC Scotland.

A few minutes later someone else came over.

'Miles, we're just going to reserve a table upstairs. Would you like to join us?'

I had been saved. And I had been saved by cricketing legends.

The *Test Match Special* lot arrived soon after this, and a group of about 20 of us ended up in the rooftop restaurant sharing one long table. At the opposite end to me sat Athers, my hero. At my end were sitting Simon Mann, Peter Baxter and Mr Who The Fuck's That? At one point I made a small joke that made Simon and Peter laugh. When they had stopped laughing Mr Who The Fuck's That? leant towards me and said quietly, 'That was a very profound thought from the man from radio bollocks.'

*

Mr Who The Fuck's That? was the first man I saw the following morning. He was still eating when I finally made it down for breakfast, nursing yet another hangover. Dining with him was a rather serious journalist with a habit of wincing that I'd met the night before. If he'd been a character in a PG Wodehouse novel he would have been called Stiffy Melvin. They were sitting together in a booth, and as we all now knew each other it seemed impolite to ignore them. I chose the most comforting options that the buffet had to offer and then walked across to their table.

'Mind if I join you, gentlemen?'

'Yeah. Fine,' said Mr Who The Fuck's That? 'We're going in a minute though.'

Of course you are.

'You'll have to climb behind me,' said Stiffy. 'I've only just sat down.'

As it was a booth, there was no other way round. And so that I could get past and into a spare seat, he leant in towards the table, and I stepped up onto the banquette with my plate, and with a little difficulty squeezed behind him and then clambered down into my seat. Then they ignored me.

They chatted about the state of the game throughout the world. Occasionally I offered up a fact to support something that one of them had said, for which I would receive a muttered thank you. If I was feeling particularly brave then I might even venture an opinion. The looks that I would receive in exchange for such behaviour would probably have been no different if I had been belching or trying to play footsie with them.

One of the receptionists came over and informed us that the bus to the ground was about to leave. If he was expecting to be thanked for passing on this news then he was sadly mistaken. They both reacted as if he had calmly walked over to our table and asked us all to sniff his fingers.

Stiffy slowly turned towards the man. 'I've not said anything before about it, but what you're charging each of us to travel to the ground by that bus is an absolute disgrace.'

'Sir?' The receptionist nervously shifted his weight from one foot to the other.

I, meanwhile, had no idea that we were being charged extra to use the bus. I assumed it was already covered in the big sum that I had paid to Sunsport. Still, whatever it was, it was unlikely to be an amount determined by this employee.

'It is. It's a disgrace.'

'I am sorry, sir.'

'It is actually,' said Mr Who The Fuck's That?, chomping on a sausage like it was a nipple.

'I am sorry about this, sirs. You must speak to the manager about this.'

'Well I might just do that,' said Stiffy. 'I wouldn't expect to pay that much in a London taxi.'

Bloody hell. Maybe we were being overcharged. I just stared at my plate, embarrassed by this stand-off.

'Sirs, shall I ask the bus to wait for you?'

'No,' said Melvin. 'I don't want to take the bus. Not at those prices. Just order us a taxi. That will probably be cheaper if we share.'

'You don't want to use the bus, sir? You want me to order a taxi?'

'No. Yes.'

'Sir?'

'No to the bus. Yes to the taxi.'

'Yes, sir. Thank you, sir.' And then he scuttled off. If he had had a tail, it would have been clamped quite firmly between his legs. When he had gone, Mr Who The Fuck's That? shook his head and said 'fucking hell' before continuing with his sausage.

The receptionist returned a few minutes later. 'I have hailed a taxi for you, gentlemen. It is outside.'

'Thank you,' said Melvin. 'That will be cheaper.'

He and Mr Who The Fuck's That? rose from the table and wiped their hands on their napkins. I stayed where I was.

'Are you coming?' demanded Melvin.

'I'm all right, thanks.'

'You don't want to share the taxi with us?'

'No,' I said, and returned to eating my breakfast.

'Suit yourself then.' The pair of them headed for the exit. As they were leaving I heard Mr Who The Fuck's That? growling and muttering the words 'fucking hell' over and over.

*

In the event, I shared a taxi to the game with Peter and Angela, the couple from the Barmy Army that I had met a few days earlier. They were in high spirits, and felt that England were in a strong position. They certainly had a healthy lead, would probably have declared overnight and India would certainly have to bat out of their skins to knock off the 368 required for victory. The pair had also managed to enjoy a lot more of what Nagpur had to offer than I had, heading out most nights to bars and restaurants, and partying with other fans. I had not seen this side of Nagpur at all, spending most of my time trying to look busy and faffing about with various aspects of cricket bureaucracy. I hadn't come to India to have a party after all. I'd come to try to become a journalist.

My inbox was full of messages from the *Western Mail*. They liked what I had sent them, and someone in their IT department had set up the blog for me and posted the first article. There were messages containing various passwords that I needed to use to access the thing, and instructions so that I would be able to post pieces myself and upload photos. They also wanted me to send photos of myself, and to write a biography. I had never seen a blog before, but it all looked professional enough to me. The great thing about it was that it was accessed via the *Western Mail*'s website. I wrote up a few other ideas that I'd had and posted them to the site, as well as playing about to see what else was possible. It appeared to have lots of other features, but I couldn't make any of them work. Nevertheless, even if I was only tinkering, all this typing and tapping would be giving off the right impression to the other inhabitants of the press box. In fact, one journalist actually uttered the words 'You look busy, Miles' as he walked past.

'Well,' I said, 'that's because I am.' And then gave one of those 'you know what it's like, right' sort of looks.

And then, despite having started the day with a hangover, and enduring a rather unpleasant breakfast, I watched the game in a good mood. I was now doing something that could be associated with journalism, and I had a pass to look forward to when we got to Chandigarh. But what would the score-line of the series be when we got there?

It looked like it could all go England's way when Matthew Hoggard knocked back Virender Sehwag's off stump before he had scored. India then went completely onto the defensive, and batted for two sessions without even a hint of aggression. By tea, after four hours of play, they had taken their score to just 131–1. Rahul Dravid and Wasim Jaffer had both batted with inordinate care, but with 237 runs still required for their victory and nine wickets required for ours, a draw looked the most likely outcome.

But after tea, everything went a bit bonkers. Once Dravid had reached his 50 (which took 168 balls), he suddenly went onto the attack, and hit ten runs from the opening over of a Harmison spell. Then he was bowled by Monty Panesar for 71, and to everyone's surprise the Indian all-rounder Irfan Pathan came out to the crease and started hurling his bat at everything. Flintoff came on to try and calm things down but was instantly hit for a four and a six. Jaffer was then removed but not before he had scored his first ever Test century. To replace him, though, came not Tendulkar but Dhoni, who also looked hell-bent on aggression. Harmison had Pathan caught at mid-on by Strauss, but that did finally bring Tendulkar to the crease, who started hitting Flintoff about, and then spanked a Blackwell over for 16. With him in his customary imperious form, and his love of runs at Nagpur, a sense of panic began to spread around the English members of the crowd. Out on the pitch, our players also began to look less sure of themselves. Surely India weren't going to get away with blocking it for four hours to lull us into a false sense of safety and then go berserk the minute that our lot started to look a bit floppy after a day in the sun? Thankfully not. Harmison had Dhoni caught at slip, yorked Harbhajan Singh soon after and suddenly everyone out in the middle was shaking hands. That was it, then. All around the box journalists who had hardly dared move from their seats for two hours, started getting up and stretching. It might have been a draw but there was still a real buzz around the ground. Such was the suddenness and, briefly, effectiveness of India's counter-attack that there was a palpable sense of relief when it all ended. Even so, the scorecard would show that England had had the best of the game.

*

Immediately in front of the pavilion a band of men had hurriedly set up hoardings covered in yet more logos in order for the official post-match presentation to take place. Several people from the box nipped downstairs and began making their way across the outfield to get a good view of events, and so I hurried after them, first grabbing my camera and then, thinking about creating the right impression for those around me, I went back for my notepad and pen. I galloped down the stairs, and then turned left towards the pitch, the route I had taken across it the day before the game had begun. This time a soldier blocked my path. 'Pass, please.'

I flashed him my temporary pass.

'I'm sorry. You need a proper pass.'

'This won't do?'

'I am afraid not. Must be proper. Like this one,' he said pointing at one that a passing journalist was flashing at him nonchalantly.

Oh well. At least I wouldn't have these sort of problems when I got to Chandigarh. I returned to the press box to watch the presentation from there.

These affairs always look pretty silly when you're at the ground unless you're very close up. They are arranged for the benefit of the TV cameras, and so whilst they look perfectly fine from the comfort of your own home, when you see them live they seem oddly shabby and chaotic. A bunch of players who would rather be knocking back beers in the dressing room and enjoying each other's company have to stagger about and clap politely while someone with a microphone thanks various sponsors. No one receiving or giving trophies ever seems to have any idea where they should be standing, and stressed-looking assistants with clipboards have to run around and tempt people to have their photos taken in front of the right thing or next to the appropriate person. No one in the crowd can hear a thing. Where I was sitting at the Oval when we won the Ashes it wasn't even possible to see the presentation, as the stage was facing the opposite side of the ground. So even though I was there at the time I never got to see Michael Vaughan raise the urn aloft, only a load of confetti cannons going off behind some sheets of plywood. Here, though, I could see Matthew Hoggard go up to collect what could only have been the Man Of The Match Award. For this he was given the usual cheque, and also the keys to a little motorbike that he immediately started to drive around the outfield, as the crowd and other players cheered him. Someone, somewhere, with responsibility for Health and Safety was probably having an embolism.

*

The press conference that followed was even more cramped than usual. Two areas had been partitioned off for various networks to conduct exclusive interviews, and so space was at a premium. I took my usual place at the back near the door and in front of the windows. The conference room was slightly below ground level, and outside children crouched down on the walkway to peer in through the barred windows to see who they could glimpse.

'Hello!' they shouted. 'HELLO!'

At first I tried to ignore it, but when they started banging on the windows I turned around.

'Hello,' I said.

'You English?'

'Yes.'

'England play well!'

'Thank you.'

'You will struggle next time though.'

'Really?'

'Yes. In next game we'll have two proper spinners. You have one. We will win.'

'We'll see,' I said. 'What did you think of Alastair Cook?'

But my question was drowned out by an excited shrieking. Another child had started banging on the windows.

'Geoffrey Sir!' he was yelling, and pointing behind me. 'Geoffrey Sir.'

I looked around and there indeed was Sir Geoffrey, being led into one of the partitioned areas to be interviewed by former Indian paceman Javagal Srinath. He was wearing what costume shops would probably be able to sell as 'The Geoffrey Boycott Outfit': slip-on shoes, slacks, an oat-coloured blazer and a panama hat. When I am of age, I too shall dress this way.

'Geoffrey Sir! Geoffrey Sir!' They chanted.

Boycott looked over to the children and tipped his hat.

'Hello, lads.'

They all cheered. He had made their day.

He then began his interview with Srinath behind the screen. I could not hear any of Srinath's questions, but Boycott's answers were given at full volume, as if he was a man addressing a mob from the vantage point of a soapbox. All round our area of the room people started tittering about the unnecessary volume at which he tended to speak – a volume that made him the centre of attention even when he couldn't be seen.

Despite the tittering though, there was also a growing restlessness in the room. Because of the post-match presentation, and undoubtedly some dressing-room chat, everyone had been waiting for quite some time now for someone to make an appearance at the press conference. People had writing to get on with, and deadlines to meet.

Eventually there was some fuss in the corridor outside, a bit of bustling, and the vast figure of Andrew Flintoff appeared in the doorway. Here was the man whose exploits had so thrilled the nation the summer previously. For the first time in a generation a cricketer had come along and captured the public's imagination in such a way that he had achieved a level of fame that transcended cricket. The man was a hero. And so when I saw him walk into the same room as me I just couldn't stop myself. I shouted, 'Heeeeeeere's...Freddie!' In an instant, I knew that was not the sort of behaviour that was expected from journalists in a press conference. As soon as I made my outburst, heads swivelled around and I could feel the heat of a dozen staring eyes. 'Who the hell's this overexcited fool?' Jumping around like a demented fan at a stage door is simply not the way that a journalist in this situation would behave. Everyone else in the room greeted his arrival with a weary, 'Well, come on then, we're all waiting' sort of an expression. I felt my cheeks redden as Flintoff walked past me. Everybody else in the room looked very serious about it all. And, of course, so they should have done. These people might have one of the best jobs in the world but, even so, whatever you do sometimes only feels like business. I had momentarily forgotten that I was in a room of people who were all at work.

Flintoff sat behind the microphones and started to answer questions. However, even though he was being amplified, he was still being drowned out by an unamplified Boycott at the other end of the room. The longer Boycott spoke, the louder he got. At first Andrew Walpole, sitting alongside Flintoff, looked irritated by the interruptions. But as they got ever louder and it became clear that Boycott was not a man who could be easily silenced, Walpole's mood transformed into resigned amusement.

It is quite something to hear a man speak with such certainty about everything he is asked, even when some of the questions can only have been of a fairly general nature. But Boycott does not seem to be a man who has ever been hampered by indecision, and was speaking at a volume you could only conceivably speak at if you knew not only that you were right, but that people simply had to hear what you had to say. Boycott has talked an awful lot in his lifetime, but I doubt that he has ever uttered the words, 'Ooh, I don't really know.'

For his part Flintoff, when I could hear him, sounded in good spirits. Nearly all sportsmen have been through some sort of media training now which enables them to reel off platitudes without a moment's hesitation. But he said that England had not really been taxed by India's late onslaught, only a little surprised. He also had praise for Monty Panesar, who he described as 'a dream to captain'.

We all filed out of the room, Boycott still in full flow, demonstrating the sort of stamina that would make even Ken Dodd envious.

*

Everyone else had work to do, so I went and stood behind the pavilion with the fans to watch the players get onto the team bus. There was a sizeable crowd of young Indian fans, but as well as the usual Indian guards, the players' safety was bolstered by three security guards that had been hired by the ECB for the tour. Their presence, and indeed their cost, had raised quite a few eyebrows in the press corps. They were very firm with the young crowd, indicating where they were allowed to stand and shouting at them if they attempted to get any closer. They escorted each and every player from the back of the pavilion onto the bus and none of them were to stop for photos or to sign autographs.

This businesslike atmosphere was not something that I had really considered before I embarked on my trip, and after I had hailed a rickshaw and given the driver the hotel's address I sat back and reflected on what I had learnt so far now that our time in Nagpur was coming to an end.

One of the first things I considered was that the business of pretending to be busy was turning out to be absolutely exhausting – much more tiring than genuinely being busy, I imagine. The continual pretence seemed at times to be shattering. All day long I had to try and make it look as if I knew what I was doing, and that I had a right to be there. This meant, inevitably, that I was spending a huge proportion of every day imitating the people around me. I had to come across as competent and trustworthy, and the sort of person that, if I was in the right place at the right time, could be relied upon to do a decent job. That's how I hoped to make it to the next level. I would carry a notebook and pen at all times so that I would look ready for work, even though I didn't really have anything to take notes for. If other people were grumbling about someone then I would join in. If everybody else were to laugh at a joke then I would laugh too. I needed to quickly assess any atmosphere that developed and then attempt to become part of it. I even began a habit of saying, 'I'm just off to file a bit of copy,' and would then go upstairs and watch the telly for an hour, before coming down and saying, 'Ooh, the wireless is a bit slow' or some other suitable journalistic whinge.

And the reason, I realised, that I was finding mimicking the behaviour of those around me wearisome, was because what they did had turned out to be bloody hard work. The reason that cricket writers sometimes have no sympathy and at other times have every sympathy for the players' touring and playing schedule is because they all go through nearly exactly the same thing. They spend just as much time away from their families, for instance. Everywhere the players go, they go. When the players are playing in matches, they're there too, watching and writing and reporting. When the players are practising they're there as well, trying to spot what's going on, see who looks in good form, and who looks in trouble. What is the team likely to be? Is the captain or coach taking anyone aside and having a quiet word with them? Every press conference is attended by just one or two players. But all of the journalists have to be there. No one wants to be the person that misses out. And presumably no one has an editor who would be sympathetic if theirs was the paper that missed out. Even the silly little junkets that the players go to, the little launches and signings, will also be attended by correspondents and reporters. And then they wait around for hours in the hope of getting some new quotes, a fresh insight of any sort; even a minor exclusive in exchange for the italics at the bottom of their piece telling the reader that *Monty Panesar was speaking at the launch of the Hula Hoops petition for a Redrafting of the LBW law.*

Most of the journalists on this tour had also toured Pakistan for two months over Christmas. It was a frequent question on first meeting others: 'Did you go to Pakistan? No? Oh, you lucky thing.' It shouldn't have been a surprise that people sometimes came across as tired, jaded or cross. It's a struggle to continually find things to write about and have an opinion about them.

I would need to work much harder from now on if I genuinely wanted to fit in with these people. I just had to do what they were doing. If the consensus of opinion was totally against my own personal feelings, I would go along with it – because the brutal reality is that there are players that the public love that people within the game hate, and there are players the public aren't keen on that are well loved and respected within the game. There are people I admire and hold dear that the people who were now around me could not abide – if I heard something that surprised me I had to register no shock.

I also had to stay alert. It wouldn't do to keep getting drunk like I had been in Nagpur. If you're not where everybody else is, they either assume you're up to something else or that you're lazy. Everybody works to the same patterns, they're at the games at the same time obviously, and they're writing at the same time to the same deadlines. Everything they do is completely in sync with one another. They probably fall asleep, shower and have bowel movements at exactly the same time as each other. They get hungry at the same time, they get thirsty at the same time. As a new face, I imagined that I might be some sort of refreshing presence, a bit of new blood to freshen up the relentless tedium of touring. And to some people I was. But to others I was someone to be suspicious of.

'Who are you? Who do you work for?' Everybody wants to be in the know all the time. They need to be. And, quietly, they all read each other's stuff. Nobody wants to be the only cricket writer not to have known a certain fact or made a particular connection. They are, usually in a light-hearted way, competitive, and they pester each other for titbits. But on top of that there are certain rules that they abide by. If one gets a particular scoop that will put the others to shame, more often than not it is shared with a few others. First, so that the person who has achieved the scoop is not ostracised by the others out of rancour. Secondly it makes sense for the facts you have or at least think you've discovered to appear in other publications as that gives the appearance of, or often works as a substitute for, verification. There was turning out to be rather a lot to this journalism lark.

And what of my objectives for the trip? I thought, as we pulled up outside the hotel. I had not yet written an article for a newspaper, although my writing was now at least appearing on a newspaper's website. I certainly hadn't made any radio broadcasts – in fact, I had not received a single response to any of my emails to BBC Radio Scotland; I certainly had not been offered any other work.

On the upside, however, no one had said, 'Aren't you the bloke from *Balamory*?'

*

Kevin and Simon were sitting together at a table in the corner of the rooftop restaurant, and waved me over. I sat down with them, picked up a menu and then Simon said something that took me by surprise.

'Miles, have you ever been on television?'

Oh God.

'Sorry, Simon?'

'Have you ever been on television?'

'Er, possibly. Why?'

'Well, I was in a car outside the hotel this morning, and when you came out of the hotel, someone said, "Who's that bloke?" And I said, "That's Miles Jupp from BBC Scotland." And he said, "I'm pretty sure that that's Miles Jupp from *Balamory*."'

'Right,' I eventually responded.

'So…did you used to be in something called *Balamory*?'

I didn't normally make any effort to conceal the fact that I had appeared in a kids' TV show from people. But at this stage in the proceedings I really didn't think that it would help if the journalists on the tour knew that I was really an actor and comedian. Surely it could only lead them to view my presence with mistrust and suspicion. And quite rightly so. If people thought I was an ambitious young journalist then they might give me a spot of work to do if they were in a fix, or, at the very least, they might respect me. What I didn't really want people to know – not yet – was that I was a frequently out-of-work actor who was trying to become a cricket journalist via the absurd method of simply pretending to be a cricket journalist. How many other people now knew? And what would be the wider implications of this? My cricketing opinions were unlikely to be given much respect by someone whose children spent most mornings watching me prancing around in a pink kilt and talking total nonsense to a robot called Nobby. I hadn't attempted to disguise this; I had just sort of hoped that no one would notice. After all, months and months often went by without my being recognised.

'Well, Simon,' I eventually said, 'yes. Yes I was in *Balamory*. Long time ago, though. When I was an actor, very briefly. Before I got bitten by the journalism bug. I'm very much a journalist now, obviously.'

'Obviously,' said Simon.

'What's *Balamory*?' asked Kevin.

'It's a children's TV show,' I explained.

'Is that the one with all those coloured houses in it? I've seen that. It's Scottish, isn't it?'

'It is,' I said.

'And you're in it?'

I nodded sheepishly.

'Wow. But you've become a journalist?'

Hmmm.

'Yes.'

'Oh,' said Kevin. To my surprise he didn't seem to think that this was an odd way of going about things.

'Why do you seem so embarrassed about it?' asked Simon.

'I just don't really want people to know about it, that's all. I just think it would seem a little odd that I was here. People will think I'm just a pretender getting in the way when they have things to do.'

'No they won't. They'll probably think it's interesting.'

'Well, I think it could be a real obstacle to me achieving anything on this trip. So please, please, don't mention it to anyone.'

I held his gaze. I really meant this. I did not want my cover to be blown any further.

Simon, however, didn't seem to understand the importance of this.

'Don't worry, Miles. People will find out, won't they?' he said. 'Some already know. That's how I know. People were talking about it in the taxi this morning. Shall we order?'

No more was said on the subject, and instead the conversation turned to the next day's journey to Chandigarh. I joined in with the chatter, but inside I felt dreadful. Simon and Kevin were relaxed about what they had learnt, but it made me feel fearful, despairing even. I felt like a soon-to-be unmasked Anthony Blunt sitting at a dinner party listening to another guest saying, 'Oh, get over yourself, Anthony. No one gives a toss about communism any more. You'll feel so much better when your treason is out in the open.'

Chapter Nine

Our flight the next day was to be an early one, and thus anyone travelling onward to Chandigarh had been instructed by our dear tour operator to leave their luggage outside their hotel rooms overnight, and then to assemble in the lobby at half six to receive our boarding cards. I could see the logic in this – the luggage would be checked in in advance of our arrival at the airport. But even so, it seemed somewhat counter-intuitive to one's normal approach to security. Your luggage is generally considered safer in the room than in the corridor, and it is partly for this reason that you are provided with a lockable door between your possessions and any prospective thieves. It also would be hard to assess the success of the scheme until we were well into our journey. If everything went to plan, you would open your door first thing in the morning and find that your suitcase was no longer there. But this is also what you would find if it had been pilfered by some grubby opportunist. None of us would be able to completely relax until we had reached the luggage carousel at Delhi where we were scheduled to change planes.

A scrum of us duly appeared by the hotel's entrance at the appointed time looking sticky-eyed, sore-headed and slightly grumpier than usual. Once the tour operator's paperwork and roll call had been completed we were then informed we would now have to wait the best part of an hour before our bus to the airport would arrive. Rather like approximately three-quarters of all announcements made over the tannoy at British mainline rail stations, this news was largely greeted by a chorus of men shaking their heads and saying, 'Oh, for fuck's sake.' But my annoyance was more about the fact that I feared that this may not be ample time for the completion of any outstanding administrative tasks people had left to do. The previous night, whilst attempting to pay the bill I'd accrued for my meals and drinks, I'd spent 25 minutes at the front desk watching a receptionist painstakingly tot up all the amounts, and then checking and rechecking many times. Having spent so long displaying such a flair for rigorous detail though and talking me through the various charges, he then surprised me with the words, 'Okay, and I'll just round that up.'

'I'm sorry,' I said happily. 'Did you just say that you're rounding my bill up?'

'Yes, sir,' he said, looking more than happy to confirm that this was indeed the case.

'You're rounding it *up*? You're charging me more than the total that my bill comes to?'

'Yes, sir,' he said, still smiling and then opening his arms as if to ask if there was any other service he might be able to offer for my convenience. Perhaps I'd like to pay a special surplus fee for checking out of the hotel in person?

'How does that work? How can you round it up?'

The smile stayed firmly on his face, but he was clearly beginning to view me like an elderly relative who needed to have everything explained not only slowly, but repeatedly. No, Gran, I'm afraid you can't play DVDs on a Betamax.

'Sir, listen. I am rounding it up, but the thing is you see. It is not actually much money.'

'Yes, but it's...my money,' I said sounding wounded, wronged, outraged even.

The receptionist smiled at me and a familiar chuckle to my left alerted me to the presence of Victor Marks, the former

Somerset and England off-spinner who is now the cricket correspondent for the *Observer* and a regular summariser on *Test Match Special*. He was enjoying watching my battle with the receptionist; a battle I had already lost. Indians win most arguments of this sort, I imagine, because they possess, or at least appear to possess, infinite patience. British people only tend to get through a few exchanges in these sort of stand-offs before they blink, by which I mean explode into a disproportionate fury, from which there is nowhere else to go other than realising how cross you have suddenly become, and then the colour in your cheek is no longer caused by rage but embarrassment, and before you know it you're quietly reeling off phrases like 'I'm so sorry. I realise it's not your fault, obviously.'

Life hasn't taught me much, but I do know that arguing with hotel receptionists is like watching footballers arguing with referees: it never changes a bloody thing. They are not making considerations based upon an ethical scale, they deal only in fact.

'It costs eighteen pounds to use the Internet for a day?' you might ask someone behind the reception desk at a standard chain hotel in Britain.

'Yes, sir.'

'But that's ridiculous! Eighteen pounds? For a whole day? I only want to use it for an hour!'

'Well I'm afraid we only charge by the twenty-four-hour period, sir.'

'I'm not even going to spend twenty-four hours in the hotel. I couldn't if I wanted to. I wasn't allowed to check in until two, and I have to be out of my room by half past ten.'

'Yes, sir.'

'I'm sorry. I realise it's not your fault, obviously.'

'No problem, sir. Would you like the charge added to your bill?'

'Yes, please. And sorry for getting angry.'

'Really, sir. It's fine.'

*

Once our bus had arrived it sped straight to the airport past the vast and imposing Pride hotel where both teams had been billeted. Outside it stood the huge air-conditioned coach that had carried the England players to the ground every day. Its grandeur and size had been the subject of many a journalist's grumbling over the last few days, and probably not without some justification. Even outside a hotel as fancy as the Pride, it looked strangely out of place alongside a smattering of people carriers, and a few rows of modest saloons. This looked like the sort of cavernous and multi-lavatoried thing that enormous parties of rich but arthritic old folks travel hundreds of miles in to go and watch West End musicals. It was certainly far more luxuriant than was required to carry 20 sweaty men and their kit a distance of a few miles. But then that seems a curiously British thing to make a fuss about. Quite often the actual cost of something isn't what bothers us. Rather like St Paul having the laws of his conscience engraved upon his heart, it is as if a lot of British people always carry an inner Alan Bennett, who makes them recoil whenever they encounter anything 'a bit showy'. 'A luxury coach? Around India? Mam would never stand for air conditioning. So much easier to lean your head out of a tram and feel the breeze.'

When our own bus stopped at the airport, most of the press corps scooped up their hand luggage and leapt off eagerly, perhaps keen to be clear of Nagpur as soon as possible. I took my time, however, and had only just gathered up both of my bags and got to my feet when the driver shut the doors, turned on the engine, and then hit the accelerator with some glee, as if Nagpur was pleased to be rid of the press corps.

'Hang on!' I yelled from the back. 'I'm still here! Stop!'

He was nothing if not obedient, and immediately slammed on the brakes with the same vigour as he had just hit the gas. I have never had especially good balance, and coupled with this was also carrying a bag in each hand and thus had no means of steadying myself. Instead, I started to hurtle down the central aisle, my feet barely touching the floor. I glanced off one upright rail, and then collided hard with a seat, which made me drop a bag. The seat took a little of the pace off me but didn't fully stop me, and thus I succeeded in tripping over the bag that I had just let go of, and falling headlong into the aisle, landing on the other bag which I was carrying. I stayed down until the squealing of the brakes had stopped and could then hear the driver laughing heartily. I looked up to see him grinning in the mirror at my unique brand of panache-free acrobatics.

'I stopped,' he giggled.

*

The first leg of our journey was on one of those planes deemed small enough to have propellers on the wings rather than engines. Apparently propellers are actually the safer of the two, but their appearance somehow instils rather less confidence, perhaps linked to memories of war films set in the desert in which you see grizzled men with sand in their eyes and bullets whizzing past their ears desperately struggling to hand-start the things.

The press were the first aboard and we were all placed toward the rear of the plane, which then sat on the runway for a while as we waited for the rest of the seats to fill up. I had a seat next to the aisle, and leaning out across it I peered out of the opposite windows to try and get a glimpse of who the other passengers might be, and to see if their boarding might be imminent. There, striding towards our plane across the scorching tarmac, was the England squad and their entourage. Soon I could hear the pitter-patter of their approach, which turned to a rumble as they climbed up the flight steps and then, one by one, came into the cabin.

I found the thought that we were all sharing a plane together unbelievably exciting. Inside me a star-struck fan was leaping up and down with joy, but after the embarrassment of my 'Here's Freddie!' moment in yesterday's press conference I did everything in my power to look as unmoved as I possibly could, even looking about me a little to demonstrate to anyone around me just how unbothered by the team's appearance I was. Whether or not I was successful in my attempts to conceal my excitement as hero after hero emerged I really have no idea. It is not unlikely that I looked as if I was desperately trying to hold in an enormous fart.

The team all appeared to be in high spirits, and were chatting freely as they boarded. But their talk quickly simmered down as soon as the frontrunners looked up and clocked the assembled press who they would be sharing their air space with. The immediate looks of distrust and suspicion that spread across some of their faces was almost chilling.

Captain Freddie Flintoff was leading the troops, and he wore aviator shades, which enabled him to stare right through everyone before placing his batting helmet in his overhead locker. No sooner had the England team sat down on one side of the plane, then the Indian team boarded. The prospect of flying with all this lot started to send me slightly giddy. The Indian cricket team are probably the country's biggest megastars, and I felt a childlike sense of glee about travelling on a plane with such superfamous people. And what if we crashed? I could imagine the terrible news being read out on Radio 4 by Peter Donaldson:

'Good evening. The entire English and Indian cricket teams were wiped out today in a plane crash. Also on-board were twenty-one journalists and, for reasons nobody is quite sure of, Archie The Inventor from *Balamory*.'

With the exception of the odd player attending a press conference, this was by far the closest that I had got to the cricketers themselves, and I relished being in the company of Dravid and Tendulkar. In 2004 Dravid had been employed, by a mystery donor, to play for Scotland in the National Cricket League and I had really looked forward to watching him play at the picturesque Grange club in Edinburgh. The boundaries there are so small that I thought even he might feel encouraged to try and clear them, but on the only occasion I managed to get down for a game I arrived to find that he'd already been out for a duck and was sitting with his feet up watching the game. That day I'd been disappointed, but now that he was playing against England I'd be happy to see him dismissed cheaply time and time again.

Though we had now been up for hours, it was still early in the morning and most of the players and journalists dozed. I glanced up from time to time to observe how international cricketers behaved in transit. Freddie had crashed out as soon as he'd sat down, although Shaun Udal read a broadsheet with some reading glasses perched on the end of his nose, occasionally beaming around the plane like a benign uncle on an unexpected day trip. At the age of 37 and not having played for England for a decade he was perhaps still a little surprised to find himself on successive winter tours. Liam Plunkett, who must have got up much earlier than everybody else in order to have enough time to gel and style his hair, was now so wide awake that he was able to tackle a copy of *Loaded*. And future England captain Kevin Pietersen spent much of the journey sucking on boiled sweets, before taking them out of his mouth and throwing them in an attempt to make them stick in Virender Sehwag's hair.

Victor Marks sat on my right, and like a kindly tortoise beginning to stir after months of hibernation, he showed signs of waking as we approached the runway at Delhi. I asked him if he'd ever been to Chandigarh before and he answered in the affirmative, before implying in his typically self-deprecating way that it was just one of many venues on this continent where batsmen had been queuing up to spank his off-spinners out of the ground.

'And what of Chandigarh?' I asked. 'Is there much to tell?'

I do not, I promise you, spend my days addressing people as if I am being played by Dame Maggie Smith. But there was clearly something about Victor Marks that brought out my theatrical side.

'Well, it was designed by Le Corbusier of course,' he said, 'which they're rather proud of. But as I remember it looks rather a lot like Stevenage. I may be thinking of somewhere else though...'

'Milton Keynes perhaps?'

'Yes, perhaps.'

I was unable to find out if it was Stevenage or Chandigarh that looked like Milton Keynes, because at that exact moment we hit the runway at a rather more obtuse angle than we perhaps ought to have done, and proceeded to bounce along it at such a rate that it felt as if one of my eyes might burst. I grabbed onto something (perhaps it was Victor Marks) and clamped my eyes firmly shut as the plane jerked from side to side. My ears were filled with a cacophony of rattling windows, slapping tyres, and a short, low emission of vowels, which signified that a group of largely middle-aged men had all just lost their stomachs.

Eventually, like someone who has recently introduced prune juice to their diet, the plane's movements became smoother. I opened my eyes to take in how green around the gills our party had become. I could hear a splendid selection of sickly groans from around the cabin. The players were going to stay on this plane all the way to Chandigarh, whereas we were disembarking here to change onto a different – presumably cheaper – flight. But having experienced this landing, no residual jealousy of the teams' onward travel arrangements remained amongst our party.

As soon as we had taxied to a standstill, there was the sound of 22 sets of seat belts being unclipped, and we all lunged for the overhead lockers in an English sort of a frenzy, and then filed hurriedly past the subdued players, desperate for the opportunity, no matter how brief, to stand on terra firma.

*

In the event we stayed on the ground at Delhi for far longer than we might have anticipated. Our luggage had to be retrieved from the plane and then checked in again, and our group spent an hour loitering by the carousel waiting for its re-emergence. I got talking to Angela and Peter from the Barmy Army who also turned out to have been on the flight, and indeed turned out to be chums of Freddie from back in Manchester.

'It must be great fun being a cricket journalist,' Peter said to me.

'Oh, it is. It is,' I said.

'Indeed it must be,' I thought.

The first movement of the carousel revealed that someone had just been dropped from the India squad: An enormous kit bag marked with the name 'VVS Laxman' passed through the rubbery curtains and out onto the carousel. There were a few 'Ah's from the journalists. Clearly Laxman had paid the price for a disappointing game, and would not be continuing his journey with the rest of the squad.

We finally passed out of the baggage hall and into the bright March sunshine where we were met by a tour operator, who was waiting for us next to a kiosk selling Father Christmas key-rings. Then we were led to another terminal and straight to another check-in desk. This particular airline was stricter than the last lot, and were quite firm that each passenger was only allowed one item in the hold. This represented quite a dilemma to a group of 22 people attempting to check-in 37 bags and boxes of equipment. Immediately several little arguments broke out, and a number of journalists put themselves forward to restore order, which only prompted further rows.

'We need fifteen pieces of luggage that can be sent on later,' we were told by the lady behind the desk.

'Any equipment has to take precedence,' bellowed one broadcaster.

'I've got some golf clubs,' said Christopher Martin-Jenkins, who was immediately rounded on.

'Not that sort of equipment. Fucking golf clubs! I mean cameras and sound kit. Things we need to do our bloody jobs.'

'I understand what you're saying. What I'm saying is that I am volunteering my golf clubs to be sent on later. I can probably manage without them for a couple of days.'

'Oh. Right. Sorry.'

Other pairs locked horns in a similar cross-purposed vein, as if this was the mating season for journalists, and this strange little ritual simply had to be adhered to. Amidst this peculiar dance of confusion a voice suddenly shouted out sarcastically, 'Oh God. As if this trip couldn't get any worse…' and all eyes turned to see a wiry, mischievous man with twinkling eyes advancing upon our group. The Scottish actor David Hayman would have been the perfect casting to play him in a biopic, but he would have to do some voice work first because he greeted our company with the words, 'Hello, gentlemen. Now, what's all the trouble?' in a rich, strong Welsh accent. People looked thrilled to see him, and his arrival brought about a temporary calm as hands were shaken and shoulders slapped. 'Edward!' some people shouted. 'Bevan!' said others. Ah, so this was the infamous figure whose name I had kept hearing. So often when I had told people that I worked for the *Western Mail*, they had said brightly, 'Oh, then you must know Edward Bevan.' 'Ah, yes. Edward Bevan,' I would say, smiling and nodding and wondering who he was.

'Edward! Hello!' said Peter Baxter. 'Edward, you need to meet Miles Jupp. Miles, this is Edward Bevan. Edward is the cricket correspondent for BBC Radio Wales. Miles is the cricket correspondent for the *Western Mail*.'

Oh dear.

'How do you do!' I said brightly as I proffered a hand.

'The *Western Mail*?' he said, as he took my hand firmly. 'I didn't know that they had a cricket correspondent.'

Oh dear, oh dear, oh fucking deary dear.

'Right,' I said. 'Yes, yes.' And nodded understandingly as if this was a common misunderstanding. 'At the moment I'm mainly doing stuff for the website. They're er…they're really very keen to expand things in that area.'

'Ah. Well, good luck with that. I like all the lads at the *Western Mail*. How's everyone doing? Ian? Griff? And David? Is David still there?'

I pondered this tricky question for a while, and then smiled broadly.

'Edward,' I said. 'Everybody is extremely well, thank you. Now, if you'll just excuse me I really do have to visit the facilities.'

When I returned from standing needlessly in the loo for two minutes, David Norrie from the *News Of The World* had taken advantage of the distraction caused by Bevan's arrival and quickly solved the luggage issue. There was a stack of 15 items next to the counter and everything else was being loaded onto the conveyor. Norrie looked a little like an ageing rock star – sunglasses, spiky hair, a small dash of triangular beard under the lip. He was handing out the correct boarding cards to everyone. I had still not yet met him, but nonetheless he seemed to know who I was. 'This is yours,' he said, handing me a card with my name on it.

*

In the departure lounge I joined a lengthy queue in order to buy two samosas, one to eat, and another one to accidentally drop into Simon Mann's lap as I sat down next to him. He did his best to be polite about it but developed a slight twitch when he noticed that my clumsiness had resulted in a serious amount of oily residue on his cream shorts.

On my other side sat Peter Baxter, who quietly enquired as to how I was finding my trip.

'Is it how you imagined it would be, Miles?'

'I suppose I thought it might all be a little...jollier,' I confessed.

He was very understanding about this, and explained that although the press corps travelled as a group that 'did not necessarily mean that they were a team'. Really, they were a group of rivals cramped together under one lumpy umbrella. That's why a stink had kicked up so quickly over the luggage. People just wanted to fend for themselves, and not necessarily have to worry about each other.

On the flight I sat next to Norrie, although we didn't exchange a single word.

A humid bus then took us to the hotel where an enthusiastic group of staff ushered us into a line and then welcomed us by placing garlands of jasmine flowers around our necks and then gently applying red tilaks to our foreheads with a warm finger. Some journalists looked uncomfortable with this ritual. Others, like Derek Pringle, threw themselves into it with gusto.

I thanked the staff and then withdrew to my room to enjoy some personal space after the journey and to panic about how to play the next few days. I wanted to make a fresh start in Chandigarh, to win around some of the more suspicious media types. I was also keen to secure my press pass and some work to justify it. None of these hopes proved particularly easy to achieve.

*

Connecting to the rather weak wireless signal, I checked, unsuccessfully, for any word from BBC Scotland. I also submitted a piece for my *Western Mail* blog. And then, with an hour or so before the sun was due to set, plodded out of the hotel to see what there was to see in Chandigarh. I had seen so little of the city of Nagpur. It hadn't helped that our hotel there was on a main road without much in the way of pavement, and thus the prospect of a stroll was not an appetising one. Although not actually cool, the temperature was a lot milder than in Nagpur, and the hotel was situated on a street with a wide pavement along which I could toddle. It was a very pleasant place for a spot of gentle ambling and shopping, despite there being far more creatures buzzing around and biting me than I would normally have liked. Along the pavement, people sat in groups chatting and smoking together, and every few yards there was a little stove on which sweet-looking coffee might be bubbling away, or samosas and pastries being kept hot.

Chandigarh is a planned city, and operates on a grid system. There were a huge number of shops in the area around the hotel and not just on the ground floor. All of the buildings were a uniform three storeys high, usually with different shops on each level. You might look up to see an optician's positioned above a clothes shop which itself was sitting over a barber. What one saw most of, however, was shops selling mobile phones or places that offered a photo developing service. Nearly every other shop appeared to be either of these, as if the people of Chandigarh's real interest was the purchasing and photographing of mobile phone equipment.

As I walked The Rutles' song 'Shangri-La' played in my head on a loop. But as I sang along to the chorus I substituted 'Shangri-La' for the name of our home for the next seven nights: 'You can be whoever you are in Chandigarh.' The song's opening lyrics were also curiously pertinent to my situation: 'Did you ever get the feeling / That the truth is less revealing / Than a down-right lie? / And did you think your head was hip / To certain things it's not equipped / to qualify?' Was this song about me? Was it about a man in a foreign land, pretending to be a thing in order to become it? And trying to ignore what he was? And maybe beginning to wonder if any of this was really such a good idea? And what did it say about me that my life was better summed up by a Beatles pastiche than anything Lennon or McCartney had actually penned?

But I hadn't just come out to wander the streets without purpose. Before leaving Britain I had not managed to find an adaptor plug, and my journalistic workload had been so light thus far, that I had managed to get a whole week's use out of my laptop's battery. A man at reception had given me directions to a shop where I could find what I needed.

'It is not far,' he said, 'but you do have to cross quite a busy road.'

He was right to warn me that this road would be something of an obstacle. But he was wrong to describe it as only being 'quite busy'. The road was simply astonishing. There were eight lanes of traffic, made up of every conceivable kind of vehicle. There were cars, buses, taxis, trucks, vans, carts carrying hay and weaving in and out of every available gap were rickshaws, bicycles with three passengers, tuk-tuks carrying whole families, cattle, and men carrying logs. There was a cacophony of horns, and the air was thick with exhaust.

I instantly knew that there was no way that I possessed the necessary reactions, stamina or foolhardiness to make it across this road without a serious incident. I must have stood there for a full 15 terrified minutes. On a couple of occasions I had tried to sum up some courage and taken half a stride into the road in an attempt to make a crossing, but each time a sudden feeling of panic enveloped me and I leapt backwards onto the pavement to cower once more. Frustratingly enough, I could see the shop I wanted to go to just on the other side of the carriageway.

I was really puzzled as to how I might succeed in my mission, and was on the verge of calling it off and walking sadly back to the hotel when an idea popped into my head. There was a cycle rickshaw progressing towards me on my side of the road, and so I waved at the driver and shouted. He stopped and I clambered into the back.

'Where to?' he said over his shoulder.

'Can you just take me to the other side of the road, please?'

'Really? That's all you want me to do?'

'For now.'

He shrugged, and as I sat back in my seat, he started to honk his horn and began the procedure of changing lanes and executed an enormous U-turn that must have taken over ten minutes. When we finally reached the other side, he pulled up outside the shop.

'Wait here, please.'

I dashed into the shop, bought what I needed, and had leapt aboard again within a couple of minutes.

'Where now?'

'Back to the other side, please.'

And so he completed a 27-point turn and plonked me back right where our journey had started.

'Thanks,' I said as I handed over the fare, and a tip. 'I couldn't have got across without you.'

'This was strange,' he said, as he pedalled off into the traffic once more.

I returned to find that my bed had been turned down, and rose petals scattered onto my pillow and sheets. I shared a quick quiet supper with Simon and Kevin in the hotel restaurant and we were joined by a chap I'd not noticed before called Gary. I wasn't entirely sure what newspaper he worked for, but he told me that he'd spotted me in Nagpur wearing my floppy hat. I had, it is undeniable, been wearing a floppy hat in Nagpur. Perhaps his keen sense of observation and passion for the truth indicated that he was some sort of investigative journalist.

*

My policy of drinking a little more sensibly in the evenings was already paying dividends, I felt when I awoke for the first time in Chandigarh. I had only drunk one glass of wine with my dinner, and was rewarded with one of my clearest heads of the trip. I felt well rested, enjoyed rather than feared the bright shards of light that were thrown by the gaps in the curtains and felt no pain behind the eyes or dull thud in my ears. I swung my legs over the edge of the bed and then launched myself into an upright position without a creak or twinge, before walking to the bathroom with a spring in my step and a feeling that everything was all right with the world. But then, whilst urinating, I took one look at my face in the mirror that hung above the lavatory and was stunned; my forehead, my nose and my left cheek were smeared liberally with a dark red, liquid. My T-shirt, too, had splashes of the stuff all over it. What had happened to me? Why was I covered with so much blood? And just how could anyone haemorrhage quite so painlessly? Was I dead? It would certainly explain why I felt so unusually good. Everything was over. I would never have to make any difficult decisions again or tell lies. Nor would I need to dress. Or wash. Or meet people. Eating? Well. I'd certainly miss eating. But my time would be my own, I could go anywhere I fancied without needing a press pass, and I could haunt anyone I pleased. Crossing busy roads would now be a doddle. The whole death thing, although a rather sudden development, already seemed to have a great deal to recommend it.

But would I have a reflection? And why would I still have to go to the lavatory? And what was that sickly, sweet smell? I held my free hand up to my face and then ran a finger across my bloodied cheek. Surely if it was blood, it would have been dried, but this sticky substance came away on my finger. I sniffed it, and then instantly realised that what was plastered all over my face was not blood, but the squelchy remains of the rose petals that had been scattered on my pillow from the night before and which I had pulped with the heat of my head. Death had not seemed like such a disastrous turn of events, but I was already back in the land of the living before I had shaken and re-trousered.

*

I knew that Nagpur had not been the success it might have been but here, I decided as I wrote up my diary at breakfast, things would be different. My blog for the *Western Mail*'s website was now up and running, and so if nothing else I could lay some sort of claim to being here working for a newspaper. I still hadn't had any response from a single message that I had sent to my colleague at BBC Scotland, but crucially I still had the paperwork that stated that I also worked for them. Best of all, Rajun Nair had assured me that there would be a press pass waiting for me at the ground here. So before I headed off into town for the first of two days lolling about with a rucksack and a copy of the *Lonely Planet*, I would make a quick detour to the ground and make sure that I finally got my hands on the big shiny press pass that I so desperately craved.

Most of the journalists would be heading down to the ground to have a look at England's preparations and to assess any likely team changes, and my hope was that by the time the majority of them had arrived, I would be nonchalantly wearing a proper press pass and thus be subconsciously drawn to their collective bosom. I taxied to Chandigarh's ground, The Punjab Cricket Association, in the suburb of Mohali, with Kevin and Peter Baxter. There was a little bit of talk about the game, and it seemed likely that there would be some changes from the

England team that had played at Nagpur but we weren't really sure what they might be.

'I think Shaun Udal might get a game,' said somebody.

The net session, it soon transpired, was taking place at the opposite end of the ground to where our taxi had dropped us, outside a set of large and unguarded gates behind the pavilion. Neatly typed signs had been stuck up in various places pointing all journalists in the direction of a wire mesh corridor that led underneath the stands, through which we should make our way to the practice area. This corridor, though, had been divided up by a series of gates, and unlike the gates into the ground itself, each of these gates appeared to be staffed. As we approached the first ones the staff were revealed to be even more intimidating than those soldiers that we had encountered at Nagpur. These were a different breed of soldier altogether: efficient and keen-eyed, with high-waisted khaki trousers, brown shirts with epaulettes, smart regulation turbans and powerful-looking machine guns slung over their shoulders, which looked instantly more deadly than the old Lee Enfield rifles that someone had picked up in the Nagpur branch of Cash Converters.

'Yes?' said the soldier, as we approached.

'We are journalists,' said Kevin, in the exact tone of voice that I imagine heralds used when bringing a message for a king.

'Show me your passes, please.'

The other two whipped out their BCCI passes, and showed them to the soldier who nodded and then turned to me.

'And your pass, please?'

'I haven't actually got it yet, but I…'

'You need a pass to go any further. What is your business here?'

'I'm a journalist too, it's just that I've not got my pass yet. That's why I've come to the ground. I have come to the ground to collect my pass.'

I smiled at him. He did not smile back.

'You need a pass to go any further.'

'But that's why I'm here,' I pleaded.

I showed him the pass I'd been given at Nagpur, and the headed notepaper from the BBC, all of which he eyed suspiciously.

'These aren't what you need.'

'Yes, but I can't get what I need unless I can get into the ground.'

He fixed me with a long, hard stare, and then looked me up and down for any signs of weakness or trouble. I hardly dared to blink under this scrutiny.

In my peripheral vision I could see that Kevin and Peter were standing back, both staring at their feet and occasionally glimpsing at their watches. I couldn't tell if they were embarrassed on my behalf or getting irritated that I was slowing them down. Meanwhile I tried to hold the soldier's stare while he sucked air through his teeth and then slowly exhaled it.

'Okay,' he said. He turned and opened the gate, ushering Kevin and Peter through with a polite smile. Once they had passed him, he dropped his smile and gestured to me to follow them. Fifty metres further down the corridor we encountered an identical situation.

'What is your business, please?'

'We are journalists,' said Kevin again, still anxious to convey his message to the king.

'Show me your passes, please.'

'Guys, you'd better go on without me,' I said. 'This might take a while.'

The other two thanked me, flashed their passes and were ushered straight through. Meanwhile I took out my headed notepaper and the Nagpur pass again, and then went through the same rigmarole, the same explanations, the same stare, the same sound of breath being sucked through the teeth before a muttered 'Okay' and a quick flick of a pair of glassy eyes telling me that I could continue my passage. For the moment.

In total I passed through five of these checkpoints, each soldier more suspicious than the last, each stare a little colder, before I finally passed through the last of the gates, out from under the stands and into the training area. I stood for a moment taking in the scene, drenched in a nervous sweat. The first of six or so nets was just 30 yards from where I now stood, and the England team had already embarked on an arduous session. Monty Panesar was bowling to Kevin Pietersen in one net, whilst in another one Freddy Flintoff was drilling a number of local spinners back over their heads. A rope had been set up to keep the press at a safe distance, although just the other side of it England's coach, Duncan Fletcher, was giving our reserve keeper Matt Prior some practice with the gloves. This involved Fletcher using a thin bat with rubber flaps so that every ball he faced was edged straight behind him to be pouched by the eager Prior. A nearby Geraint Jones, his own keeping practice apparently over, looked on anxiously. It was his own place that Prior was chasing.

As well as Kevin and Peter there was already a small smattering of other journalists sitting around on plastic chairs, and the Sky Sports News team had set up their tripod and were filming pieces to camera. Also present were a number of Indian officials there to greet and oversee, and yet more soldiers making sure that no one got any funny ideas, sonny. There was a trestle table covered with cups and saucers, pots of coffee, and jugs of milk. It was all set out as if we were soon going to be standing around nattering about what a splendid sermon the vicar had just given.

There was also another cloth-covered table bearing a sign that read 'Accreditation'. So I marched over and told the Indian official manning it the news that I was expecting a pass. There were already a selection of passes laid out on the table, and so I scanned them, looking for one that bore my name. I could not see one.

'What is your name, please?'

'Miles Jupp. I'm with the *Western Mail* and BBC Scotland.'

'I cannot see one here with your name on, I'm afraid.'

'Right. Are there any other passes anywhere, do you know? Is there a separate pile for freelancers maybe?'

'I do not think so, no.'

Oh, come on. Please.

'It's just that I was expecting one. I spoke to one of the BCCI officials in Nagpur and he told me that there would definitely be a pass here for me.'

'Well, there is no pass for you, I'm afraid.'

'Right.'

I put my hands on my hips and slowly felt a wave of fury rising within me. I knew I wasn't necessarily in the right here, but all this you-can't-have-a-pass-no-actually-you-can-have-one-no-on-second-thoughts-don't-have-a-pass-I've-changed-my-mind-again-you-can't business was starting to do my fucking nut. 'Everything will be fine,' I had been told by the nice man at Nagpur. At the time I was ready to shower him with kisses, but now I wanted to dash back there and give him a bloody shake. Had he had any intention of passing on my details to his colleagues at Chandigarh or was he just fobbing me off, tired of having to plough through emails from a man banging on about the importance of keeping the people of Wales in touch with vital cricket news? Perhaps he was forgetful, and the forms necessary for my pass to be processed were still buried deep in one of the messy piles of paperwork that littered the offices of The Vidarbha Cricket Association...

'Mr Jupp?'

The official behind the desk was trying to get my attention, and snap me out of my inner monologue.

'Sorry. Yes? What were you...?'

'I was saying that even though there is no pass for you here, I do not think that it will be a problem.'

'Really?'

'We can issue you with a new pass.'

Oh, the flirts. All this toying with me had to *stop*.

He directed me to stand against a whitewashed wall behind me and then took my photograph with a digital camera. Then he asked me to write my full name and employer down on a piece of paper. This time I did not write 'BBC', as so far those letters had spelt only bureaucratic difficulty for me. Instead I just put 'Miles Jupp, *Western Mail*'.

'Please, Mr Jupp, take a seat. I will be back shortly with your pass.'

I sat down on one of the white plastic seats with a keen sense of anticipation. Again it appeared that I was just minutes away from finally getting my hands on that pass. A busload of other journalists had clearly just arrived, as at that moment a swarm of them flooded into the practice area. Damn it. I wanted to be already wearing my pass by the time that the majority of people had got here.

'Hello, Miles,' said Derek Pringle wandering past. 'Everything good?'

'It's all good,' I said. 'All good.'

But just two minutes after he had disappeared, the Indian official that I had been speaking to reappeared. He was not, however, accompanied by a pass. He was instead scurrying along trying to keep up with a huge, barrel-chested moustachioed man, who looked like an Indian version of Obelix in a blazer. He was steaming towards all of the journalists with a face like thunder, holding the piece of paper that I had written my name on.

'Miles Jupp!' the large man bellowed as he neared us. 'Who is Miles Jupp?'

'I am,' I said nervously getting to my feet.

'You are Miles Jupp?'

He looked at me with a level of disdain that was almost magnificent, as if I'd got his unmarried daughter pregnant and had then cheerfully approached him to ask for a loan. He was like a coiled spring. Something noisy and frightening was about to happen.

'Yes. It's me.'

'You. You are Miles Jupp from the *Western Mail*?'

'Yes.'

A vein in his left temple started to pulse and his mouth started to twitch. His eyes began to bulge. Next to him the man from behind the accreditation desk was giving me a twisted stare that I interpreted to mean either 'You're fucked' or 'You might still have some time. Run! Run from this place! Run from this place before this man reaches inside you and pulls your still beating heart out through your anus and then squeezes it with his teeth until it bursts and your lifeblood is splashed all over your lifeless, pointless form.' He really did have a terribly expressive face, this fellow.

'Well,' Obelix said. 'You cannot have accreditation.'

'But I—'

'No buts. I have strict instructions.'

'About me?'

Oh God. What if someone had reported me? Had I been exposed as a pretender? Was I going to be hanged like Perkin Warbeck?

'No. I have not had strict instructions about you. I have had them about all freelancers. No more passes for freelancers.'

'But I was specifically told that there was a pass waiting for me here.'

'Well there isn't. There isn't any more space. You must apply for one through the BCCI.'

'But I've already done that,' I snapped back, surprising him a little, and me even more.

This angered him, and he took a step forwards, leant down towards me so that his face was close to mine.

'I am telling you formally...' he began slowly and quietly. Then he exploded again. 'NO PASS! NO PASS!'

His hot breath blasted away the last of the drops of nervous sweat that minutes earlier I had been drenched in.

'But can you just tell me why?'

I wanted to hear the answer. I needed to know what he had to say. Could I not have a pass because of some administrative cock-up, or because someone had notified them that I was a fraud and not deserving of accreditation? There was no answer to these questions though. He just erupted, like a man who has had to answer too many cold calls that day.

'JUST SHUT UP! SHUT UP AND STOP ASKING ME THINGS. THAT IS IT. NO PASS.'

'But—'

'SHHHUUUUT UUUUP!'

And with that he turned on his heels, and stomped back whence he had come. The first official gave me a quick, apologetic glance and then scurried off after Obelix. Perhaps it was his responsibility to lead Obelix into darkened rooms after moments like this, and apply a cold flannel to his forehead. But as he departed, clearly intent on calming down, my own anger rose and all sense melted into the red mist that now enveloped me. I lashed out and kicked over a plastic chair. I derived some small satisfaction from seeing the thing cartwheel away, and shaped to kick the next one down, ready to make my way along the row and mow them all down like a lone drunk who won't be satisfied until there are no traffic cones left standing. I was just swinging my right foot back and lining up to make contact when I realised that a silence had descended over the area. I stopped mid-kick, and turned around to see that everybody was now staring at me: all of the other journalists, all of the Indian officials, and all of the soldiers; some of the England team had stopped what they were doing in the nets and were now looking over in my direction to see what the fuss was.

I was in a rage. I had now been promised a pass twice and still hadn't managed to get one. Okay, so I might not actually be a journalist. And yes, I didn't really have any actual journalism to do. It was also the case that to get this far I had already told a number of lies. But at least I had had the manners, the honesty, the decency and the integrity to make a point of always lying through the correct channels.

'What was all that about?' asked one correspondent.

'What an officious bastard,' I moaned to no one in particular. 'Anybody could put a blazer on, and then march around cocking things up for people.'

'Yes,' said David Lloyd from the *Evening Standard*, 'I imagine even you could do that.'

A helpful official had picked up the chair that I had sent flying and put it upright again. So I sat down on it, put my head in my hands and sulked. My feelings of frustration were exacerbated tenfold by the distance I was from home. I was, though, now even more determined than before to get my hands on a pass again. In fact, I wanted more than that. I wanted to get into print. I wanted to make a broadcast. And I wanted to be paid for it. Not for the money itself, but just so that I could say in all honesty that I had worked as a cricket writer and broadcaster, and could feel that I had earned my spurs. And I had to get a pass so that would happen. I needed to get as close to the action as only a pass could allow me, or I would have nothing to write or broadcast about. There was no angle from which you could view my situation without me looking totally fucked.

I was later told that the England coach, Duncan Fletcher, had watched my angry chair kicking and found it hilarious. Apparently it is the only thing that he has ever found remotely amusing.

*

As the practice session drew to a close, I caught a glimpse of Andrew Walpole accompanying some of the England players to interviews, and so I followed him. Once he had chaperoned the last of his charges, I explained what had just happened, and the predicament that this left me in. He listened sympathetically.

'Come on then, let's go and talk to the bloke.'

We found the large, grumpy bloke in one of the tunnels that led down to the side of the pitch and Andrew spoke to him on my behalf.

'I've got a young journalist here who really needs a press pass. He can't work without it.'

'There isn't space for him,' said Blazer Man, and walked off again.

'I'm really sorry,' Andrew said.

Perhaps this was it, then. If I was going to watch the second Test it would have to be from the stands. I wouldn't have the option of going to any press conferences or watching any of the legends in action behind the scenes. I was just back to being a plain old punter.

'There'll be a press conference at the team hotel tomorrow afternoon,' said Andrew. 'Come along, and I'll see what I can do.'

Well, that was something to cling to for the moment. As Andrew headed off in the direction of the pavilion, the rest of the press corps came down the tunnel I was in and swept past me, led by yet another Indian official.

'Where's everyone going?'

'Pitch.'

'Right.'

Of course, that's what proper cricket journalists did; they went out into the middle of the stadium before the game to examine the wicket that it would be played on. Then they could write interesting things about its condition in their preview pieces: 'The wicket here at Mohali looks dry, and will surely start to break up if the sun stays out.' Or: 'There's still a bit of green at both ends, and there's a little moisture about, but if the openers can see off the new ball this track should flatten out into an absolute belter.' I often read these sorts of descriptions in newspapers, and probably nodded knowingly, but in all honesty I never really understood exactly what people were on about and how such things could be confidently predicted. Sometimes the ball seemed to spin because the pitch was wet, and other times because it was so dry. Sometimes the pitch was good for batting because it was so fast, and yet other times this was more helpful to the bowling. To me, time spent listening to talk about the pitch was no better than time spent guessing what the weather might be like: an inexact science. All I ever learnt from watching Geoffrey Boycott sticking his car key into the cracks was what type of car he drove. If anybody said anything about the pitch I would just nod, and if they asked me a direct question I would try and dodge it, by shrugging and going, 'Well, it's all there, isn't it?'

I joined the group and the Indian official led everyone as far as a gate at the edge of the pitch marked with the words 'No Admittance'.

'Wait here, please,' said the official and disappeared, leaving us with a security guard in a white shirt and black tie who was deep in conversation on his walkie-talkie.

A couple of people attempted to pass through the gate, but the security guard broke off from his walkie-talking to stop them.

'Please wait. We must wait for that man to return. Then you may go out there.'

There were a few mutterings from the press corps, perhaps even a hint of dissent. The security guard didn't look like the sort of man who could have physically prevented more than 20 people rushing past him. Before any mutiny could spread, though, one of the smart khaki soldiers with an automatic weapon appeared by his side, and smiled curtly at the group. Everyone stood down, and cheerful conversation broke out around me. I was feeling gutted though. I was in a worse position than I'd been at this stage before the first match. At least I had some sort of pass for that one, and the promise of work. That work, though, had not materialised. And I still had no pass. All I had gained since then was a blog and an electrical adaptor plug, neither of which were really much to boast about and both of which had cost me over the odds.

A gentle cough over my left shoulder alerted me to the presence of a journalist who had sidled up to me for a bit of a chat. From what I had experienced of him so far he seemed nice but possibly a little prickly.

'So, you were having a bit of trouble with your pass?'

'That's right.'

'I saw your little…exchange with our friend back there.'

'Yes, he was a bit serious.'

'Yes, heavy-handed.'

'Mmm,' I replied.

'Of course, you shouldn't have to deal with all that stuff, it's not your job.'

'Sorry?'

'Well, it's not up to you to handle all that stuff, is it? It should be dealt with by whoever you work for.'

'Oh, right. Absolutely,' I said.

'Who do you work for again?'

I told him.

'That must be tough,' he said. 'I mean, BBC Scotland probably don't take all that much stuff do they?'

'It's er…it's not been frantic, no,' I mumbled.

'And even the *Western Mail*. I doubt they're mad keen. You'd probably have been all right if Simon Jones hadn't got injured.' He laughed, and so I chuckled too.

'But seriously,' he continued. 'That must be difficult. Pretty hard to support yourself just working for people like that. You don't work for anyone else do you, or I'd probably have come across you before now.'

'Well...'

'I mean, you'd need a little more income wouldn't you. Do you cover any other sports?'

'No, no. I do some writing that isn't journalism.'

'Oh really?' This intrigued him. 'What sort of stuff?'

Hmm. The last thing I wrote were some lines for the pantomime that I'd done in Aberdeen. Before that some sketches for a disastrous sketch show at the Edinburgh Festival. Nothing that really suggested that I was a proper, legitimate journalist.

'Well, I try to keep it pretty light.'

'I see,' he said, ominously. Then he gestured out towards the pitch with a quick tilt of the head.

'Anyway, what about here then? What do you reckon?'

What did I reckon about what?

'Well it all looks...quite nice,' I offered.

'I don't mean what do you think it looks like! I mean the game,' he snapped.

'Right, right. Well it's sort of difficult to know, isn't it? Without having got to inspect the wicket yet.'

'Yeah, but even so. Have you any thoughts about the team? Do you think we'll make any changes?'

'I don't know really.'

'You don't know? You must have some thoughts. Otherwise what are you going to write about?'

Never mind what am I going to write about. I have nothing to write for. It was like asking a drowning man what his favourite swimming stroke is. Or a tailor asking a lady what side they dress.

'Er...'

'Well?'

'Well, what are *you* going to write about?' I countered.

He scoffed at this question.

'I'm not going to tell you what *I'm* thinking about writing. Especially not if you don't know what you're going to write about. You might be tempted to nick my ideas.'

Yup. Definitely prickly. But what *did* I think about the game? What might the team be? There wasn't all that much wrong with the lot that had just played. What could I say that would make me sound insightful? Possibly something about Ian Blackwell not having had the strongest of debuts...Then it came to me. Something someone had said in the taxi on the way over.

'Okay,' I said. 'I'm probably going to write that I think that Shaun Udal might get a game.'

'What?'

'Shaun Udal. He could well play here.'

'Do you think so?'

'Yes, that's what I reckon.'

'You think Udal's going to play? How do you know that?'

'Well I just...think...you know...that he might. This pitch takes spin apparently and he's...you know...a spinner. So I just thought...that...that he might.'

'There's something you're not telling me, isn't there? That wouldn't be enough to go on. If you think he's going to play you must have a valid reason. You've got a source, haven't you?' he said accusingly.

'A source?'

'Yeah. Someone's clearly told you something. Who was it?'

'Hmm?'

'Who was it? Who's your source?'

'I honestly don't have a source,' I said.

'There's an etiquette to all this, you know. If you've got some information, it's probably a good idea to share it with the rest of the press corps.'

'I really don't have a source.'

'Is it a player? One of the coaching staff?' he demanded.

'Look, I promise you—'

'Hello everyone!' The Indian official had now reappeared. 'Please follow me out, and I will show you the wicket.'

The security guard opened the gate, and the official walked through it, with the press corps hot on his heels.

'Passes, please!' shouted the guard and everybody showed them as they filed past.

My interrogator, Mr Prickly, bustled off towards the gate, but not before he'd prodded my chest with his finger.

'I will find out, you know!'

Again I joined the back of the mob, and tried to scuttle through the gate unchecked. A hand reached through the group, and held on to my shirt. He might not have looked much, but the security guard had a surprisingly strong grip. I stopped, and let everyone else pass.

'Is there a problem?' I asked.

'Your pass. Where is it?'

I couldn't go through the whole performance again.

'I don't have one. It doesn't matter.'

'You don't have one? Are you a journalist?'

'Yes, but I don't have a pass at the moment.'

'Is there someone who can vouch for you?'

My 'colleagues' were already halfway out to the middle.

'Let's just leave it,' I said. 'It doesn't matter.'

I walked back through the wire mesh corridor, each gate being silently opened by the same soldiers who had reluctantly let me through earlier. I emerged from the tunnel at the same time as the

England team emerged from the pavilion and stepped onto their luxury coach. As no other journalists were around, I was able to take a few photos of them. Some of them carried random items of kit; perhaps a bat or some shoes. Andrew Flintoff, for reasons I shall never know, was carrying a pot of paint.

Then I took a rickshaw back to the hotel on my own.

Chapter Ten

'What happened to you?'

I was just finishing some lunch in the lobby café when the rest of the press corps returned. Kevin had sat down opposite me.

'That was a fucking disaster,' I told him.

'No pass yet?'

'No.'

My struggles with bureaucracy had become a little soap opera that Kevin was really starting to enjoy.

'That was a bit dramatic at the ground.'

'What?'

'That bloke shouting at you.'

'Right.'

'And you kicking the chair. You don't get to see that sort of behaviour very often on these trips.'

'Well, I was just getting a bit cross.'

'I could see. Do you want a drink?'

'A Coke, please.'

'Certainly. That's on me, by the way.'

'Thank you. That's a great comfort.'

Not as comforting, though, as the joy of watching Kevin try to get the attention of the waiter.

'Hello, sir, you would like your bill?'

'No, I haven't had anything yet.'

'Oh. Well, what would you like to eat?'

'Nothing.'

The waiter looked at his notepad, and then back at Kevin. 'What would you like?'

'Two Cokes, please.'

'Two Cokes. And for you, sir?' the waiter asked me.

'One of them is for him,' said Kevin.

'Right. Two Cokes. One for you. One for him.'

He thought briefly about writing this down on his pad, and then thought better of it.

'Two Cokes. I'll get someone to come and take your food order.'

'But I don't want any...' Kevin began as the man disappeared, but then returned to my problems.

'Anyway, what are you going to do?' he asked.

'I can only wait, really.'

'What for?'

'There's a press conference tomorrow. Walpole says I should come to that and he will try and help me,' I told him.

'That should be okay. He's a good man.'

'Yes. He seems very helpful.'

'BBC Scotland probably ought to do more to help you.'

'Yes. It's tricky really. Tricky.'

I was in a despondent state, and my mood was only lifted by Kevin attempting to pay for the drinks. Each time he explained to a different waiter that he wanted to pay for two Cokes, we would be brought two more glasses of the stuff. This happened twice, and with four full glasses on our table Kevin started to become agitated.

'I just want,' he told the original waiter, 'to pay for two Cokes.'

'You want more Cokes?'

*

My original plan of having a look around Chandigarh had been scuppered somewhat by my failure to collect my promised press pass. Returning to the hotel empty-handed left me in a grumpy stupor, and I was in no mood to do anything much. A walk around the city would have been a far better way of working off some of my frustration, but instead I took the decision to return to my hotel room and mope. The press conference at England's team hotel was not until tomorrow afternoon, and thus I had a whole day to wait before I knew if I was going to end up with a pass or not.

Upstairs I got into my bed and slept for several hours. Then I turned on my computer, and attempted to write a happy-sounding piece for my blog about what a fun place Chandigarh had been so far. It was all lies. The real fun started when I attempted to log on to the hotel's wireless network and then post what I had written to the website. The signal was incredibly low in the rooms, and continued to cut out every few minutes. I had propped my door open in an attempt to 'waft in' a few more bars of reception, but it did little to help. Four times in succession, I got to the point on the screen where it told me that my file was uploading, and then a fresh message would appear telling me that I was not connected to the Internet. When it happened for a fifth time, I slammed my fists down on the table and started shouting. In a way, it was what I needed. I had had an infuriating day so far, and the hotel's wireless connection was presenting me with an ideal opportunity to let off some steam.

'You fucking thing. You stupid fucking thing. Just work. Just fucking work. Just fucking fucking work you fucking fuckheaded fucking fuck.'

These are the words that tend to escape from my mouth whenever a piece of machinery that I'm trying to operate fails to do that which I would really rather like it to. I can't say that words like these have served me well. I can't call it a technique, either, because it rarely does anything to help. It is not a thought-through, rational response to a problem. It's a grumpy man being driven over the edge by his unrelenting fury about things that probably don't matter all that much. Over the years my anger has helped me to shatter two PlayStation controllers, to break the hard drive in a laptop in half and, in an example of splendid middle-class rage, take several chunks out of a kitchen table with the handle of a pasta maker that simply wasn't doing what it was supposed to.

The hammering of my fists on the desk and the shouting did nothing to alter the wording on my computer screen. So I clicked on the 'connect' icon again and moved on to the next, harder and louder, stage of my ritual.

'Oh come on.'

THUMP.

'Just fucking connect, you fucking fuck.'

THUMP.

'Come on, you piece of fucking shit. What's your fucking problem, you fucking shitty fucking dick!'

THUMP. Press the 'connect' icon again.

'Oh just fucking connect, will you? How hard can it be? Just do what I fucking tell you!'

THUMP.

'Please, you piece of shit. Just connect. Just fucking connect. Connect to the fucking Internet.'

THUMP.

'Aaaaaargh.'

THUMP.

'Come on!'

THUMP.

'Please…'

THUMP.

'…will…'

THUMP.

'...you...'

THUMP.

'...just...'

THUMP.

'...fucking...'

THUMP.

'...connect...'

THUMP.

'...to...'

THUMP.

'...the...'

THUMP.

'...fucking...'

THUMP.

'...pissing...'

THUMP.

'...shitting...'

THUMP.

'...fucking...'

THUMP.

'...Internet?'

THUMP THUMP THUMP.

I waited to see if this had helped. The screen refreshed, and then I saw the words 'You are not connected to the Internet'.

'Oh for fuck's sake...'

'Er, is everything all right?' said a voice.

I quickly turned to my right to see the BBC's chief cricket correspondent standing in the doorway, and wearing a concerned but sympathetic expression.

'Oh, Jonathan. Hello. Just having a bit of trouble with the Internet.'

'I see.'

'I can't seem to connect. Quite a weak signal.'

'I think you'll find that the signal's rather stronger out on the landing. There's quite a few of us working out here.'

'Oh. Thanks.'

He gave me a friendly smile, and then retreated back onto the landing. I followed him out and there, sure enough, were he and three or four other journalists sitting cross-legged on the landing. As I came out of my room those with headphones in looked up and gave polite nods of acknowledgement, those without them eyed me with a hint of surprise, possibly fear.

'Ah, there's a bit of signal out here is there? Super.'

I fetched my own laptop, and then sat down with the others. I couldn't have moved more than 15 feet, but the signal was now showing at almost full on my screen. I was instantly able to post my blog, and then started to have a rummage through all of the emails that I had ignored since my arrival, and browsed the Internet. All around me, the others tapped away, and some journalists disappeared and some new ones took their place. The cast on the landing kept revolving, but the number of characters remained the same. Over the course of several hours, most of the press corps joined us on the landing: your Derek Pringles, your Stephen Brenkleys, your David Gowers, your Scyld Berrys... journalists of every rank and type were taking turns to sit or sprawl out under the flickering fluorescent strip lights, looking fed up with the world, fed up with life. Sighing. The loneliness of touring was getting to people.

At one point a small fleet of hotel staff arrived to turn down everybody's beds and to scatter rose petals on them. Most of the doors were wide open, as if we were the cast of *Friends* enjoying another kooky night in together. One door was shut, and a member of staff knocked gently on it for nearly a minute. He was just about to slip his master key into the slot when the door opened and the man was startled to see Ian Botham appear before him looking like a sleepy Falstaff. The man was so startled that at first he said nothing, but just stood staring at Botham.

'Hello?' Botham said eventually, in order to break the silence.

'Your bed, sir?'

'My bed?'

'I'm to prepare your bed, sir. For sleeping.'

'It's okay. I'm already sleeping.'

'Are you sure, sir?'

'Yes. Really. It's fine.'

But the man seemed incapable of absorbing the information, or perhaps of just turning his back on a legend like the one before him. I don't know if there's an official world record for 'longest time taken to convince hotel staff member that one's bed simply does not need to be turned down', but it seems unlikely that it has ever taken anyone longer to communicate or understand this fact. This bizarre stand-off lasted for an age, all the time Botham's face becoming all the more hangdog and his eyes narrowing in despair. Eventually Botham closed the door. The man stood there, still thinking. Then, in a last-ditch attempt, he leant towards the door and shouted, 'Are you sure, sir? What about chocolates?'

*

My moderate attitude towards alcohol consumption had not lasted long, and I woke late. Not that I immediately had much to wake up for; the press conference I needed to attend would not be until two in the afternoon. I lay in bed wondering what I had drunk, and who I had drunk it with, and I despaired. I was so many rungs down the ladder from where I had wanted to be by this stage. There is not a word that means the opposite of 'vertigo', but there certainly should be, because I was starting to experience the exact feelings that it would describe. The *Western Mail* relationship sounded like it could go no further than the blog that I was already writing. I had to be able to get somewhere further with BBC Scotland. If there was anything I could tell them about the tour that would excite their interest, then I could yet be asked to make a broadcast. I shouldn't just be punting at the sports department at BBC Scotland, I should try and make contact with some of the people in entertainment I had encountered. I had made regular contributions to *The Fred Macaulay Show*. I should see if they would be interested in chatting about something, anything. Even if it was only about *Balamory*.

But although I awoke glum and anxious, within minutes of having showered and dressed I was laughing. I had gone and sat out on the landing with my laptop and emailed a producer on *The Fred Macaulay Show* I knew with a few ideas for their show. It was then that I started to have a look through what my colleagues in the press corps had written so far from Chandigarh. And to my great delight Mr Prickly had written a piece about how a source had indicated to him that Shaun Udal would probably play. I might not have been credited, but at last – I had made it into print! When, later that day, I was told that Shaun Udal would definitely not be playing I was absolutely beside myself with joy.

*

Our hotel in Chandigarh was much bigger than the one in Nagpur, and thus the lobby was big enough to contain a café as well as several separate seating areas; perfect for people-watching. My intention in Chandigarh was to keep my head down a little, especially after Simon had asked me about *Balamory*, but this meant I was now even further out of the loop. There had also been very few communications from the press office's message service, and so I was beginning to wonder what, if anything, everybody else was up to. I sat in the lobby café drinking coffee, and reading *The Looking Glass War* and for well over an hour saw no one. Where were they all? Perhaps they had all headed off for some fun without me? I couldn't go knocking on anyone's door because that might reek of desperation. I'm quite sure that many people may well have been putting on a front, but most people appeared to know exactly what they were doing all of the time. There was not really room for the sort of dithering that I usually specialised in.

Eventually a smattering of journalists started to appear in the lobby. Scyld Berry from the *Telegraph* caught my eye.

'Do you want to share a car with us?'

'Yes,' I said. 'That would be great.'

I put my novel in my bag and hurried over to them, wondering where it was that this car might be going.

'I know it's a bit early,' Scyld said, 'but we might as well give ourselves enough time.'

'Absolutely.' I said.

Not a clue. David Lloyd from the *Evening Standard* was in our party, and we were also joined by Kevin. A fleet of ageing white hatchbacks were assembled outside the hotel, their drivers standing alongside.

'Who's for Berry?' asked Scyld, like a man proudly presenting homemade ice cream to an eager table of diners.

'Sir, please.'

A man waved us all over, and we clambered in. Scyld, the tallest of us, took the front passenger seat. I was in the middle in the back, my bag held tightly in my lap.

'Can we have you for the afternoon?' said Lloyd. 'Can you take us everywhere?'

'It's no problem, sir.'

How many stops would we be making? Were we shopping? There was lots of chat about the game, but none about where we were going. I recognised a lot of what I saw on the journey from the previous morning. I realised why when we and a number of other journalist-crammed taxis pulled up outside the ground. We were dropped at the same gates as yesterday, but this time they were manned by two soldiers. As soon as we were out of the car one of them spoke.

'Passes, please.'

The others all got theirs out, and hung them around their necks. I didn't even have my BBC Scotland letter with me.

'I shall wait for you here,' said the driver.

'Yeah, about half an hour I should think,' said Lloyd.

'Half an hour. Here. Yes, sir.'

I made a play at fumbling in my pocket and my bag for a pass. Kevin knew I didn't really have one, but the others didn't.

'Actually,' I said. 'What is it that we are all here for again? Is it just more nets?'

'It's the press box,' said Berry. 'We're just going to see what's what.'

'Oh, the press box? Right. I went yesterday,' I said.

'Did you?'

'Yeah. It's…er…it looks…good.'

'Right.'

'If that's all you're doing, I'll go and get on with some other stuff,' I said, taking out my mobile and waving it about importantly. 'I'll meet you back here in half an hour.'

'Okay.'

As they all turned to go into the ground, Kevin looked at me in the way that you look at people who you know are trying to cover up their drinking. I walked for 30 seconds until I reached a bench that had a view of the gate, then put my phone away and took out my book.

*

By the time our car had set off again, all of the other passengers had reserved their seats in the press box for tomorrow's start to the game. I was yet to find out whether I could even secure access to the press box. At least we were now on our way to the team hotel where I would have a chance to meet Walpole and see if he had managed to find a way of helping me out.

'Which hotel is it please?'

'The Taj,' said someone, 'Do you know where that is?'

'Oh yes. This is in sector 17. Is not far.'

Because of Chandigarh's grid system, it was divided into blocks and sectors. This gave it a faintly science-fiction feeling whenever you were giving directions. We soon pulled up outside the hotel, which was clearly part of a luxury chain, and unquantifiably more fancy than our own. It was vast and imposing, and just across the road from a splendid rose garden, and the city's main museum. As we parked, the team's luxury coach pulled in just ahead of us and out tumbled the team, still in their blue and red practice strips, and many of them bedecked with their earphones.

'Right then,' said David Lloyd as we clambered out. 'Lunch.'

'Shall I wait here?' said the driver.

'Please. Couple of hours, probably. Okay?'

'Okay.'

This seemed a wonderful way to proceed through a working day as a journalist. Car to the ground, car to a fancy hotel for lunch, quick press conference, then car home again. In India, of course, even today this is still an affordable and practical way to behave. Even in Britain this is how so much of Fleet Street operated until sometime in the '90s, I imagine.

The players looked in relaxed mood as they descended from their bus and jogged into the hotel. But once some of them had returned from their rooms ready for lunch to see that they would be sharing the lobby buffet with the press corps, you could see their expressions tighten. There was little interaction between the players and the press corps. Up by the noodle bar Simon Hughes and Duncan Fletcher were deep in conversation, although I had not managed to get close enough to hear whether they were discussing cricket, noodles or buffets in general.

Kevin Pietersen walked past the table for two where Kevin and I sat, and looked downcast at his dining companions.

'Does anyone talk to each other?' I asked Kevin the journalist.

'Yes, sometimes. It depends who it is. I mean, Matthew Hoggard will always talk to me. I've known him since he was a teenager. Other people are a bit more guarded, I suppose.'

'Does anyone ever ignore you completely?'

'Not often. Sometimes you ask someone if they want to do a quick interview and they say, "No, you're all right." That really annoys me.'

'Really?'

'Really. All right, Paul?' he suddenly called over my right shoulder.

I looked behind me, and saw Paul Collingwood was indeed approaching our table. He said nothing, and carried on past us.

'Bloody hell,' said Kevin. 'That is rude.'

'Is he someone you know well?'

'I've interviewed him a lot. I mean he's said hello to me heaps of times before.'

'Maybe it's because he's about to eat?' I offered.

'Because he's about to eat?'

'Yes.'

'Why would that make a difference?'

'Well, sometimes it's not very nice when people watch you eat.'

Kevin was eyeing me as if I'd suddenly starting speaking in French.

'What are you talking about?'

'It's true.'

'People don't like you watching them eat? You're watching me eat, and I'm coping with it. That's just nonsense. It's mad.'

'But put yourself in their position.'

'We are in their position. We're in the same restaurant.'

*

I scoped out the function room where the press conference would be in good time, and then hung around in the long corridor that led to it. Most of the English press corps and a lot of Indian journalists piled into the room to get a good seat, but I wanted a chance to quietly tackle Walpole on my own. Other than Kevin, every time someone had asked if my press pass troubles were resolved I had said 'Oh yes' in a breezy fashion, as I imagined that still not having one a week into a tour would make me look pretty amateurish. Almost as amateur, in fact, as me actually being an amateur.

By one minute to, every other journalist in the building was waiting in the function room, and so when I saw Walpole round the far corner and start heading along the corridor there were no other journalists about. He was accompanying Matthew Hoggard to the press call.

'Andrew?'

'Hi there.'

'Any luck at all with the...?'

'Yeah, hang on a minute...Matthew, if you just head on, I'll catch up with you in a moment.'

Hoggard shrugged and carried on, and Walpole stopped.

'I had another word with someone at the BCCI and they're adamant. You just can't have one.'

I heaved a sigh of disappointment. I had hit the end of the road.

'But...' he continued and then he stopped and glanced about. 'I really shouldn't be doing this, but I've been through the bag of passes I've got, because there are some people who had asked for accreditation that haven't ended up coming out here, and you can have this one for now – until the BCCI get this sorted.'

He pulled a press pass from his pocket, and placed it in my hand.

'It's not strictly speaking allowed,' he said, 'but I can see what a bloody miserable time you're having. And you won't be able to work without it.'

'Thanks, Andrew,' I said, pocketing the pass.

'Now good luck with it. Wait up, Hoggy,' he called and then jogged after our eccentric floppy-haired swing king.

I stood there for an instant and was momentarily flushed with joy. Mainly, though, I felt relief: relief that I hadn't come all this way for nothing; relief that I could pass through the same doors that the rest of the press corps passed through; relief that I could get into the ground and the press box and the press conferences; relief that I hadn't travelled this far only to have a door slammed shut in my face.

I followed Walpole and Hoggard and rounded the corner into the packed function room. It was a room the size of a cargo container and there must have been well over 50 people there. Hoggard and Walpole squeezed past everybody to get to the desk at the front, although there were so many cameras that had been put in place by Indian television companies that it was impossible to see either of them once they had sat down.

I could see that a lot of the English journalists in the room looked pretty cross with this arrangement. Hoggard, as he often does when anywhere other than in the middle of moorland, looked like he didn't really want to be there but still managed to maintain an attitude of bemused detachment. Every time Walpole asked who had a question, one of the Indian television crews shouted out one. The first couple of times that this happened, a number of English journalists put their hands up. But the camera crews seemed unaware that there were other people behind them and ploughed on with their questions.

'Mr Hoggard, the Indian team contains many left-handers. What for you is the difference between bowling at right-handers and left-handers?'

Hoggard pondered this for a while.

'When I'm bowling at left-handers, I just tend to bowl a little bit more to the right.'

'Thank you, Mr Hoggard.'

By now all the English journalists were sitting or standing with their arms folded, and showing no interest in the proceedings. They had looked around at each other and formed some sort of consensus of inaction. When the last of the camera crews had asked Hoggard a question, Walpole asked if there were any other questions. There was silence.

'No questions at all?'

Nothing.

'Okay, guys. I hear you.'

This all seemed extremely odd to me. What was the point in coming to a press conference to sit there and say nothing? I did that nearly every day, obviously, but these people were real journalists with proper articles and reports to write. The Indian crews all packed up their kit, and everyone began to exit the room. Hoggard and Walpole remained at the desk, while the Indians headed off and the English loitered by the door to the room.

'What's going on?' I asked Kevin.

Kevin was getting very used to being asked what was going on by me, but took great care in his role as interpreter.

'Well, it's the TV people, isn't it?'

'How do you mean?'

'The print journalists don't really like having the press conferences hijacked by TV crews who just want to get a few quick sound bites.'

'That's all right, isn't it? I mean, everybody could have had a turn, couldn't they?'

'They don't like it. If the room's full of cameras like that no one else can get near the table. People want to ask detailed questions and get long answers. They can't do that if the players have to keep reeling off sound bites to silly questions.'

'But can't they use the sound bites too?'

'No. They'll be all over the television, won't they? They want to get stuff from the players that's only for the newspapers. There's a competition going on. Everybody's fighting for survival.'

'So what will happen now?'

'They'll make Walpole take them off somewhere else with Hoggard and sit and have a proper chat with him.'

'Right.'

'But they don't want the TV crews to know that that chat will be taking place. Because they'll want to come and film that too. The different media all need their own material.'

Walpole and Hoggard suddenly stepped from the room and set off down the corridor. Everyone else gave chase to find out where this impromptu print-special would be held. I followed half-heartedly, unsure if I wanted to go to another moody meeting, even if it would mean a chance to watch Hoggard in action – demonstrating his matter-of-fact Yorkshire bluster one minute and then launching into a set of eccentric musings the next. Besides, if every different medium should get its own material, I should wait for my chance to have a special press conference devoted entirely to amateur hacks writing blogs for the websites of Welsh newspapers. As we sped through the lobby I opted out of the dash. I didn't need any quotes. I had got what I had come for. Everybody else carried on to the opposite corner of the lobby to pass through a set of metal detectors, and I sat down on a giant sofa to people-watch.

A smattering of England players were now there, getting ready to enjoy an afternoon off. Andrew Strauss was leaning by the hotel's entrance in flip-flops and a polo shirt, looking like he was waiting for a shopping companion. Matthew Prior was in conversation with two gentlemen who, it sounded like, had travelled a long way to bring him some fresh wicketkeeping equipment. Alastair Cook headed off to the lobby's business centre to send a few emails. He certainly had some news to tell his friends.

Now that there were no other journalists about, it was safe to get out the press pass that Walpole had given me and examine it properly. I pulled it slowly from my pocket with its lanyard that I so treasured. To have a pass with a lanyard attached seems a small and pathetic victory, but it felt like a massive achievement. The bright blue lanyards emblazoned with the words 'BOARD OF CRICKET CONTROL INDIA' were the most eye-catching aspect of the passes that I envied everyone else's possession of. Now I too had an official pass, even though it had somebody else's name on it. And somebody else's photo. I do not consider myself to be a particularly vain man, but I wasn't especially flattered when I first examined the photo of the man Walpole had described as the one who he thought I looked most like. I might have persuaded Walpole that I was a journalist, but I certainly hadn't convinced him that I was much of a looker. The journalist whose pass I had been given may well not have turned up on tour because he had received a better offer of work modelling for someone who made balloon animals. Still, this pass represented my best chance of getting into the press box for tomorrow's game. If I was one member of a group of people flashing their passes at a busy time for the security guards, then this would stand me a chance of gaining access to the media enclosure. But it also took the extent of my fibbing up by a few notches; tomorrow when I tried to get into the ground I would not just have to pretend that I was a journalist, I would have to pretend that I was a particular one. I was no longer merely exaggerating what I did; I was going to be an imposter.

Chapter Eleven

It had rained a lot during the night, and at breakfast no one appeared to think it very likely that the game would start on time. Not that I actually spoke to anyone during breakfast. There were no places left at any of the tables occupied by journalists, so I ended up sitting on my own, pretending to busy myself with my diary and just picking up scraps of conversation whilst picking at some chicken sausages.

I was feeling short on confidence. There was no guarantee that my purloined pass would get me into the press box. I would be able to get into the ground by just buying a ticket, but travelling and staying with all of the press corps but then not making an appearance in the press box would arouse yet more suspicion about my credentials and motives. And the more paranoid and vulnerable I felt, the more hardened and suspicious the faces of the rest of the press corps seemed to me. I decided, though, against travelling to the game with everybody else and trying to just flash my pass as part of a mob passing through security. I didn't want any of the other journalists to see me using somebody else's pass. I was also keen to avoid being refused access to the ground in front of everybody else. Who knew how serious a crime it was attempting to enter the media enclosure by carrying a pass that was not my own? Could I be dragged off in a half nelson to face questioning? It wouldn't look good for Andrew Walpole either. The other journalists might guess that it was from him that I had obtained the pass. I would, of course, try not to drag his name into any of it if I did end up facing an interrogation. But what if I revealed it under duress? I could probably handle the odd nipple-clamp or matchstick under the fingernail, but I wasn't convinced that I could cope with being water boarded. I'd probably blurt his name out, and within minutes he would find himself being flung into the neighbouring cell. Over time we would gradually build up the same sort of unbreakable bond that began to form between Brian Keenan and John McCarthy during their years in captivity together, and on our eventual release there would be book deals, chat-show bookings and the possibility of an appearance on *Desert Island Discs*. But even so at the end of it – and I'm sure that John McCarthy, if asked, would probably agree with me on this – I would feel I could have done without the fuss.

*

A number of journalists had gathered near the hotel's entrance. The natural leaders amongst them, and a few of the others who fancied themselves as being key to any decision-making process, were trying to organise everybody into groups to make their way to the ground together in taxis. Keen to avoid being swept along with everybody else I opted to make judicious use of the lobby's generous lavatory facilities, and then lingered there with my laptop and kit until I felt sure that the coast was clear. I ventured out to find that all of the journalists had indeed now disappeared. But so too had all of the taxis that were usually gathered outside the hotel. I wandered out into the street with my kit slung over my shoulder to see if I could flag one down. I hadn't brought my guidebook down from my room with me, and wasn't completely sure what direction I should be walking in to make my way to the ground. I considered everything I could remember about travelling to and from the ground over the last few days and so eventually opted for a right turn and began to walk briskly away from the hotel. The rain clouds were dispersing and the sunlight was just beginning to break through.

Ten minutes later, I had still not seen a taxi or a rickshaw and the sun was completely out. Ten minutes after that I was drenched in sweat and tripping along the uneven pavement cursing everything that I encountered. The shoulder strap of my laptop case was cutting into my neck, and my shoes were nipping my ankles. I cursed every vehicle that passed me for not being a taxi, and groaned each time I had to blink the salty sweat from my eyes. The game would be starting in less than half an hour. All I could do was to keep walking along this perfectly straight road until something happened. A white car approached on the other side of the road, which looked like one of the taxis we had taken the day before. I stepped out and tried to hail it. For this I was rewarded with a honk and a swerve, and so leapt back onto the pavement. The yellow car behind it slowed, though, and a friendly-looking man leant out of the driver window.

'You are looking for a taxi?'

'Yes.'

'I am a taxi.'

'Oh great.'

I opened the back door and clambered in.

'Could you take me to the cricket ground, please?'

'You want to go to the cricket?'

'Please.'

He chuckled.

'You were walking the wrong way for the cricket.'

'Oh.'

He executed a quick U-turn, and then sped back the way I had been walking and staggering. Two hundred yards beyond the hotel we passed a taxi rank where tens of drivers were leaning against their cars, their engines idling.

*

There was still a sizeable number of fans on the street outside the stadium when we pulled up. I looked around in vain for any signs directing me to a media enclosure, and then walked past a queue of Barmy Army members all looking relaxed and chirpy.

'Miles!'

I turned round. It was Peter and Angela again.

'Hello!' I said. 'How are you enjoying Chandigarh?'

'Great,' replied Angela. 'You look lost.'

'I am. I had a bit of trouble getting here.'

'You keep getting separated from the group, don't you?' said Peter.

'Yes, I seem to.'

'I think all the journalists go in through that gate over there,' said Angela, pointing me in the direction of a different entrance a hundred yards further on.

'Oh thanks.'

'You'd better hurry. It's all right if we're late, but you can't be. This is your job!'

'Well...'

'See you around,' waved Peter.

'Cheers,' I muttered, and hurried on.

Even if they believed that I really was a journalist, they must by now have decided that I must be a rather incompetent one. I was headed towards the gate, but pulled up 30 yards short of it in a panic. The gate was being guarded by two officious-looking policemen, both of whom were armed with machine guns and who were painstakingly checking passes. It was this last aspect – the fact that they appeared to be paying such close attention to the passes – that caused me to panic, and not the fact that they were armed. Even if they decided not to let me in, I was reasonably confident that they wouldn't rub salt in the wound by then opening fire on me.

I pulled out the pass I had in my pocket and squatted down to re-examine it with my back to the media enclosure gate. Somehow the man in the photograph managed to look even less like me than he had the day before; his eyes were a different colour (to mine, not each other); his hair was a different colour to mine. The only things that we definitely had in common were skin colour and head shape. Presumably we also shared an interest in cricket, but I couldn't be certain about this because he hadn't gone to the bother of actually turning up. And looking first at the pass and then back at the officious policemen, I realised with a jolt of horror and shame that if this pass was going to help me get where I wanted to go, then I would have to disguise myself. The first part of my disguise I had, inadvertently, been working on for some weeks. The man in the photograph was clean-shaven, whereas I was wearing a reasonable amount of beard. It wasn't the same colour as the man in the photograph's hair, but that didn't concern me too much as it isn't the same colour as my hair either. I rummaged around in the laptop case for my floppy sun hat, plonked it onto my head and then yanked it down as hard as I could manage without pulling its brim off. I put on my sunglasses. And then I finished off my disguise with a rather ambitious touch, which was to attempt to copy the facial expression worn by the man in the photograph. He hadn't given me a great deal to work with, as he had a blank, almost dozy look that would be hard to emulate with my eyes concealed. What he had done, however, was have his mouth slightly open at the moment the photograph was taken. This was a tic that I could definitely emulate. I slipped my pass over my head and neck, got up and slung my laptop case over my shoulder to turn and face the entrance to the media enclosure. And as I walked towards the two men, I allowed my jaw to go all loose and droopy. I doubt this would have done much to enhance my beauty, and as I discovered when I reached the gate, it also detracted from my ability to speak with any real coherence.

'Hey-wo. Iz worse tharmydia intranze?'

'Excuse me, sir?'

I tightened my mouth long enough for me to say, 'Is this the media entrance?' and then let it go slack again.

'Yes, sir. This is media entrance. Your pass, please?'

I pointed to it on my neck.

'Can you turn it around so that I can see the photo, please sir?'

I looked down to see that the lanyard had become twisted, and thus the side facing him merely described England's tour itinerary, and gave him no information about who I was, and why I was here.

'Saw-ee,' I said and nervously turned it the right way round, so that our open-mouthed friend was now staring back at him.

He looked at the photograph for a while, slowly tilting his head to one side, and then to the other. I focused on trying to look relaxed whilst also holding my mouth open. Then he leant in towards me, and took the pass between the forefinger and thumb of his right hand and peered at it. He was examining it so closely that I thought he was going to sniff it. The other policeman then leant in as well, glanced at the pass, shrugged and then walked slowly away.

'Okay,' said the thorough one eventually, 'You may go in.'

I clamped my jaw shut in relief, only just preventing myself from pumping the air in celebration of the fact that I had got into another ground, that my subterfuge had been successful and that my versatility and skill had enabled me to morph, at barely a moment's notice, into looking like how a slightly different man would look if he had a ginger beard, wore sunglasses and a hat and had developed a slack jaw.

The policeman pointed me in the direction of the rather grand pavilion, where presumably the press box would be located. Its rear entrance had a colonial look to it. There were whitewashed pillars on either side and an arched porch was emblazoned with the lettering 'Punjab Cricket Club'. Colourful plants in pots had been placed either side of a set of steps which ran up to the doorway. At the top of these steps stood a lone policeman, and as I climbed the steps towards him, I once again loosened my jaw. He examined my pass with only a little interest, before uttering the magic words, 'You may go in', and ushering me through the heavy wooden and glass doors.

It was dark inside the pavilion, and I removed my sunglasses to take in its size and splendour. The floors were covered with terracotta-coloured tiles, the white walls were emblazoned with framed photographs of great cricketers of the past and present, and there were huge palm plants in vast pots. There were a few sofas and armchairs dotted about the place. I stood for some moments enjoying its cool and airy feel, and welcoming the respite from the brightness and heat outside. The match, I knew, was about to start and yet it was oddly quiet. Where was I supposed to go now? A door at the far end opened and a man in a blazer and tie approached me at a canter.

'Welcome to the Punjab Cricket Club. May I help you at all?'

'Hello,' I said. 'I'm a journalist.'

'A journalist? You must be quick, sir. You know the game is about to start?'

'Yes, yes.'

'If you are journalist, you must have been in our press box before, yes?'

'I've not actually.'

'It is upstairs. Third floor.'

He pointed to my left, where a doorway led to a wide flight of stairs. I now saw a typed sign helpfully blu-tacked to the wall at waist height confirming what the gentleman was telling me.

'PRESS BOX 3RD FLOOR. (UP)'

I thanked the man, and then took off up the stairs two at a time, anxious not to miss the start of play. The staircase was just as empty as the lobby. I could hear no sound other than the echoes of my own footsteps thumping up each flight. It was only when I rounded the corner to take the final flight of steps that I encountered another person: a Punjab Cricket Club official in a blazer and tie standing guard outside the entrance to the press box. Next to him was a sign that read 'All Passes Must Be Shown'. As I climbed the final steps and started to wave the pass in his direction I suddenly remembered, too late, that I no longer had the sunglasses on. In their place, therefore, I developed a squint.

The man looked at the photo on the pass, then at me, and then back at the photo. I squinted harder.

'Are you okay?'

'Hmm?'

'Your eyes, sir. They are okay?'

'Fine, yes. Why?'

'Why do you have them closed like this?'

'Oh. Yes. That. I have a problem with them.'

'You said they are fine.'

'Well, they are fine normally. It's just something wrong with them at the moment.'

'What is problem? Something in them? Can I look for you?'

Why did this man have to be so helpful?

'Oh no, there's nothing in them. It's a...disease. It's called...'

'Yes, sir?'

What was it called? There was a definite condition that I was thinking of, however the only word that was springing to my mind was 'myxomatosis'. I couldn't say that.

'It's...er...it's a thing called, er...'

'We have medical staff at the ground, sir. I'm sure somebody could examine you. Perhaps one of the team doctors?'

'No, no really. It's fine. I've had it diagnosed already. I've got drops for it.'

Drops. Of course. That triggered the word for me.

'Conjunctivitis!' I shouted triumphantly and, it must be said, rather too loudly.

'This sounds painful, sir.'

'I'm fine as long as I wear sunglasses.'

'Then you must make sure you wear your sunglasses, sir.'

'I will.'

'Anyway, please. You must come through. You know that the game is about to start?'

'Oh yes. Thank you.'

He opened the door behind him and ushered me through. Suddenly I was in the midst of a media complex, with all the writers' rooms, radio and TV studios on one floor. The place was heaving. I pocketed the press pass before it could cause me any more trouble. Another man in a Punjab Cricket Club blazer came over.

'Yes, sir?'

'Hi, I'm looking for the press box.'

'Which bit? What are you?'

'I'm a journalist.'

'TV? Radio? Writer?'

'A writer, yes.'

'What sort of writing? Newspaper?'

'Well…'

'Website?'

He pronounced the word with such a note of distaste that I didn't dare say yes to him; as if to do so would have been tanta-mount to confirming to him that I just needed a desk and a power point so that I could sit down and furiously start writing pornographic literature.

'I write for a newspaper, yes.'

'This way, please.'

He led me up some further steps, and opened a door at one

end of the back row of the raked seats and desks that made up the press box.

'If you write for website, sit near the back. If you write for a newspaper you may sit near the front.'

And off he went. I looked around the box. There were no spare seats near the front. In fact, there didn't seem to be a space anywhere. I looked around anxiously. And then I finally spotted one; near the other end of the back row. I slowly made my way towards it, squeezing my way past everyone and mouthing a few 'hello's. And when I had made it to the place that I was aiming for, there on the desk in front of me were written the words 'Miles Jupp: UK Media'.

This made absolutely no sense to me whatsoever. I had spent nearly two more days lying and arguing with people to gain access to this box, and I'd only managed to do so in the end under an assumed identity. And yet here was a place reserved for me under my real name. I glanced quickly around the room. I could see Mr Who The Fuck's That? giggling about something. I could already hear the crowd applauding the teams making their way out to the middle. I sat down, pulled out my laptop and a notebook and said hello to the people either side of me. On my right was Kevin, who wasn't usually working from the press box but from a studio. He was talking agitatedly to some-body on his mobile phone, the index finger of his left hand pushed tightly into his ear. Rod Gilmour, whom I had last seen heading off to interview Michael Atherton, was on my left.

'You just made it, then?' he asked.

'Yeah. What a journey. Taxi driver got lost.'

'Bad luck.'

'Who's won the toss?'

'England.'

'Right. And what are we doing?'

'Well, have a look,' he said, gesturing out to the pitch.

And I looked up just in time to watch the first ball of the match. I didn't, however, see the first ball of the match. All along the front of the press box there were long windows. But between each window was a little stretch of wall. And one particular stretch of wall was exactly where I wanted to be looking, directly in my line of vision between the middle of the pitch and where I was sitting. I could still see large chunks of the playing area. I could see what I saw were Indian players taking up their fielding positions, and clapping to encourage the bowler. I could occasionally see the ball skimming across the outfield and somebody sprinting after it. But what I couldn't see was the important bit in the middle of it all; the bowler delivering the ball, or the batsman trying to hit it, or the wicketkeeper trying to stop it. I could not see what one might reasonably term 'the main business area'. I leant as far as I could to my right and left, but it didn't make the slightest difference. I had made it into the box on time, but it hadn't done me any good whatsoever.

I slumped in my chair wondering what the various shouts from the crowd and tuts from the journalists all meant. There was a small TV mounted on a wall bracket away to my left, and after a few minutes of play one of the taller members of the press corps reached up and turned it on. It made a hissing noise, the screen flickered and soon it was possible to make out a picture. It was a bit fuzzy, but you could see that it was cricket. Eventually the picture settled down. The television was showing footage of New Zealand versus the West Indies.

To reach this point on my trip I had flown from Edinburgh to London, from London to Delhi, from Delhi to Nagpur, from Nagpur back to Delhi, and from Delhi to Chandigarh. That is a total of 5,702 flying miles. FIVE THOUSAND SEVEN HUNDRED AND TWO. All in order to lie my way into a room, and write for nobody about a thing that I could not see.

*

Something changed in Chandigarh. The atmosphere of the tour started to change, and I too began to feel completely different. Up until this moment I had lived every moment of the tour in detail, but now I started to experience it all as more of a blur.

I hadn't even noticed when I arrived in the box that one of the reasons why it was so crowded was that the *Test Match Special* team were sharing our facilities. The studio that Peter Baxter had set up the day before had become a victim of the overnight rain, and flooded. Thus Baxter had been forced to set up as much equipment as he could in the press box, and Mike Selvey and Geoffrey Boycott commentated on the opening session of play from the front row. There was too much noise between me and them and so I could neither see the cricket that they were describing nor hear their descriptions of it. This was why Kevin was also in the box. He was having to give his updates to BBC 5 Live over his mobile phone rather than via his usual satellite contraption.

England had somehow made it to 16 without loss. I might suddenly catch sight of the ball although without ever knowing exactly who had hit it before it would disappear from view behind another journalist's head. I eventually discovered that by leaning a long way forward and low over my desk I could get a reasonable view of a scoreboard. This was how I learnt that the score had moved on to 23 without loss. Then I saw the ball go over the boundary rope at what could have been third man or long on, depending on which end whoever it was that was bowling, was actually bowling from.

Finally, after I had been in the box for half an hour, Angus Fraser stood up and switched the television over to the correct channel and I was able to get my first glimpse of England's two batsmen at the crease. In comparison to the quality of my viewing so far, this was deeply luxurious. The delay between the live action and the footage of it appearing on screen was far more considerable than it had ever been in Nagpur, which only added to my sense of disorientation. Nothing matched up. The crowd might all make a collective gasp, for instance, while the television was still playing an advert.

I then heard a huge cheer from the crowd and a chorus of tuts break out around the box and some moments later saw on the television that Andrew Strauss had managed to get himself caught behind off the bowling of Pathan.

Kevin immediately rang through to London on his mobile, was put straight on air, and started to communicate news of this wicket over the radio waves. He was halfway through conveying the circumstances of Strauss's dismissal when an unbelievably loud voice started booming through a tannoy regrettably mounted on the wall immediately behind him. Everybody in the box winced, but Kevin, who was the nearest to the noisome creature and the person in the room who most needed silence, nearly went through the ceiling. He recovered from his shock, apologised to the listeners at home for this interruption and managed to finish his report. This task was not made any simpler by the fact that so many people were now laughing at him.

'Well, this isn't ideal, is it?' he said in a vexed manner when his ordeal was over.

Indeed it wasn't. Any practical joker in the party was now in a prime position to pass timely messages to the pavilion's tannoy operator and interrupt all of Kevin's future broadcasts. He might try to give a summary of the morning's play at lunch time only to be interrupted by the tannoy asking if the owner of a blue Datsun Y-Reg could please make himself known to the club secretary. Alastair Cook was also out not long after, although I missed this as at the other end of the box I was trying to make the coffee machine work.

I returned to my place without a coffee and wrote up some pieces about Chandigarh for my blog, and was still doing this with only half an eye on the cricket when the game stopped for lunch with England on 54 for the loss of two wickets.

*

Kevin was gone when I returned, the radio studios now having been deemed to be in a fit enough state to use. In his place, however, was Nasser Hussain. Unlike during the Nagpur game, the Sky commentary position was right next to the press box, and so various members of their team had wandered into our box during the morning session. I was delighted to see that I might be spending the afternoon session sitting next to a former England captain, although disappointed that he was occupying the seat that I had my eye on. Again, my best view would be provided by the television.

'Hi there,' I said, as I plonked myself down next to him.

'All right, mate?' he said giving me a half-smile. I'm not sure how often Nasser Hussain does smile actually. He may well have been flashing me the biggest one he has. He then started haranguing David Hopps, albeit good-naturedly, for something he had written about him in the *Guardian*.

I sat there watching Ian Bell and Kevin Pietersen bat steadily together, and sent an email to BBC Scotland, telling them that I had now arrived in Chandigarh and that the second Test was under way. Perhaps, I suggested, I could report on the state of the series on John Beattie's *Sporting Round-Up* that Saturday? Alternatively I could do an interview with a big cricket name for them, if that was appealing. Someone like Nasser Hussain, I suggested, adding that he happened to be next to me at that very moment. There was no reply. Nor was there a reply from the sports desk of the *Western Mail* to my suggestion of an article about how much England appeared to be missing Simon Jones. They didn't, so far, appear to be missing him a great deal. But I wrote in my email that they seemed to be missing him enormously.

A couple of times I caught Nasser Hussain's eye and he nodded back, but I struggled to think of anything to say. The night that we had met in the bar, he had been in a relaxed and approachable mood and I had been emboldened by beers. Here though, I felt different. Everybody was in work mode, but I knew that all I really wanted to ask him were the sort of bar room questions that a fan would ask him about moments in his career. In fact, as a fan, what I really wanted most of all was a photo of the two of us together. This, I knew, would absolutely not be the place for that sort of request, but at the same time I did not want to let the opportunity slip away. Perhaps I might be able to take a photograph of he and I together surreptitiously. And so it was I hit upon the idea of taking out my camera, and connecting it up to my computer and then fiddling around with it as if I was having some sort of difficulty with it. I could then start screwing up my face as if the thing was causing me no end of grief. That way, as if to examine the extent of the problems I was having, I would be justified in taking a succession of apparently random images. My prize for all this kerfuffle would be a picture of me sitting next to former England captain Nasser Hussain.

I set it all up, spent a few moments idly moving images from the camera to the computer, and then started fiddling around with the mode settings. This is when I started to try out a few frowns. Then I hit a few random buttons on the computer and tutted loudly. It was a big performance. I disconnected the camera and muttered 'oh, this wretched thing' a couple of times before fiddling with a few settings on it. And only then did I start taking a few random photos. I took one of my laptop, examined it, tutted and then pressed a button. Then I took a photo of the ceiling and examined it closely before making a few imaginary adjustments. I turned the camera towards me and took a photo of myself, then looked at that and made a 'not quite there yet' noise. Finally I took one of me from the right featuring an unaware Rod Gilmour, and then from the left, the money shot: Nass and me, side by side. I glanced quickly through the photos, and then turned the thing off with a weary sigh. The whole operation took nearly 12 minutes. To this day, though, I do possess a photograph of me sitting next to the former England captain Nasser Hussain in the Chandigarh press box. He is only just in shot but still manages to look quite perturbed. I take up most of the frame and am staring into the lens as if I am terribly haunted by the problems that my camera has caused me. It is an awful photo.

*

The cricket progressed smoothly enough, although without much in the way of excitement. Occasionally Kevin Pietersen played a big shot, but in the main he and Ian Bell batted without taking risks. Bell is one of those cricketers, like Darren Gough before him, who suffers that curious affliction of always looking like a schoolboy playing against grown men whenever he dons his batting helmet. This is not so much caused by his stature, but by his posture at the crease, as if always trying to make himself appear bigger than he is. It was, in the end, a schoolboy error that did for him, shouldering arms to a delivery from Kumble that was either a googly or simply didn't spin at all. Either way it took the top of Bell's off stump, and his 81-run partnership with Pietersen was over. Bell's departure was greeted with a lot of disappointed noises in the press box. Man-child or not, he had looked in supreme control at the crease. It turned out to be a terribly timed error too, as not long afterwards the game was held up owing to the bad light, and as the batsmen started walking towards the pavilion it began to rain. This brought about a lengthy tea interval, and people milled around the box looking frustrated, amongst them Michael Atherton himself, who appeared rather old and frail today. This was as a result, apparently, of his making the decision to drink long into the night with Ian Botham. Nonetheless he was alert enough to impress me during the final session. Kevin Pietersen had managed to make 64 before he was caught and bowled by the Indian debutant Munaf Patel. What was impressive was the way that Atherton said 'out' with a great deal of certainty, just at the moment that the ball pitched and Pietersen was reaching for it on the up, but before he had even made contact. That showed real foresight. Bad light then caused play to stop for the day just after five o'clock with the score on 163–4. As the players left the field, the sound of typing filled the press box, and I looked around to see everybody with their heads down, furiously composing their reports of the day's stop-start play. There didn't seem to be any point in me pretending to be busy, as no one was looking up from their work anyway. Instead I quietly packed up my things, and made my lone way downstairs out of the pavilion and out onto the street.

*

It had been something of a top-heavy day. My main concern in the morning had been about getting into the ground and the press box, but once I had nervously, and perhaps ludicrously, triumphed in that battle, there had been little more by way of excitement. My view of the game was absymal, the cricket itself had been stop-start and often stodgy and the atmosphere was muted. The complete lack of email response from my potential employers to anything that I had suggested to them, and the consequent lack of any meaningful work I could do, left me feeling cut off and adrift.

Heaps of people were spilling from the ground at the same time as me, but there was no sense of hubbub, rather there was the sort of hands-in-pockets flatness that often follows a day's play that has been forced to finish early. For spectators there is almost nothing as frustrating as a game having to stop for 'bad light'. Devotees of other sports might find the idea of stopping just because it's raining a little pathetic. If you're familiar with cricket's nuances, though, or have played the game, then the need for cessation of play during showers is understandable. And at least rain is something sort of tangible. 'Bad light' is just a bloody annoyance. It doesn't even sound like a proper reason for anything, it just sounds like an opinion. It's like a vague and flimsy excuse that a lazy painter might make after coming home from a day at the easel with yet another blank canvas. 'Well I was all set up to do a lovely landscape, of course I was. But it was the light, you see. It was just...bad.' What could be more frustrating, in the middle of the afternoon, than a group of professional athletes trudging off the field claiming that they're not able to see anything, when outside the ground cars and buses without their headlights on are cheerfully being driven around and millions upon millions of people are going about their day and managing to avoid walking into lampposts and each other even without the general levels of visibility being enhanced by the presence of floodlights? Given that there are blind people who play cricket to a very high standard, the idea that bad light is a legitimate reason for stopping play is ludicrous.

Chandigarh that day had also become a city in which I was incapable of spotting and hailing a taxi. Much as when I had left the hotel that morning, I had no idea in which direction I should be walking, but this time there was at least a crowd to be dragged along by. After ten minutes of walking in a straight line, though, most of the crowd had dissipated and slipped off down other junctions and once more I was left alone and lost. The area I was in wasn't quiet or intimidating, but it was infuriatingly devoid of identity. As vast swathes of Chandigarh are identically planned, everywhere you find yourself looks like everywhere else you've ever been. I stopped several people and asked if they could point me in the direction of my hotel, the name of which

I was a little unsure of. It was something to do with central London, I thought, but what exactly? The Piccadilly? The Mayfair? Every person I stopped asked me the same question: 'Which sector is it in?' and every time I was forced to reply, 'I don't know.' I was like someone that had come a cropper late at night on a stag do in an unfamiliar city and who had been abandoned by the group. Except it wasn't yet six in the evening, and I had little to celebrate. I walked past several bus stops and looked at the signs on them that listed their destinations. All of them were just lists and lists of numbers correlating to the various sectors, and the longer I stared at them the less sense they made, as if the humidity and ever increasing despair had brought on a bit of the old late-onset dyscalculia.

I stood on the corner of one of Chandigarh's many junctions and began to curse. I cursed the fact that I had been separated from the herd; I cursed that I had left the hotel without my guidebook; I cursed the bad light that had curtailed the day's play; I cursed my lack of work; I cursed the strap of my laptop case sawing into my neck; I cursed whoever had booked us into whatever our hotel was called; I cursed BBC Scotland; I cursed the *Western Mail*; I cursed Chandigarh; I cursed India.

The straight line that I had been walking thus far had brought me no joy, and so I turned to my left and began walking along another road. This time I soon saw a taxi and a rickshaw, but they both contained passengers. I did however find another bus stop, and this one also contained a destination called 'Terminus'. That was something. I was sure that I had seen the word up in big letters somewhere near the road I had crossed to buy my electrical adaptor. I decided that when this bus came along I would get on it.

It was a further ten minutes before the bus arrived, but the more I thought about it, the more I was convinced that 'Terminus' was familiar to me. There had been a small shopping

complex along the road from where I'd had such difficulty crossing. Perhaps that was called 'Terminus'? In fact, I had a hazy
recollection of seeing some sort of bus station across that road.
When the bus finally came and I leapt eagerly aboard I double-
checked everything with the driver.

'You go to "Terminus"?'

He looked a little puzzled by this question.'Yes.'

'Can you tell me when we are there?'

Again he looked puzzled, but then shrugged. 'Yes, okay. If
you need.'

'Thanks,' I said and started down the aisle in search of a seat.
It was a crowded bus, but I fancied I could see a space or two
near the back. Having been felled so unceremoniously by the
driver at Nagpur airport, I was anxious to make sure I was in my
seat before we set off again, and so started down the aisle at quite
a lick. Two ladies with large shopping bags blocked my path and
I tried to squeeze past them.

'Excuse me, please. Sorry.'

'Stop, stop,' said one of the ladies. 'Our bags. Be careful.'

I stopped, and they slowly began to pick up their bags.

'Sorry, I thought I could just step over them.'

'Please. No.'

'I'm sorry.'

'Now you go.'

It wasn't actually the bags, however, that had been obstruct-
ing my path. It was the ladies themselves. Again I tried to
squeeze past them, but it was a task that was made harder by the
fact that they were each now carrying their bags at waist height.
I pushed gently past the first lady but there was no way past the
second one without removing the laptop case that was slung over
my shoulder. I stopped between the two ladies, neither of whom
yet appeared to have moved an inch apart, and cautiously lifted
the strap of the case over my head. In order to do so I had to

hold my face uncomfortably close to the second of the two ladies. She looked at me in horror with her mouth screwed tightly shut and I started to panic that I was now deep in the midst of some horrendous cultural misunderstanding. I couldn't travel like this all the way to Terminus. Besides, the bus hadn't set off again yet. The thought that I might be offending these ladies, and indeed any other passengers on the bus – some of whom I could now hear tutting – triggered a sudden outbreak of sweat. I froze on the spot wondering quite what I should do. I could hear a voice from nearer the front of the bus shouting something. And then a voice nearer me was raised.

'Excuse me, mister.'

Were they talking to me? I froze. I could hear yet more tutting, and then the voice came again.

'Mister?'

The lady who I was face to face with slowly raised her hand and pointed at me.

'You,' she said accusingly.

I turned around and then leant out to one side to see the source of the voice. Behind the posterior of the first of the two ladies I was sandwiched between was sitting a smartly dressed man in his early forties. He had a cotton satchel on with writing on its side, and looked like he was on his way from a conference. His eyebrows were raised as if to suggest that he had something he needed to say to me. Had my behaviour offended him so much that this diminutive fellow was going to order me off the bus? Or perhaps it was some sort of logistics conference that he was on his way home from. In which case he might have a solution as to how I might disentangle myself and my laptop case from these two appalled ladies and their shopping.

'Yes?' I said.

'The driver.'

'I'm sorry?'

'The driver. You must speak to the driver.'

I looked up and back down the aisle. The driver was leaning out of his booth trying to get my attention by flailing his arms around. Other passengers were turning to stare at me.

'Yes?' I said, in what I hoped was an apologetic voice.

'Ticket,' said the driver. 'Money. You must pay for the journey.'

In my excitement at finding a way back to somewhere near the hotel I had managed to completely overlook this traditional part of bus journeys the world over and had just arrogantly sauntered down the aisle and instead got on with the business of getting in other people's way and invading their personal space. I felt crestfallen, but could never have achieved the levels of despair that became etched across the faces of the two ladies that I was wedged between when they realised that I would need to extricate myself and squeeze past them again.

Indian people are, I am sure it is fair to say, far more polite than British people tend to be, but as I jostled my way back past the first lady and her shopping I could tell that I was beginning to try the patience of everybody else on-board. In my panic I pushed the first note I could find into the palm of the driver.

'You want change?' he said, almost accusingly.

'Well, only if it's not a problem.'

'You have something smaller?'

He handed me back the note I had given him, which I could now see was for 500 rupees.

'Sorry, how much is the ticket?'

'Fifteen.'

'Right. Sorry.'

I rummaged around in my pockets, found the two coins I needed and handed them over.

'Thank you, sir.'

'You will tell me when we are at Terminus, won't you.'

'Yes,' he sighed and then started up the engine. I turned back to face the rest of the bus. People were either staring straight at me or out of the window whilst biting their lips. I briefly considered going in search of a seat again, but the faces of the two ladies that I had been wrestling with told me that this would most certainly not be happening. Instead, I stood in the aisle and stared at the floor.

We made a number of stops, and people got on and off, but I remained where I was until eventually at one stop everybody else got off the bus. I heard the engine being turned off, and looked up to see the driver climbing out of his cabin.

'This is Terminus,' he said.

I looked out of the window, but all I could see were other buses.

'Sorry, where is the shopping centre?'

'Shopping centre?'

'Yes, Terminus shopping centre? That's right, isn't it?'

'Terminus is where all the buses stop. That is Terminus.'

'Oh. Thanks. And sorry about the ticket thing. I just forgot.'

'Okay, sir. Goodnight, sir.'

He got off the bus, and so I did the same and followed him across the tarmac, wondering where I was. And then, above the buses I suddenly saw the big letters spelling out the word Terminus that I'd had a hazy recollection of and everything finally clicked. I was such an idiot. Terminus wasn't the name of a shopping centre at all. The letters were there because this was the Bus Terminus, where all the buses stopped. I could have got on a bus at any of the stops that I had walked past and I would have ended up here, just along the road from where I had bought my electrical adaptor. Once I got across that road again I would be just five minutes' walk from the hotel. And I was opposite the entrance to a subway. I walked down its steps, along a tunnel, and resurfaced on the other side of the road, just 50 yards away from where I had hailed my cycle rickshaw three days earlier. I walked along the road, and around the corner near the busy junction and along the pavement I had walked down on my first night in Chandigarh, past the men sat out on canvas chairs arranged round hot-plates, smoking and eating samosas. They looked relaxed and jovial. They also looked at home, and I envied them for it.

*

Everyone else from the press box had already returned by the time I walked in through the doors of our hotel and into the lobby. A few were loitering by the reception desk making dinner plans. Kevin Howells and Peter Baxter were on their way into the bar for a drink, and asked if I wanted to join them. So I dashed up to my room, showered off the dirt and frustrations of the day and slipped downstairs again to join them. When I reached the table Peter was in the middle of describing a recent visit to Geoffrey Boycott's room.

I had been told by my father's cousin Steve that Sunsport booked every single member of the press corps' travel and accommodation apart from Geoffrey Boycott's. He, either through thriftiness or paranoia, always opted to organise his own arrangements. This was why one never saw him on the buses and planes that the rest of us shared, or encountered him in the evenings at the hotel. While we were all staying in this hotel, or the rather fancier Taj hotel where the players were, Boycott had secured himself the use of an apartment within the ground itself. The night before the Test, Baxter had visited the ground to give Boycott a copy of the commentary rota for *Test Match Special*'s coverage of the game. Boycott had answered the door dressed only in a long T-shirt, and then invited Baxter in for a cup of tea. Baxter settled into an armchair, but it was only when Boycott had given him his tea and settled down in the chair opposite that it became clear that Boycott had no underwear on. Baxter, of course, said nothing and Boycott appeared completely unaware that he was airing rather more than just a few opinions.

'It was extraordinary,' said Baxter. 'I didn't know where to look.'

'Well, Miles is really no better,' said Kevin and gleefully related to Peter how much of myself I had displayed to Simon and him so soon after we met.

'Goodness,' said Peter. 'Everybody's at it.'

Afterwards Kevin and I ate in an Italian restaurant in the basement of the hotel. It was fine, but we could have been anywhere in the world. At our table we sat with Tim Abraham, the reporter from Sky Sports News, his cameraman Graeme and a photographer called Tom Shaw. We played a game called 'Top Threes' in which you have to name your three favourite things in any category. Often it was surprisingly hard to narrow a list down to three. Sometimes it was harder to even think of three. Everybody got abused for at least half of their selections, although Tim Abraham received dog's abuse for his choosing Level 42 as his favourite band. I got shouted down for choosing *Airplane* as one of my favourite comedy films, which seemed harsh. No choice was greeted with such derision all night though than when Graeme, after much consideration, decided that his favourite ever film was *Bird On A Wire*, the Action/Adventure/Comedy starring Mel Gibson and Goldie Hawn. I laughed a lot while we played, and I had needed to. But as I climbed the stairs to my room I wasn't laughing any more. The evening's fun and banter had provided only a temporary change in my mood. I knew this was the sort of fun I could probably have had in a Wetherspoon's, not travelled 5,702 miles for. It was beginning to dawn on me that this whole trip was nothing like the clever idea that it had seemed.

*

I felt in no rush the next morning, and made my way to the ground alone again and in my own time. I sat down in the press box in time to see Andrew Flintoff survive a huge LBW appeal off the bowling of Kumble. At least the box was a little less crowded that day, and I had been able to shunt up a place and actually see the middle of the square. England's score had moved on by three runs before I'd arrived and Paul Collingwood had also been hit on the hand by a fast delivery and received a lengthy inspection from the team physio. Flintoff had also become a father again overnight, and had a new son called Corey who he was yet to meet. I logged on to the box's Wi-Fi to check if there was any noise from BBC Scotland. There was silence. Someone at the *Western Mail* had at least sent me something: a short email to say that they were happy with the way that the blog was going, and that it was 'worth carrying on with'. I sent a reply saying how much I was enjoying writing it, and if there was anything that they might be interested in me writing for the actual paper then I would be only too happy to provide it.

I looked up from my computer in time to see Collingwood flick Munaf Patel off his legs for a beautiful four. I turned to watch the replay on the television, which was now showing uninterrupted coverage of our game but in black-and-white. There was also a new figure in our midst: a cuddly and shiny blond man who turned out to be a sports gossip columnist. Someone had mentioned him the night before and warned me that it was unwise to say almost anything within earshot of him. I had assumed this to be a joke, but watching the way people behaved around him now, I began to wonder if people's mistrust was heartfelt. He was sitting at a desk in front of a blank sheet of notepaper looking around the box and just waiting, it appeared, for someone to let slip something scurrilous – like a dog waiting by a dining table for scraps of greasy meat to be flicked in his direction. Quite a few people stopped to say something to him, but they were nearly always making a joke about how much they disliked him. He looked as out of place as I felt.

With the score on 180, England lost their fifth wicket. Paul Collingwood, with 25 runs to his name, was drawn into a forward defensive by a delivery from Kumble that bounced a lot, turned a little and clipped the very top of his off stump. The general consensus in the room was that this was not really a dismissal that the batsman should have been blamed for. 'Great ball,' someone said and the majority of those present concurred. Even so, it still mean that yet another England bats-man had got themselves in and then got out when looking well set. This certainly irritated Geoffrey Boycott, who had walked in at the back of the box and started chuntering about 'soft batting' while everybody was watching the slow-motion black-and-white re-run of the dismissal on our monitor. Everybody's attention turned to him and his rantings. 'This is just roo-bish,' he kept saying.

'I suppose you think it might all be better if you were the coach,' said Peter Hayter, rather bravely.

Clearly Boycott was in no doubt on this point whatsoever, and looked incensed that anybody could even speculate other-wise. He pointed a finger at Hayter. 'If I was the fucking coach then they might be fucking better.'

'They couldn't pay you enough,' said another voice.

This infuriated Boycott further.

'Two hundred thousand pounds a year the current coach gets,' he said. 'Two hundred thousand.' Then he turned to the gossip writer... 'You should write about that in your column.'

The columnist raised his eyebrows, but then an unexpected tone of doubt crept in Boycott's voice. 'Er, actually you might want to check that first.'

This was a timely piece of editorial advice. Only that morn-ing I had been reading an Indian newspaper that had carried a syndicated article by Sir Geoffrey himself. They had titled the column 'Yorkshire Pudding' and the byline photograph was of Greg Chappell.

Boycott's anger had now abated, and he and the columnist fell into a lengthy conversation mainly about 'some very nice cheeses' that had been sent out to Delhi for him. As he rhapsodised about his dairy goods, the cricket suddenly picked up a little. In the gloom Geraint Jones square cut Kumble hard for three, and then square drove Munaf Patel for a four that absolutely hammered into the advertising hoardings on the boundary edge. Flintoff then lifted Kumble neatly over mid-on for a four, before sweeping him so fine that it hit the rope directly in line with the stumps. This brought up England's 200, but also signalled the start of the drinks break. Having had drinks, the umpires then offered the batsmen the choice to come off for bad light and they took it.

*

And that, it turned out, was that. Because it then began to rain. And it rained, and it rained and it rained. And as the rain fell, so did the mood in the box. At first it felt like just a little break; a chance to get up and walk about a bit, and for people to lean across each other's desks and chat about things. David Hopps described how an Indian journalist had asked Andrew Walpole if Flintoff would be available for an interview about the joys of fatherhood. When told that he was not, the journalist had asked if he could interview Kevin Pietersen on the subject instead. Meanwhile Derek Pringle confirmed that he'd had a small part in the film *Chariots Of Fire*.

But as the rain break dragged on, the levity slowly leaked from the room. People were becoming restless and fidgety, and still had word-counts and deadlines to meet. I watched a correspondent two rows in front of me trying desperately to concoct a sentence about the arrival of Flintoff's son. 'Andrew Flintoff's wife has given birth to a son...' he started, and then paused to think about where this sentence might then go. He tutted, deleted the line and started again. 'During the night, Andrew Flintoff became a father again...' he started before he lost confidence and deleted that too, and tried a new tack. 'I'm sure Mr and Mrs Flintoff are as delighted about the new arrival as any young couple...' he began, then stopped and sighed. I watched on with a mixture of amusement and pity as he repeated this routine another seven times, before finally admitting defeat, deleting the last of his attempts and shutting his laptop with an exasperated sigh.

Other people were browsing the Internet and starting to bicker amongst themselves. I saw one journalist walk past the gossip columnist and jab him hard in the soft flesh beneath his ribs, purely out of boredom. He jumped slightly, turned to see who had done it and then looked forlorn.

Somebody announced that lunch was being served, and so everybody trooped downstairs and skipped through the rain to the clubhouse alongside the pavilion where hospitality was being provided. The food was splendid, but the atmosphere was beginning to sour. I joined at least two conversations just at the moment that they spilled over into rows.

'All right, chaps.'

'Hello, Miles. No, Donald, I think you'll find it's you who's being a shit.'

I tried to tag onto another conversation, but it soon turned into a post-mortem of a falling out that one of them had recently had with another correspondent.

'I think I'd better head back and watch some more of the rain,' I said, hoping that it would be a vaguely jokey line with which to extract myself from the conversation. It fell extremely flat, with both of the other parties looking back at me as if I had just said, 'You're both boring. And I doubt your wives are much fun to be with either.' They looked at me for so long that I ended up apologising quietly, before withdrawing and returning sadly to the pavilion. I rechecked for any emails from the *Western Mail* or BBC Scotland, but there was nothing. Instead I wrote a piece for the blog about what a laugh it all was, and then sat back wishing that was the case.

No one could do anything. Writers had nothing to write about. Broadcast reporters had nothing to report on. And commentators had nothing to commentate on, but would probably have been able to fill the spare airtime anyway with inane waffle, and increasingly desperate anecdotes that had nothing to do with anything:

'I didn't know Graham Gooch could play the harp.'

'Tell you who makes a great gazpacho: Viv Richards.'

The arrival of the rain had brought with it a complete change of feeling, as if it had got into people's bones. Again I struggled to judge the mood of some of the conversations around me. David Hopps and Paul Coupar were discussing the fact that Hopps's profile in India was much higher than it was at home.

'How big are you here?' I asked. 'Have you ever been on the front cover of the Indian edition of *The Puzzler*?'

I laughed at my own flippancy, but he did not. He just turned to me and said, 'Don't take the fucking piss,' and then resumed his conversation. I blushed, and cursed myself for not just keeping quiet.

Either something had changed, or I had been blind to it before. I became more aware of a niggling in the air, and of competitiveness and resentment.

'How come some people have moved to a better hotel?'

'Have you heard they've given him a podcast now? Has he asked you to be on it? He hasn't asked me.'

'Do you know what he gets paid for that column? It's outrageous.'

In an attempt to keep the crowd happy, the man operating the ground's PA system was playing every record he could get hold of. U2's 'Where The Streets Have No Name' was followed by the British National Anthem. It was the first tune for a while that Derek Pringle hadn't danced to, and it certainly did nothing to rouse me. I was starting to feel something worse than frustration; I felt sad.

It was just not how I imagined it. When I had been sitting at the Oval and looked up and saw that press box, I had seen all these journalists and imagined a great sense of team spirit. So many of the people in the box with me now would have been the people in the box that I was looking up at, and I had imagined them to be a group of people who travelled the world together, working and hunting as a pack. I imagined that this might all be fun. Of course, the reality is that working in a press box is akin to working in an open-plan office in which everybody is employed by a rival company.

And yet. When play was finally called off for the day at half past three, everybody else in that box put their heads down and got on with touch-typing 800 words, full of fact, comment and insight born from years and years of professional service. These people, I knew, were the cream of the crop, the masters of their trade – all hard at work. And all I was doing was sitting at the back playing Minesweeper.

*

That night I drank a skinful of red wine whilst having dinner with Kevin and Simon Mann. But when I retired to my room I still felt wide awake, and sat up in bed watching *The Big Indian Comedy Show* on the television. I could not understand a word of it, of course, but it was a big glitzy, light-entertainment show and everybody appeared to be having a good time. Their enjoyment, however, was not remotely infectious. The rain hammered against the windows, and there was the odd rattle of thunder, which made the bedside light beside me flicker on and off. I felt lonely and devoid of purpose. In the press box that day whilst idling away the afternoon I had checked the distance between Chandigarh and Edinburgh. It was 4,116 miles, and at that moment I could feel every single one of them.

Chapter Twelve

I woke the next morning, with a hangover, to a text message on my phone telling me that the England team were going to stay at their hotel until the weather improved. I turned over and tried to go back to sleep, but it was impossible. My head was pounding, and my joints ached. Worst of all was the pain I experienced whilst thinking about the situation I was in. Sports writing gigs, I could now see, were assigned weeks, maybe months, in advance. I couldn't just turn up and take a limited-overs approach to this journalism lark; I was going to have to play the long game. All I could hope was that by staying around and looking busy I could still get to know people and maybe they might think of me in the future. But after Simon had secured the *Balamory* confession from me, that had made things harder still. I felt uneasy. Since Simon and Kevin had spoken to me about being an actor and a performer, very few people had actually said anything about it. Vic Marks had said to me, 'So you're a comic, are you, is that right?' which was hardly aggressive. But I didn't know who did and who didn't know this easily Google-able information. Nor about how they might react if they did. Nor whether I could still convince people I was now a journalist if I turned up and got on with stuff. I was in completely uncertain territory. All I knew was that I didn't have a great deal to do. Even if the lack of cricket was frustrating, yesterday had probably been the day when I looked most at home in the box because nobody else had anything to do either.

I was just on the point of falling back to sleep when I received a fresh text message telling me that, on second thoughts, the game was in fact going to be getting under way at ten o'clock. Anxious not to miss another start I grabbed the quickest of showers, pulled on some clothes and hurtled down to the lobby to see if there was anybody else that I could share a taxi with. Scyld Berry was just on the way out of the front door.

'Scyld?'

He popped his head back through the door with a quizzical look. 'Yes?'

Somewhere he had found an extra half syllable to stick into the word, so that it hung in the air for longer than it should have.

'Are you going to the ground?'

'Ye-ees.'

'Can I share your cab?'

'Ye-ees. You're going to the ground, are you?'

'Of course.'

'Where's all your stuff?'

'Hm?'

'Are you not taking anything to the ground with you?'

In my haste I had rushed out of the room completely forgetting to pick up my laptop case or even a notebook. All I had on me was the press pass, some banknotes in my pocket and a pair of sunglasses on. I looked like I was heading out for a couple of hours of gentle sight-seeing, not for a regular day's work.

'Ah, well. I just thought that I'd...erm...'

What did I just think?

'Or do you not write anything for the Sunday paper?' said Scyld.

'For the Sunday paper?'

Of course. It was a Saturday. Anything that people wrote today would be published on Sunday. Some papers had specific Sunday correspondents, and didn't use their usual daily columnists. Scyld had kindly provided me with a way out of the dilemma he had posed me. I didn't need a laptop on a Saturday. I could just turn up and watch the cricket. I didn't even need to look busy. What a relief.

'That's right,' I said. 'Absolutely correct. Nothing to do on Saturdays but watch.'

And then a man who told us he was a former 'Punjabi Police Commando' drove us in a taxi to the ground so fast that the first thing I had to do when I arrived was to go and find a lavatory to be sick into.

*

Because it was a Saturday, the box had a different make-up to it. Anybody who wrote for a Sunday paper was entitled to take one of the seats nearest the front with the best view. Some of the daily reporters hadn't even turned up, but nonetheless the box was still crowded. There had been a bit of rainfall whilst I had been in the midst of my own brief shower but nonetheless the game still got under way at ten o'clock and I was sat in a good seat just three rows back when Geraint Jones and Andrew Flintoff, our not-out batsmen, strode out to the crease.

Flintoff started well by driving Kumble through mid-on for four, but then edged one just short of Rahul Dravid at slip. Kumble had two huge appeals for bat-pad catches off Geraint Jones turned down, and so to celebrate his survival I made my way to the back of the box in search of a cup of coffee from the machine. Geoffrey Boycott was standing in front and when I leant forward to take a cardboard cup he growled, 'No coffee' at me. Rather than this being an order though, it turned out to be a piece of information. 'Machine doesn't work.' Within moments of these words being spoken by such a recognisable voice, a number of the pavilion staff came scurrying over to mend it, and they had it working within minutes.

'You go first,' I said to Geoffrey once it was up and running again.

'No, no, young man. You look like you need it more than me.'

'Thanks.'

That was kind of him. I poured myself a cup, and took a sip.

'How does it taste?' said Geoffrey.

'Fine.'

'Right then. In that case I'll have some.'

As I returned to my seat David Gower came into the box, and started chatting to the people in front of me about a political argument that had been going on amongst certain members of the Sky commentary team. It sounded as if some of Michael Atherton's gentle explanations of social justice might have been going a little over Ian Botham's head. Either that or he was choosing not to listen.

'Both was playing the role of the United States,' explained Gower.

'Is Atherton a big socialist?' somebody asked.

'He's a Notting Hill socialist,' Angus Fraser suggested.

Out on the pitch, meanwhile, a war of attrition was being played out, and after an hour of play England had managed to advance their score by just 29 runs. Flintoff, although clearly having to work hard, was looking solid but Jones was struggling to pick anything that Kumble sent down to him. His biggest success came when he missed a ball down the leg side and it ran away off his pad for four leg-byes. He also managed to edge one delivery through the slip's grasp for four, but mainly he tried to play defensively off the back foot, which solicited a frustrated 'ooooh' from Kumble every other ball. Shortly after the drinks break Jones nudged Harbhajan Singh, who had removed his sun hat to reveal a rather stunning yellow patka, into the leg side for a single which finally brought up his and Flintoff's 50 partnership. In reality it had taken only 84 minutes of play, but the fact that it had been spread out over an entire day of real time made it seem so much slower. Twenty minutes later Flintoff, who had first come out to bat two days ago, reached his own half-century by scampering through for a single when a leading edge ballooned up in the direction of an empty short cover. He was only one and a half Test matches into his captaincy career, but so far it was making him play in a very mature way, the added responsibility becoming him well.

He also brought up England's 250 by power-sweeping the debutant Chawla to the midwicket boundary. Jones then got in on the act by paddling Harbhajan hard through square leg for four, which delighted me. Flintoff then hit Chawla for two sixes over long-on; the first of them little more than a checked drive that flew hard and flat to land just over the boundary; the second one a far more brutal spanking that cleared the fence and finally came to land high up in the stand. Jones also took a liking to Chawla, powering him through midwicket to become the (now here's a statistic) eighty-seventh Englishman to score 1,000 runs in Test cricket. Not long after that a single for Flintoff off Harbhajan brought up the pair's fifth century partnership in Tests, and as if to salute the pair the ground was suddenly bathed in bright sunshine.

With the score on 282–5, Rahul Dravid took the new ball and threw it straight to Irfan Pathan. But it was Munaf Patel at the other end who made the breakthrough, leaping high to parry a drive from Flintoff in his follow-through and then catching it cleanly when it came down again. Flintoff's 70 was a real battler of an innings, but his dismissal came at an unfortunate time, just a few overs before lunch. As the players trooped off with the score on 286–6, Michael Atherton came into the box and stopped to chat with Simon Hughes.

'What's this about you having a podcast, Yosser?'

'I have, yeah. Would you like to be on it?'

'Not especially.'

*

I bumped into Simon Mann on the stairs.

'How are you feeling?'

'A little rough,' I said.

'You certainly seemed to enjoy your wine last night.'

'Yeah. It's quite hot in the press box.'

'You should go upstairs then. Go up one more flight and there's a Chairman's Enclosure. It's open to the elements, you could get some fresh air.'

And so after I'd found something to eat, that's exactly what I did. I climbed up to the top level of the pavilion where instead of a cramped and humid press box there was an array of raked seating sections in the open air and a number of corporate boxes. In keeping with the colonial feeling of the pavilion, these contained groups of people dressed in smart linen suits taking tea. I plonked myself down in one of the seating rakes next to a speaker from which I could hear the voice of Nasser Hussain, chatting away about something in their commentary box. Scyld Berry appeared and took a seat beside me in time for us to see Liam Plunkett glove a short ball from Patel down the leg side and be snaffled behind by Dhoni for a duck. This brought Matthew Hoggard to the crease.

'I imagine that you're a sort of literary Matthew Hoggard,' Berry said to me, somewhat unexpectedly. I had absolutely no idea what he meant by this. It didn't sound especially like a compliment, but nor could it be classed as an insult. I decided that he asked it as a test, purely to see how I responded, and so I chuckled.

Geraint Jones then square drove Patel to the boundary fence to bring up his sixth Test 50 but the 300 mark was achieved via the unlikely method of a Hoggard sweep. Three hundred sounded like a lot, but it was by no means enough yet. Simon Mann had said at dinner last night that England needed a bare minimum of 350 in this innings, and so Hoggard would need to stick around and Jones had to start scoring some quick runs.

But it was not to be. Jones played a forward defensive to Kumble soon after and the ball took his inside edge, bounced once and then agonisingly trickled back onto his stumps. His dismissal was an important breakthrough for the Indians, but I was taken aback by the massive roar from the crowd which greeted it.

'Is Geraint Jones very highly rated here?' I asked Berry.

He seemed amused by the idea.

'That was Kumble's four hundred and ninety-ninth wicket. They're hoping to see his five hundredth now.'

'Ah yes. Of course.'

And then with his very next delivery Kumble trapped Steve Harmison in front with a flat, straight ball and the place absolutely erupted. Everybody was up on their feet, applauding and cheering. Klaxons and horns were sounded. The Indian team all raced to greet the leaping Kumble and swarmed around him offering hugs, handshakes and high-fives, before briefly raising him aloft as he acknowledged the response of the delighted crowd. Four other bowlers – Warne, Murali, McGrath and Walsh – had taken more, but Kumble was the first Indian to reach 500 wickets and it was a moment for everyone in the ground, perhaps even the departing Harmison, to savour.

*

I had met Kumble once. It was 1995 and he was playing for Northamptonshire for a season. He was ludicrously good, and took over a hundred wickets that summer. Tom Harrison and I had been friends at school when we were seven, and I don't remember either of us having the slightest interest in sport at all. Yet over the years we each separately developed a massive love for cricket, and in our teens would go and watch games together. So much did we love cricket in fact, that having spent a day at the Oval watching England hold out for a draw against the West Indies, we then travelled to Uxbridge for three days in a row to watch Northamptonshire playing Middlesex (whom Tom supported) in what turned out to be a crucial top of the County Championship table encounter. During play we sat as close to the sightscreen as we could, but we would hang around near the pavilion during the intervals to get autographs and try and chat to players. On our final day there, we finally got a chance to meet Kumble and ask for his signature. He signed very carefully and slowly, and thus left a silence that I felt needed filling. I eventually opted for 'I've come all the way from Northamptonshire for this.' This probably sounded like a sort of complaint – the kind of thing you might say if you'd driven a party of young children all the way to Alton Towers only to find out that it was closed. Anil Kumble gave me a confused look, signed Tom's book and then headed off to the pavilion.

'Why did you say that?' asked Tom.

'I don't know,' I replied. 'Do you think he thought it was an odd thing to say?'

Tom thought for a bit and then said, 'He was probably thinking "And I've come all the bloody way from India."'

Looking at the glorious scenes out on the pitch and seeing the cheering fans, it felt good to know that I had at last reciprocated.

*

Panesar nervously blocked the hat-trick ball, but prodded at the next, a googly, which flew comfortably to Dravid at slip. Kumble had taken three wickets in four balls, and England had lost their last five wickets for just 17 runs. I nipped downstairs to use the lavatory, but when I returned to watch India's innings from the same location, my way out onto the top tier was blocked by an Indian official.

'You are going where, sir?'

'I was just going to watch from one of the seats out there.'

'You are a guest of the Chairman, sir?' he asked brightly.

'Well I...'

'Do you have a ticket for this area?'

'I have a pass,' I said, and took it from my pocket to show him.

'Oh,' he said, not looking pleased with what he was seeing. 'You are journalist.'

'That's right.'

'This is not the place for the journalists to watch the cricket.'

'I've just been watching it from here.'

'No, sir. Journalists do not watch here. Please follow me.'

And then he put his hand on my arm and began to lead me back down the stairs from where I had just come.

'It's fine,' I told him. 'I know where to go.'

'It's okay,' he told me. 'It is not a problem.'

And then he led me back down the next flight of stairs, and to the doors that led into the cramped press box.

'Here is the press box. Everything you need is here.'

'Thank you,' I said.

He held a door open for me, and watched as I walked in. Then he smiled at me curtly and closed it behind me. It had been a hell of a struggle just to get into the box in the first place. Now I was finding it equally hard to leave it.

I took one of the few spare seats, next to Rod Gilmour. The general feeling in the box was that 300 all out was not likely to be a big enough score, and there was some surliness generated by how quickly England had capitulated in the innings once the big breakthroughs had been made. As India started up their second innings, Rod let me use his laptop to check my emails, my paranoia having led me to think that the one day that I didn't bring my laptop would be the one day that BBC Scotland or the *Western Mail* got in touch and asked me to do something for them. There was, however, nothing from either of them.

What I had received, though, was a lengthy email from my friend Alan Blaine. Alan was just on the verge of leaving Britain to spend a few weeks travelling in India. Alan and I had both been in the same year at Edinburgh University and, indeed, studied on the same course: Divinity. Alan had never really done a great deal of work during our time there together. I remember in our first term at university bumping into him on his way to go and hand in an essay that he told me was three weeks late. At the time I thought that it was a slightly pathetic effort to be that late to deliver the first piece of work we had actually been set. But, over the next few years, it came to pass that handing in an essay three weeks late was actually Alan's finest academic achievement. He handed things in several months, or even terms, late. He was put back a year at one point, in the way that a difficult nine-year-old might be. The academic upshot of the four years he spent enrolled as a student at the university was a laminated certificate of attendance. Alan simply had far too many extra-curricular passions to leave time for reading and writing about theology. He appeared in an inordinate number of plays at the university's theatre, and read countless sporting biographies. He was devoted to the music of INXS and, though he always protests that this was not the case, was terribly good with the ladies. Since leaving university he had spent his summers driving passenger boats full of tourists along the River Ouse in York, whilst pointing out items of historical interest to them over the boat's PA system and occasionally colliding with bridges.

His greatest love, though, was elephants. Something traumatic had happened to Alan during birth, and he spent the first few weeks of his life sharing an incubator with a toy elephant. Alan's survival was touch-and-go, apparently, and despite the fact that countless doctors, nurses and consultants had played an enormous part in getting him through this sickly phase, Alan always seemed to attribute his survival to the presence of the elephant. And that was that. He was indebted to them forever, and obsessed about them. His favourite book was *Travels On My Elephant* by a man called Mark Shand who had once travelled

800 miles across India from the Bay Of Bengal to Sonepur on the Ganges on the back of an elephant he had bought, and who he named Tara. At the end of their epic journey together he took Tara to a place called Kipling Camp in Kanha National Park, a nature reserve in central India where she still lived. What Alan most wanted to do when he arrived in India, therefore, was not to see the Taj Mahal, or the Red Fort of Agra, or the beaches of Goa. He wanted to go and visit this elephant. And in his email, he was asking if I wanted to go with him. Now I knew quite a bit about Alan's travel plans already; he had told me about them when he asked if he could borrow the money to pay for his flights. It would be amazing, he said. We would not only meet Tara, but we could even swim with her. Alan had looked at the dates of the Test matches and could see there was definitely a bit of a gap between this Test and the final one in Mumbai. I sent him a quick message saying that I would think about it. I had already thought about it, though; it sounded stupid. I had come to India to become a cricket journalist and to try and get on with that crowd, not to go gadding about in the middle of nowhere like some loon on a never-ending gap year.

I watched the rest of the day's play in the press box. Virender Sehwag, as if to make up for all the hours of play that had been lost to weather, set off at a canter. But he had only made 11 of his characteristically flashy runs before he fended at an awkwardly short ball from Harmison and edged it behind to Geraint Jones. Dravid replaced him and was characteristically defensive, and together he and Jaffer put on 77 runs before, with the score on 96, Jaffer drove softly at a ball from Panesar and was easily taken at cover by Flintoff. The roar that greeted Tendulkar's walk to the crease was almost as loud as the noise made for Kumble's five-hundredth wicket. He did not last long though. He had made just four when he tried to fend off a brutal ball from Flintoff that flew off an edge and was caught by Strauss at slip. It had taken the best part of 40 overs for India to take their score to 103–3. This was certainly not anything like watching fireworks, but it did mean that the game was finely balanced.

David Gower came into the press box on a break from his commentating duties, and wandered around cheerily and charmingly to chat with people. I raised an eyebrow at him as he passed, wondering if he would even remember me from back in Nagpur.

'Hello. How are you getting on?' he asked.

'Oh, struggling on,' I said, trying to convey the jokey impression that I was struggling a little rather than a lot.

'Very good.'

Then I remembered hearing that he had an interest in wildlife, and so dangled what little I knew about Kipling Camp as a conversational carrot.

'Actually, though,' I said, 'a friend's just invited me to go and spend a few days at a place called Kipling Camp. Have you heard of it?'

'Kipling Camp? Oh yes. That was Bob Wright's place. I first went there twenty years ago.'

'Oh right. Do you think I should go?'

'If you've got the time, then definitely.'

'My friend says that, if I went, I'd get to swim with an elephant.'

Gower looked amused by this notion.

'No, no. That's dolphins.'

'There are dolphins?'

'No.' He smiled. 'It's dolphins that you swim with. You bathe with elephants. It's a crucial difference.'

'Oh, I see. Well, as long as I don't get the end with the taps.'

Gower emitted a small chuckle, then nodded and withdrew courteously like a well-practised courtier excusing himself from the presence of Louis XIV at Versailles. He returned to the Sky commentary box and I resumed looking about the place with nothing to do and a sense of unease.

By a quarter past five the box was filled with the tap-tapping of people desperately writing up their reports of the day. At moments like this the box is at its most quiet but also at its most alive. Then a message was relayed to the box that Andrew Flintoff would not be making an appearance at that evening's press conference. This prompted a number of annoyed outbursts, which I have to say I found to be ungracious and unreasonable. It was surely perfectly understandable that he wouldn't be keen to go and face the press at the end of a day like this. That morning he had finally completed a dogged innings that had straddled three days, and then had to field in the heat for several hours, as well as marshalling the troops and sending down rather a lot of rapid overs himself. Of anyone in the England camp he would have had by far the most on his plate, and all in the knowledge that back home he had a son that he had yet to meet.

Yuvraj Singh batted as slowly as Dravid, but with the score on 134–3 he suddenly drove hard at a wide, pitched-up Hoggard delivery and Ian Bell at short cover took off and stretched out a hand high to his left, the ball already seeming to have sped past him. There was a brief silence as his fingers first touched the ball, and he and it appeared to hang in the air together until he fell and tumbled and then stood up with the ball held aloft to let us know that it had really stuck. This was a flash of brilliance that had come almost from nowhere, and was a reward for the persistence of England's bowlers. There was not much play left in the day, and Dhoni came out to bat at a time completely unsuited for his style of play. His strike rate in one-day cricket was, at this point, 166.7, which meant there was pressure on him from the crowd to knock the skin off practically everything he faced. He batted largely with restraint, although he did smash one ball from Flintoff that travelled to the point boundary at an astonishing speed. The umpires called play with the score on 149–4, and the players all trooped off the field. Everyone around me was still hammering away at their keyboards, and so I quietly stood up and slipped away unnoticed and unnecessary. I had no intention of going to any press conference anyway as I had already found the atmosphere in the box claustrophobic enough. I really did have to get out.

At the bottom of the stairs I walked into the cool hall of the pavilion and was struck by the sight of a huge figure. It was Flintoff himself, a man of such epic proportions close up that the leather armchair on which he was sprawled looked ridiculous in comparison. He was drenched in sweat, his face reddened by both the heat and by his own exertions. He was smoking a cigarette, and gulping at it as if it was thirst that it would quench and not a craving for nicotine. He looked completely and utterly shattered, like an embattled Cyclops. Just minutes before I had seen this man standing tall and upright, and proudly applauding his players as he led them off the field after a long and battling day that had left the game so finely poised. His own contributions had been pivotal to the position England were now in. Now, though, away from the glare of the sun and the cameras, he had let his shoulders and his guard drop and he looked almost to be without bones, like a heavy overcoat that had dropped from a hook and then lay on the floor in a formless heap. Various other figures – administrators and officials – passed by where he sat and didn't so much as flick a glance in his direction, just carried on with whatever their business was, paperwork to fill in or a drinks function into which to usher guests. I stopped for a moment though, unable to take my eyes off him. I found it almost upsetting to see him looking like this; the hero of the previous year's summer, an unstoppable and irrepressible god, suddenly not all-powerful but instead merely human. If someone looked like this at the end of a party, a kindly soul would carefully remove the glass from their tenuous grasp, and lay a blanket over him and push a cushion under his head, before turning off the light. This though was a man just past the halfway point of a series with no chance yet of any sort of respite. And upstairs there was a box of people wondering why this man couldn't be bothered to speak to them.

*

I set off, hands in pockets, in what I now knew to be the direction of the hotel. I walked and I walked and I walked. There was no way I could walk all the way back to the hotel before nightfall, but I walked until I was so hungry that I could go no further, and then stopped at a stall by the side of the road. I pointed at a couple of chapattis on a hot griddle and some unidentifiable curry, paid some money and was handed my meal on a paper plate. There was an awning in front of the stall, but no chairs, and so I sat down cross-legged on the pavement, my back against a tree, and I ate my food in silence.

For three days now I had done the same thing: I'd got up, I'd gone to the ground, I'd seen as much of the cricket that I was physically capable of, waited without success for news from my potential employers; I'd written my blog and pretended that I was a happy, busy journalist. But I had to face up to the stark reality that I really wasn't any of those things. All along the challenge seemed to be about getting into the press box. But just getting into a press box didn't make you a journalist, any more than shouting out heckles from the back of a room made you a comedian. It wasn't just that I didn't have any proper journalism work to do; more worryingly it was becoming clear that I didn't think like a journalist, I didn't feel like one. I felt in awe of the real journalists. So many of them appeared to me to be go-getters; the sort of people who could walk into a room with a single aim and not leave until they had achieved it. I'm the sort of person who would walk into a room, take one look, think 'Naaah' and walk out again. I didn't have their drive, their focus, their instinct.

Take the one piece of serious cricket journalism that the *Western Mail* had actually charged me with getting: Get a quote from Flintoff saying how much England miss Simon Jones. I'd asked the press officer if there was any possibility of an interview, he had said that there wouldn't be and that was that. I had just left it.

Of course what I should have done was just go to a press conference that Flintoff was attending, stick my hand up and ask: 'Are you missing Simon Jones?' Presumably, even if only out of politeness, he would have said, 'Yes, of course,' even if he then went on to say how good the rest of the bowling attack were and that he had every confidence in them. I would already have had the answer I needed, and thus, I would have been able to write up the story that they wanted. That's what a proper journalist would have done: innocuous question, innocuous answer, 500 words, name in print, job done, get paid, officially a cricket writer. But none of this had occurred to me until a week too late.

But I knew that it wasn't just the fact that I had not so far made any advances in the world of cricket journalism that was making me feel so sad. There was something else. Even without stuff to be getting on with, I had still been able to get into the places that I wanted to. I had sat in a press box for an entire game, and had been in touching distance of, and spoken to, so many of my cricketing heroes. But the reality was that being constantly surrounded by people for who all this was just part of the daily grind, a routine that had to be endured, was having an unforeseen but profoundly depressing effect on me. As the motorised traffic roared past me and the bicycles and rickshaws squealed along, the horrible thought dawned on me that seeing the game from this angle meant that cricket was losing its magic for me.

And on top of all that there was something else bothering me. I felt odd. It wasn't about work or even about cricket. It was about people. Finding myself drinking with Gower, Botham and Hussain…that was fantastic. But it was also…strange. Lending Atherton a biro. Great. But also a little weird. These people were megastars to me, but I had put myself into a situation in which I could probably have looked up and seen one of my childhood heroes bobbing about in my line of vision for at least ten hours of every waking day, just wandering about doing perfectly normal things: sending text messages, asking for directions to the lavatory, removing lint from their sweaters…Every time that I saw one of my heroes going unfussily about their daily business, their stardust sparkled a little less.

Working alongside and amongst them, or even just pretending to, had taken them off their pedestals and put them into real life. My real life. And I really wasn't sure that I liked it. It wasn't as if these people had been disappointing, far from it. They had been charming, interesting and even interested. But they had been normal. I wished that I hadn't seen Flintoff slumped in that chair like a vanquished dragon. And I was suddenly glad that my hero Michael Atherton had essentially said nothing to me. One of the things I've always liked about him was his quiet, his restraint. I would rather only hear him talk about biros or memory sticks than invite me to join him in a jacuzzi with some strippers or sit me down and tell me his regrets. He had kept his distance and I was glad of it.

Those men with their raised batons outside the pavilion in Nagpur had been right all along. 'Keep back! Keep back!' they had barked at us. But they weren't protecting the players, they were protecting us. 'Keep back! Keep back! Don't get too close to your heroes!'

I stood up and dusted some flour from my trousers, threw my plate into a bin and hailed the first rickshaw that came along.

The colours, the sounds and the smells that had so intrigued and frightened me on my other rickshaw trips were barely there during this journey. 'I'm out here for a month,' I thought. 'I've come here because I love cricket, and because I thought this would be a magical journey.' But now I could feel that this trip was beginning to make me hate the thing I loved and cherished. I had thought I was ready to take my relationship with cricket to the next level, but in fact I had overdone it. Good God, what on earth had I done?

And as I slumped in the back of that rickshaw chundering along highways amidst the stinky fumes, it dawned on me that I would need to take some sort of a step back. There were people that I needed to keep some distance from. I had to keep away from the very people whose company I came to India seeking to enjoy. If I didn't act now I could ruin one of the things that I loved most in my life, possibly forever.

*

I returned to the hotel determined to make a conscious effort to avoid any of my heroes and began heading up to my room. I was going to have a bath, sit down and write something about India and then dine alone and read my book. But as I gloomily and wearily climbed the stairs with my head hanging low, I heard a voice from above.

'Hello there!'

I looked up, and saw that there walking down the stairs, wearing a fresh shirt and with a smile on his face, was David Gower. I just couldn't get rid of him.

He stopped.

'Hello, David.'

'What are you up to?' he asked.

'Well I'm just…going up to my room.'

'Ah. I'm on my way to the bar.'

'Right.'

'We're all going to be in the bar.'

'I see. Well, I've just got a few things to be getting on with in my room, actually.'

He looked slightly taken aback. 'Well I'm…sure that you do. But once you've done whatever it is that you've got to do in your room, then hopefully we'll all see you in the bar.'

'Yeah. Maybe, David. Maybe.'

And I just left David Gower standing there on the stairs and I walked on past him, locked myself in my room, and then sat down on the end of my bed and thought: 'I've just turned down a drink with David Gower.'

Doubts and uncertainties were swirling around inside my head. And then suddenly, amidst all these doubts and uncertainties, I became painfully aware of one, absolute fact: which was that I needed to get to the lavatory extremely quickly. I thought momentarily about the food that I had eaten from the stall by the side of the road and then charged into the bathroom, dropped my trousers and collapsed onto the pan in the certain knowledge that something absolutely appalling was about to happen.

*

I opened my account with a fart of such intensity that you would probably have been able to lean against it. This was instantly followed by a bowel movement that was so unbelievably violent that it asked some serious questions of my sphincteral elasticity. And then it just happened. Everything that I had ever eaten or that had grown inside of me started to sluice from my system.

It was a relentless, horrific assault on all of the senses. What I was producing in terms of consistency would have been an acceptable substance for perhaps dressing a salad with. But in terms of smell and I imagine taste, it would have been completely inappropriate. If someone had given you a slice of quiche that smelt like that, you would certainly have struggled to appear grateful.

And it just wouldn't stop. Occasionally my guts appeared to be announcing an intermission, but they were just playing tricks on me. I'd be on the verge of letting out a sigh of relief and then suddenly a fresh wave would be upon me. I was soon stuck in an horrific cycle of shit, wipe, start to stand, grimace, sit again, shit again, wipe again, start to stand again, grimace again, sit again, shit again...

Seven hours later I was still sitting on that lavatory, hunched and sweating, the same thoughts passing through my head like a ticker tape.

'What the fuck am I doing? What the fuck am I doing here? Over five thousand miles from home, alone and gaping on a toilet in the Punjab region, emptying myself to death on a doomed tour, in a vain dream turning so sour that I can practically taste it. I'm an idiot, a loser, a failure. I am utterly useless. I serve no purpose whatsoever, unless there happens to be somebody out there who wants to use my bowels as an egg timer. Providing it was for timing an egg that for reasons I am incapable of imagining they wanted to boil until the heat-death of the universe.

'Whatever it is that you imagine yourself to be trying to achieve, you are not. You are FAILING. You started out with very little work, and you have lost it. You failed to organise your press pass. You are in no position to generate future work. You have aroused suspicion, you have struggled to fit in. You're gaining access to games under an assumed identity, busting a gut to get into a room you barely want to be in any more anyway.

'You're a twenty-six-year-old man without a single commitment in your diary; no stand-up, no acting, no writing – everything has gone to shit. This plan, such as it was, has been ludicrous, stupid and lazy. This was not a clever, daring adventure; this is a pointless, ill-conceived, reckless, arrogant and lonely waste of time and money.

'What the fuck are you doing with your life? What is wrong with you? What even are you? What am I? What am I? What am I?'

It was, in so many ways, the most existential shit that I have ever had.

At long last, there was a hiatus of sorts. I did a final wipe, let out a sigh, and then slumped forward and put my head in my hands. Then I remembered where my hands had been and took my head out of them, and pulled up my trousers and hopped to the sink, gagging and spluttering. I washed and dried my hands, splashed cold water onto my face, and then headed back into the bedroom that I had suddenly sprinted from what was now many hours ago. I took a few slow and unsteady steps towards the bed, but was then struck by a fresh, stabbing pain in my left-hand side that was so intense that I dropped to my knees immediately. Then another piercing pain came from my right side and flashed across my whole stomach. My hearing became muffled, and I realised that my sense of depth was warped, as the bed appeared to be further and further away from me. I watched it retreating, and then everything – even the throbbing in my ear – stopped and I collapsed forward, falling full-length onto the floor. And as I lay there with my face in the carpet, I began to think about everything I had ever done in my life that I regretted – which took a distressingly long amount of time. I finally added this whole experience to the list, and then remained on the floor and began emitting a low, forceful groan; the same sort of involuntary noise that I make whenever I read the words – 'a replacement bus service is operating'.

If there was any positive to be taken from the situation, it was that it isn't necessarily a bad idea to be alone and in a locked room when you are hit simultaneously by both severe food poisoning and some sort of nervous breakdown. But I now knew that I was fighting battles on two fronts. The two problems were not of equal concern, though. At least I had been warned about the potentiality of being incapacitated in exactly this manner. But I was pretty confident that the possibility of a breakdown had not been mentioned in any of the guidebooks. And of the two problems, that would be infinitely the harder to deal with. I'd already learnt on this trip that the diarrhoea side of things could be freely discussed at the dinner table without concern. The breakdown chat was likely to be a bit more awkward.

By the time that the sun started streaming in through the curtains, I was still lying spread out on the floor. I ought to have been crying, and indeed I felt like I was; my shoulders were heaving and the corners of my mouth were taut and twisted. By rights I should have been in floods. But I wasn't. Nothing ran from my eyes. Clearly my stomach convulsions had left me so dehydrated that I had even emptied my lachrymal glands along with everything else. The peculiar salty sensation that I had experienced during the closing moments of my most final evacuation of my session had turned out to be me actually shitting out my own tears.

Chapter Thirteen

I didn't go to the ground for the two remaining days of the game. And I hardly cared. In fact, even sitting on the lavatory watching the television via the bathroom mirror I still managed to get a much better view than I had for much of the time I spent at the ground.

I had experienced an incredibly uncomfortable, sleepless and mentally fragile night, and had expelled a truly horrific quantity of hot brown liquid. But there was definitely a part of me that was relieved that it had happened. Being ill gave me an excuse not to go to the game, not to have to show another man's press pass and make silly faces, not to have to squeeze in amongst a whole load of people who knew what they were doing, have a terrible view and try and look happy and busy.

According to my tour itinerary, we would all leave Chandigarh the morning after the game and make our way to Mumbai where we would check into the astonishing and luxuriant Taj Mahal hotel and have four days off before the final Test. Everybody in the press corps had been raving about the Taj Mahal, and how that was the best hotel that we would stay in by far, and that Mumbai was the best city. Many people's families would, I knew, be joining them there. It did sound terrific, but lying on the floor during the night I had told myself that I needed to get away from everyone, and I still felt the same way. I didn't want to see, for now, all the people who I associated with my catastrophic and reckless failure to become a journalist. I wanted to relax, and restore my sanity and, indeed, salt levels.

But where could I go? Then suddenly I remembered Alan's offer and was thankful for it. I would go and meet him and his elephant friend at this Kipling Camp place, and try and forget about my disastrous flirtation with the world of cricket journalism. Late in the morning, I hobbled out onto the landing to get some Wi-Fi signal and I emailed Sunsport, and told them that I had been offered another journalistic assignment at Kipling Camp between the two Tests, and wondered if they would be able to help me getting there at all?

Otherwise, I spent much of the day in bed and avoided food, but phoned down to reception at regular intervals to see if I could be brought more mineral water to help flush whatever was wrong with me away. At equally regular intervals I sprinted into the bathroom for another stint on the pan. There was little muscular control that I could exercise over events, but at least I now felt that I was de-toxing in some way, and that with every hurried step I took towards the bathroom, I was taking a step towards feeling healthy again.

When it seemed like a reasonable hour in Britain, I nipped back out to the landing to check my email. There was already a reply from Sunsport, suggesting that they could organise everything immediately. I could leave the night that this game finished, and be back in Mumbai in time for the final Test. Should they go ahead with it? Yes, I said, you absolutely should.

Then I returned to bed to ring Alan and tell him the good news.

'Miles? I'm just on my way to the airport. Can I ring you back?'

'Alan, I'm going to come to Kipling with you.'

'What?'

'Yeah, I've changed my mind. When will you be getting there?' I asked.

'Tuesday morning.'

'Well, I should be able to get there on Tuesday.'

'You haven't got long to organise it.'

'It's being done for me. It's all being arranged.'

'Great. Are you all right by the way?'

'Well, I'm a little bit...ill.'

'Yeah. You sound...odd.'

'Right. Well, we can talk about all this.'

'And there's a place for you at the camp is there?'

'What do you mean? It's a camp, isn't it? We can just turn up, can't we?'

'No. It's not like a campsite. You have to make reservations. Book a cabin.'

'Oh,' I said.

'Do you want me to reserve you a place, or can you manage that?'

'I am a bit ill, Alan.'

'Fine, I'll email them from the airport. I'll call you when I've sorted it.'

Great. Even people I didn't have to pay for the privilege were taking care of my travel plans for me.

'Thanks, Alan.'

'No, hang on, that's silly. I'll call you if there's a problem.'

'Okay.'

'So if you don't hear from me, everything is fine. Or at least it should be. It might mean I've lost my phone,' clarified Alan.

'Great.'

'See you on Tuesday. Unless there's a problem.'

'Super. I'll see you then.'

'Did I mention that this is the camp where the elephant in that book lives?'

'You did, Alan. Yes, you most definitely mentioned that.'

Not long later I checked my email again and Sunsport had sent me a new itinerary. I was to be met in the lobby the next evening as soon as the game was over and taken to the train station in Chandigarh, and then put on a train to Delhi. There I had a room reserved at the Le Méridien hotel. The next morning I would be collected early and taken to the airport and flown to Nagpur. When I arrived there, a car would collect me and drive me all the way to the camp. This seemed like a tremendously straightforward way of travelling, and would have been a more suitable way for a movie star to travel than, say, an out-of-work former children's TV actor. But I didn't care about the money. I just wanted to get away from the press corps for a bit, and stop pretending to be a journalist for a few days. I wanted to get my head together and to see a friend. Even if that friend would be more excited to see an elephant than he would to see me.

*

While I was recuperating and planning my escape, England had a disastrous day. India and England were at level pegging when I left the press box the day before, and when Dhoni was caught behind in the second over of the day to leave India on 153–5, England were in an ascendant position. Unfortunately for them, though, Rahul Dravid batted on and India's lower order fired. Pathan and Dravid took the score to 229 before Dravid lost his leg stump to a ball from Flintoff that kept low, just five short of a century. Pathan, meanwhile, brought up a half-century from just 51 balls before slicing Flintoff to Collingwood at point. When they took lunch on 269–7 honours were definitely even again. England, however, couldn't make another dent before India had passed our score. Kumble batted diligently, taking over two hours to make 32. Harbhajan Singh, however, hit seven boundaries during a breezy (by which I mean 'really fucking annoying') 36, before swinging a tad too arrogantly at a Flintoff delivery and being caught behind. Chawla scooped Hoggard's slower ball to Collingwood at backward point. Munaf Patel then hit his second ball, from Harmison, to the point boundary, and then the next over hit Hoggard down the ground for a straight six. Plunkett yorked Kumble to bring it all to an end in time for tea, but the damage had been done, and India had rallied to lead England by 38 runs. Worryingly for England, who had worked so hard to try and control the game, India had taken their score from 200 to 300 in just 111 balls.

Watching the cricket on television made me feel strangely disjointed from everything. The people whose voices I could hear commentating belonged to the same people that I had been queuing up for lunch with the day before, or seen slouching about the place. Now they were on my television again, and their mystique was, thankfully, returning. I had seen the former Australian batsman Dean Jones around the pavilion a few times, but it wasn't until I heard him commentate that I realised how extraordinary a man he was. He was a fine, perhaps brilliant, batsman. On air, though, he is totally bizarre and makes almost no sense whatsoever, just a series of unlikely and unquantifiable claims. During the tea interval he gave a five-minute presentation to camera which opened with the remark, 'Personally I reckon that over the years, bats have got better by about thirty to forty per cent.' He even had the gall to make this statement with enough conviction for it to actually sound like fact. It was extraordinary to watch a man doing little more than making a succession of wild guesses, but attaching mathematical figures to them. At one point he said, 'Back in Australia seventy per cent of bats are bought for people by their mums. Well, it's really worth getting your dad's help as well.'

The evening session made for very poor viewing indeed. Cook was caught behind in the sixth over. After 14 overs, our score was just 22–1. Eight overs later we brought up our 50, but then almost immediately afterwards Strauss took an almighty sweep at a delivery from Kumble, bottom edged it onto his own foot and watched it sail into the gloves of Dhoni. Strauss walked off looking gutted, his 13 runs having taken him 102 minutes.

Pietersen then tried to sweep Singh and missed it only for the ball to strike his wrist or his arm guard and then lob up and be caught by Dravid in the slips. Arm or wrist, the Indian appeal was successful, and England had lost their third wicket with a lead of just 17. Bell was looking tremendous out in the middle, but at the other end, however, Collingwood looked like a man hopelessly at sea. Even when he is in form it would be hard to describe his batting as aesthetic, but out of form – as he had suddenly become in this game – his batting induces panic attacks. He played and missed at several and was then dropped by Dravid at slip when he had somehow managed to score six runs. Ian Bell just had time to bring up his 50 before Collingwood, after several more edges and misses, prodded at a big leg break from Kumble and edged it low to Dravid at first slip. England 88–4. Flintoff arrived at the crease hell-bent on seeing out the day, taking huge thrusting strides to try and block Kumble.

'Flintoff's a big man,' said Dean Jones, 'but he's got soft hands.'

And it was the soft-handed Flintoff who finally brought England's hundred up, pulling a rare short ball from Kumble to the fine-leg fence. It had taken England just shy of 45 overs. It had been an awful session of batting, the only bright spot being Bell's fluent 50. But with just two overs left in the day, Bell himself displayed a sudden flakiness, poked purposelessly at a ball from Kumble and edged a hard chance to Dhoni who took it. After three near-faultless hours, his needless dismissal turned an awful session into an horrific one, and when play finished with England on 112–5, a lead of just 74, nobody on commentary had a good word to say about our display. I might not have achieved a great deal in the press box, but England certainly played a lot better when I was there.

I felt strong and held together enough to go for a little walk around what would normally have been suppertime, but was now another occasion on which to avoid food. Kevin was in the lobby when I returned.

'Have you eaten?' he asked.

'Nothing all day. I've been in bed.'

'Oh, have you? Not at the ground, then?'

'No. Too ill.'

'Lucky you. Terrible day. A waste of a good position.'

'I'm going to disappear tomorrow, Kevin.'

'Sorry?'

'I'm heading off for a bit. I'll be back in time for the Mumbai game.'

'You're not coming to the Taj? It's supposed to be amazing. Your sort of thing.'

'Well, I'll get there eventually. I'm going to go and meet a friend somewhere for a few days.'

'So I won't see you until then, I suppose?'

'Looks like it.'

'Are you all right? I mean apart from being sick and everything?'

'I'm fine,' I said. 'Just fine.'

'Well, okay then. I'll see you in Mumbai,' said Kevin, looking like he didn't believe me.

I returned to my room with more bottles of mineral water, and did my packing for the next day's journey before tentatively taking a hot bath, and then stretching out on the bed to watch some Indian television. After flicking through the channels for a while I came across a debate programme that looked like it was shot on the set of *Kilroy* but was in fact all about cricket. Sitting in the front row was Ajay Jadeja who I remembered as a big-hitting one-day batsman in the 1990s, but who now appeared to have relaunched himself as a Steve Martin-style 'wild and crazy guy'. Whenever he was asked his opinion about anything by the host, he launched into a breezy, shouty monologue, peppered with 'bloody this', 'bloody that' and 'what a load of crap' to roars of delight from the crowd. Geoffrey Boycott appeared via a satellite link, and was a completely different person. In Britain he is one of those sportsmen who, despite their undoubted brilliance, is often admired begrudgingly and who perhaps deserves more praise and respect than they receive. In cricket-mad India, where he is loved unconditionally, he is able to behave in a relaxed, smiley fashion and his jokes are greeted with laughter and applause rather than the sighs of 'Oh Geoffrey' that he might be more used to receiving on our airwaves.

The highlight of the programme for me, however, was a splendid elderly gentleman in a turban and blazer who sat on the front row and was tremendously earnest about everything. During a discussion about the behaviour of visiting teams he suddenly burst into life and made a passionate, furious speech denouncing the Australians. He singled out one particular player for special opprobrium, claiming that this person had recently stood on a table during an official dinner and sang bawdy songs before returning to his hotel 'where he did something so disgusting in the swimming pool that the next day it had to be emptied'. I found the words of this sincere and appalled old man, to my shame, completely hilarious.

*

It's hard getting to sleep after spending most of the day in bed, but lying half awake in the dark in bed is a much nicer way to spend a whole night than sitting screaming on a lavatory, or lying face down on a carpet groaning and hating yourself.

I waited until I was sure that the rest of the press corps would have left for the ground, and then went downstairs to pick at what was left of the breakfast buffet. It was the first food I had eaten since my snack by the side of the road nearly 40 hours earlier, so I went at it gently and just ate a few mouthfuls of the blandest things that I could see. It was great having the whole dining room to myself, and not having to attempt any forced chatter with people or feel the glare of their suspicion and mistrust. I drank a little fruit juice, and idly flicked through some local papers. I even had a small cup of coffee, but regretted it when I was about halfway up the stairs to my room and had to sprint the rest of the journey and fly straight into the bathroom. I emerged, cursing my own arse, in time for the cricket to start.

Poor England were in a shittier mess than my bathroom had been two nights previously. They would have to be remarkably tough to battle their way out of this one. Geraint Jones smashed the first ball of the day for four through cover-point, but then four balls later played back to a shorter ball from Patel and the ball took an inside edge and cannoned onto his stumps. Four overs later the same bowler trapped Liam Plunkett dead in front for LBW and England were just 124–7. Another four overs after that Patel yorked Hoggard to leave England 139–8. But Harmison was in a mood to hang around for his mate Flintoff, who had a dogged 27 to his name by this point. Harmison blocked diligently and Flintoff whacked the odd four to bring up another half-century off the ninety-ninth ball he faced. Harmison had resisted the Indians for nearly 15 overs and helped to add 42 before he was caught off balance by a quicker ball down the leg-side from Kumble and Dhoni whipped off the bails. Flintoff himself was the last man out, the arrival of the last man Panesar causing him, not unreasonably, to start wanting to smash everything desperately out of sight. He top edged a huge sweep off the bowling of Chawla and the catch was held, fittingly, by the destroyer Patel. England had managed just 181, and India would now have to chase down a paltry 144. When I huffily turned the TV off at lunchtime, India had already scored 28 runs without loss.

I couldn't wait to get out of Chandigarh, but that was still no excuse to be holed up in a hotel room watching television. I didn't fancy watching our bowlers being hammered around the park, any more than I fancied being in the company of the rest of the press corps at the moment that England, inevitably, lost. Even if I had been at the ground, I was fairly certain there was no way I would have gone to the post-match press interview to witness a miserable autopsy. Instead I pulled on my sun hat, and headed out onto the streets to walk without aim, and think about what I was doing and where I was going. The battering that my bowels had taken was one thing, but I also felt in shock. I was genuinely taken aback at the way that attempting to become a cricket journalist had made me feel. I couldn't believe that a situation had developed where I could be in India, and yet still not be bothered enough to actually watch the game at the ground. I felt, to my horror, really bored of cricket.

I had seen on one of my previous walks a number of barber's shops, and so went in search of one for a clean shave. A clean shave, I felt, would help me feel refreshed anew. I found a shop just minutes from the hotel above, of course, some sort of electrical shop. There were three men there, all in their forties, all with identical haircuts and moustaches, all gathered under a television that was mounted on a bracket in the corner, and all giggling as they watched the replays of the England wickets that had fallen that morning.

'Ah, you English?' one asked as I knocked on the open door.

'Yes, I am.'

'You are losing the cricket, you know.'

'So I hear,' I said.

'You don't seem bothered,' said one of the men who led me to an old-fashioned barber's chair, and draped a sheet around me. 'You don't like cricket?'

'I used to,' I said.

'Then we will turn it off.'

The television was switched off, and the two other men sloped from the strip-lit room to go and smoke on the street.

'What would you like? Haircut? Shave?'

'Just a shave, please.'

'Face massage? You can have face massage.'

'All right then, I'll have a face massage too.'

He warmed a flannel under a hot tap, and laid it over my face. Then he set to work rubbing soap into a lather between his hands, which he spread onto my chin and jaw as he removed the flannel. Then he picked up and flipped open a straight razor, and with remarkable lightness of touch set about removing my beard with a series of quick moves, gently humming to himself as he did so. He fetched a fresh flannel when he was done, and laid it over my face again. He removed the flannel once more, and began rubbing oils and cream into my face, which he then manipulated with his thumbs, pushed deep into the flesh of my cheeks, and then massaged along the length of my jaw. He was a deft practitioner.

'So why you here, if not for cricket?' he asked as I handed over some coins.

'I don't really know,' I said. 'I've just sort of ended up here.'

Back in the hotel lobby, there were vast numbers of women queuing up, I learnt, to take part in some (presumably rather early) heats for the title of Miss India 2006.

*

India knocked off the runs for the loss of just one wicket, Hoggard trapping Jaffer leg before for 17. I watched the presentation ceremony on the television, and our team looked simply miserable, whilst I did the rest of my packing and then uploaded a few quick blog postings that could be posted while I was away from the press corps. Then, at the appointed time, I went down to the lobby to get my lift to the station. There, milling about, were a few dejected fans and a couple of returning journalists grateful for an early finish. Again, checking out of the hotel was not an easy task.

'You are not staying until tomorrow?' asked one of three men on the reception counter.

'No. I'm leaving tonight. Now. It should have been arranged by the tour operator.'

'Which tour operator are you with?'

I gave their name, and the receptionist said 'Hmmm' rather ominously. Then he and the other two had a heated and prolonged debate about various aspects of my bill. It lasted 15 minutes, was conducted entirely in Hindi, and could only be resolved, it turned out, by me signing my signature on huge swathes of official-looking documents. I asked what this all meant, but was only given a selection of shrugs, and so I obediently and hurriedly signed the lot. I had no idea what I was signing. Perhaps I would eventually get home to discover that I had handed over everything I own to a syndicate of hotel receptionists whose names I may never know and for whom I might have to cook and clean until I'm 80.

Only once this mountain of paperwork had been completed, and I was told I was free to go, did someone from our travel agent appear at my elbow. I couldn't tell if he'd only just arrived, or had been hiding behind a pot plant and waiting until any mistakes at his end of the operation had been rectified. He had brought with him the train ticket that I needed to reach Delhi as well as one for my flight back to Nagpur.

'Good luck with it all,' he said as he handed them over.

'Thanks.'

'And you're making your own way back to Mumbai?'

'That's right.'

'There's a driver waiting for you outside. It's the same driver we used yesterday. He hit a motorbike, actually, so he might drive a bit slower than usual.'

Comforting words.

He then led me out to a people carrier, where a nervous man loaded my suitcase into the boot and then, whilst I was getting buckled up, the pair of them stood outside having a few quiet words, presumably about yesterday's collision. We drove slowly along Udyog Path, through an industrial area, and then pulled up outside Chandigarh's boxy train station. There was a queue of cars behind us already, so I leapt out as quickly as I could and the driver ran round to open the boot and pass me my suitcase. It was not so very different from the many occasions on which my father has dropped me at Peterborough station. Then he said goodbye, rather less tenderly than my father usually does, and sped away, leaving me suddenly, and for the first time on my trip, completely to my own devices.

Everywhere that I had travelled with the press corps we had gone around as a large group, and every time we had passed through a gateway or check-in, a man had appeared with a little sign telling us where to go. I pulled my suitcase into the main terminal, and found myself immediately in a huge bustling crowd. I wheeled around desperately through the throng and hauled my suitcase up some steps trying to find a sign whose instructions I could understand, or someone that might help. There was a part of me that wanted to panic and get cross in the way that I do when I'm lost in a British railway station. But a bigger part of me felt free. I decided to just allow myself to be swept along in the general mayhem and see where it led me. Soon, along with hundreds of others, I was standing on a bustling platform in time for a blue and yellow train to sweep into the station. There were a group of men dressed in creamy churidar trousers and red kurta tops with golden armbands, walking around and giving directions. I approached the nearest one.

'Is this train going to Delhi?'

'Yes.'

'I think I have a reservation…'

'Please wait, sir.'

Looking over my shoulder, he suddenly put his left hand on my arm, and pulled me firmly towards him, as if about to embrace me lovingly. At that moment, I felt a surge of people shove past us, and I turned in time to see a circle of soldiers scurrying across the platform towards the next carriage along, shielding a number of people who I could not see. Being dragged along with this body of men were a large number of photographers and excitable young men, all running alongside and leaping in the air, trying to look over the heads of these soldiers. A door at the far end of the other carriage suddenly was flung open, and whomever the soldiers were conveying was practically hurled aboard, and then the door was hurriedly shut behind them. As soon as this had happened the crowd dispersed as quickly as it had appeared, and the platform, though still bustling, became a little calmer. The porter, still holding onto my arm, let me go and then coughed politely as if to apologise for this interruption.

'I am sorry, sir. You think you have a reservation for this train?'

'I hope so.'

I showed him one of the tickets that I had been handed in the hotel lobby. He looked at it quickly and passed it back.

'Yes, you do have a reservation.'

'Could you tell me which carriage it's in, please?'

'Yes indeed,' he said. 'It is this one.' And he patted the side of the carriage we were standing next to twice, smiled at me, and then continued along the platform. I wheeled my suitcase along to the door, hauled it up the steps and then turned left and into the carriage. There was just one free seat in the carriage near to where I was standing and on closer inspection I saw that it had my name on it. The luggage rack above it, however, was already crammed and as I stood there and the train pulled out of the station I wondered what to do about this. There were no racks at the entrance to the carriage, only the overhead ones. Suddenly the thought of this made me fret. What could I do? I couldn't leave the suitcase in the narrow aisle as it would be in the way of anyone walking through. I couldn't go out and find a space for it between carriages, I wouldn't be able to see it, and it had my laptop inside. Would I have to put the suitcase on my seat and stand? Or would I have to sit with the thing standing upright on my lap all the way to Delhi or until somebody else got off?

I was just standing there, looking puzzled, when the man in the seat behind said, 'Are you okay?'

He was in his fifties, dressed in a well-cut suit, and had a thick grey beard that was beautifully trimmed. He had a kindly smile.

'I've just got a bit of a problem. There's nowhere to put my suitcase. It's all a bit full up there.'

I gazed up to the luggage rack, and he followed my gaze and then looked back at me.

'This is not a problem,' he said calmly.

And he stood up and he turned round to everyone else behind him on our side of the carriage and said, 'Excuse me.'

Everybody looked up at him, and he simply pointed at the luggage rack, and then at me and then gestured, using his hands like a fisherman, the width of luggage rack space that my suitcase would need. And to my amazement everybody on our side of the carriage stood up uncomplainingly and, starting with the person at the far end, each of them in turn moved their own luggage along by the required amount, gave a friendly nod in my direction and then sat down until finally there was a space above my seat for me to put my case. I did so, and then thanked the gentleman behind me. He looked back at me and shrugged, as if to say, 'This is just what we do,' and returned to reading his paper. I sat down in a state of total amazement. As someone who had spent over a quarter of a century travelling round on British public transport this was undoubtedly the most helpful behaviour I had seen on a train in my life.

I sat down next to a pretty young girl, and we exchanged a few minutes of small talk which was pleasant enough. I then listened to her for an hour and a half while she explained in vivid and excruciating detail about her conversion to Christianity. Her story was not quite over by the time she cheerfully disembarked at a place called Panipat. I was unable to follow all of what she was telling me not just because of unease, but also because throughout her tale, a regular stream of passengers would come through our carriage with cameras, and then return looking rather pleased. I became more and more curious about what was going on, but felt unable to stop this girl mid-flow, while she explained about bright lights and the sins of her past. Once she had left the train, I was finally able to speak to someone walking back through.

'What's happening in the next carriage?' I asked another Englishman, dressed in our rather splendid blue strip from the 1992 World Cup.

'It's Kumble and Dravid.'

'What? Just sitting there?'

'Yeah, they're great.'

'They don't mind people taking photographs?'

'Not at all.'

Fantastic. This would be so unlike my silly faffing about in the box trying to get a picture of myself with Nasser Hussain. Now that I was away from the press corps I could approach these two Indian legends as a fan without feeling self-conscious about it and just ask to have a photo taken with them. They must have been the people that the soldiers escorted onto the train back at Chandigarh. I walked into the next carriage, and there they were, spread out and looking relaxed and without anyone guarding them at all. They were in conversation with another man of the same age, but as I approached they looked up.

'I'm sorry, could I possibly have a photograph?'

'Of course,' said Dravid.

There was an empty seat between them so I sat in that and the man they had been chatting to offered to take my camera. We all smiled, I congratulated Kumble on his five-hundredth wicket and then I thanked them and returned to my own carriage to examine the photo. I was thrilled with it. Because I was sitting in the middle and they leant in towards me, it rather looked as if they had asked to have their photo taken with me.

*

It had been dark for a long time by the time that our train pulled into the station at Delhi, and as I stepped down onto the platform I had a sudden and acute sense of being alone and a long, long way from home. Everybody else in my carriage had leapt to their feet at the very moment that the train's driver had first started putting on the brake as we made our final approach. I was caught unaware by this, having never checked the time that we were due to arrive, and being far too used to the incessant announcements that we are subjected to on British trains, on which it is rare for five minutes to go by without being reminded by someone – speaking with a voice so loud that you can feel lesions spreading across the surface of your brain – where you are, where else you might be going and then giving you a variety of bewilderingly vague reasons why you will not be arriving there on schedule, as well as some apologies for this unfortunate situation delivered so begrudgingly that they are essentially taunts. Whilst everybody else was picking up their luggage and making jauntily for the door, I still had to faff about with books and notepads and then get my shoes back on before I could begin trying to search under seats for my biro.

It was the sight of the station having nearly totally emptied by the time that I had finally disembarked that led to this instant pang of loneliness. Coupled to this was a feeling of uncertainty about Delhi itself. So quickly had I acclimatised to having such aspects of my life organised by a tour operator, I had not bothered to look at a map of Delhi, or even write down the address of the hotel, merely committed its name to my memory.

Outside of the station there was a mass of taxis, but their drivers were hustling for work so aggressively – snatching my suitcase out of my hand and placing it into their open boot – that each time I felt instinctively that I could not trust them, and so would snatch my suitcase back again and hurry on, only for the pattern to be repeated elsewhere. As I stumbled about in the darkness, shying away from one aggressive driver after another, I began to feel panicked. In my naiveté I had failed to consider what the atmosphere might be like outside a rail terminal in one of India's busiest cities at this time of night, and the sense of menace that I might feel. There was a strong odour of urine in the air and there were people, whole families perhaps, lying on the pavements, and sitting in the gutters, and every so often a hand would grab my ankle as I walked, or I'd become aware halfway through a stride that I was stepping over a person. I felt unsettled by what I saw and I felt shamed that it made me feel that way. Of course, a sunburnt young white man with a moderately expensive suitcase and a look of total confusion on his face would attract attention in a place like this. Children grabbed at my hands and my pockets, shaking my trouser legs and making the loose change I was carrying jangle. A lady half-sitting and half-slumped against the wall of the station sat under a yellow light, and looked up at me as I tried to turn away from a group of children pulling at my shirt, whilst wheeling my case out of the grasp of a lunging taxi driver. She stared at me with eyes that were so sad and sunken that I stopped dead. 'Help,' she mouthed with her dry lips, and she held out a thin, weak arm. I dug some change from my pocket, and then leant forward and placed it in the palm of the open hand that she proffered. Her brittle, almost hollow-looking fingers closed around it. She didn't speak, but blinked her eyes and very slowly nodded her head at me. I felt ashamed and inadequate, wanting to say something but thinking of nothing other than a strange desire to apologise to her.

Then suddenly I was falling backwards away from her. Someone was pulling my suitcase from my hand. I twisted around, but let go of it as I did so and a squat man in his early forties picked it up and scuttled away with it.

'Oi!'

I chased after him as he squeezed between taxis, picking my way through the random arrangement of the cars and trying to avoid doors being opened without warning, and still side-stepping the odd strewn body. He was heading for one of the furthest of the yellow taxis, and when he reached it he opened up the boot, dropped my suitcase inside it and then opened the passenger door.

'Where are you going, please? I will take you,' he said when I reached the car, and then opened the door wider and ushered me inside.

I didn't really want to go anywhere with a man who had wrenched my luggage from me and then forced me to chase after him, but I also felt as if I had no choice. I had to get away from this place and find my hotel. I resented this man, but there was no point taking my suitcase back from him; all the other taxi drivers were probably the same.

'I'm going to a hotel. Le Méridien. You know where it is?'

'Of course.'

'How much to Le Méridien?'

'It's not much.'

'How much?'

'Is four hundred.'

'Four hundred?'

'Yes.'

I had lost all sense now of how much it was reasonable to pay for anything. What was 400 even worth? I told him that would be acceptable, and then I clambered into the back of his car, and he banged the door shut behind me. He shouted something I couldn't understand to another driver and banged his hand down twice on the roof above my head. I heard the other driver cackle and yell something back. Then my driver opened his door and climbed into his seat, and then turned and grinned at me.

'You okay?' he asked.

'I'm fine,' I huffed.

He did not turn around though and turn the key in the ignition, but kept looking at me expectedly.

'What is it?' I asked.

'Four hundred.'

'Yes?'

'You pay me now.'

'I'll pay you when we get to the hotel.'

'You pay now.'

'But that's…that's ridiculous. I'll give you the money when we get there.'

Now he turned away from me and sat with his arms folded. I looked out of the window at this strange, dark city. I felt tired. I sighed and then I took out my wallet, and saw that my smallest note was for 500. I could see him watching me in his rearview mirror.

'You have money? If you pay me then we can go to hotel.'

'Have you got change?'

'Oh yes.'

'If I give you five hundred, can you give me a hundred back?'

'Yes, yes.' Then he coughed impatiently, as if it was me who was holding things up.

I passed a 500 note forward to him, and he took it from me silently and started the engine and started to pull out.

'My change?'

'Sir?'

'Can I have my change, please?'

'At hotel. You can have it at hotel.'

And on he drove in silence, while I sat in the back and fumed, making a fist and quietly striking the seat beside me as he drove us through empty, menacing streets. Rain started to hit the windows. After driving for five minutes he said, 'Le Méridien is not a good hotel.'

'No?'

'No. Not good.'

'Right.'

'I know much better hotel.'

'It's fine, I'm sure.'

'My brother. He has a very good hotel. Is much better.'

'Well, I'm sure it's...'

'You will like this hotel. You will like it very much.'

'Well, I'm staying at Le Méridien,' I said.

'Le Méridien. Not good. Not good.'

And then he rounded a corner and pulled up outside a grey two-storey building, with an illuminated green and red sign that said 'Hotel Welcome'.

'This is it,' he said.

'This is what?'

He looked at me in the rear-view mirror.

'This is my brother's hotel. Is much better. And I have taken you here for good price. Come on.'

With incredible speed, he got out of the car, pulled my suitcase out of the car boot, put it down on the doorstep of the hotel, and rang a bell. Then he started knocking on the other rear passenger window. I was seething. He opened the door, and stood there like a New York chauffeur, ushering me towards his brother's horrible hotel.

'I'm not getting out,' I said firmly.

He peered in at me. 'But we are here.'

'I am not staying at your brother's hotel. I am staying at Le Méridien.'

'This is much cheaper. Much better price.'

I wanted to stand my ground, but that meant staying in the car. And my suitcase was no longer in the car. The driver was between me and the step my case was sitting on, outside the door that was now being opened. A near identical man came out of it. He had the same squat build as the taxi driver, and an even thicker moustache. He, though, was not dressed in slacks and a polo shirt, but some grey tracksuit trousers and a vest.

'Welcome,' he said.

'No,' I said. 'No.'

I climbed out of the car and pushed past my driver, grabbed the suitcase and dragged it back round to the boot, and started fumbling with the catch.

'What are you doing?' said the driver.

'I'm not staying here!' I shouted. 'I'm staying at Le Méridien. That's where my room is booked. That's where I asked you to take me. That's where you said that you would take me. That's where I want to go. Not here.'

I found the right bit of the catch, and the boot clicked open. I lifted it up, put my suitcase inside and then slammed it shut.

'You want to go to...Le Méridien?' asked the driver incredulously.

His brother was now leaning against the doorframe, watching this scene impassively. He did not seem at all surprised or concerned by his brother ringing his doorbell at this time of night, and then standing on the pavement being shouted at by a furious passenger. Perhaps this scene was played out on this stretch of pavement at this time every night.

'Yes, I want to go to there!' I shouted.

'But Le Méridien is the other way. It's in completely different direction,' he said.

'YOU drove us here. YOU. You drove us in this direction.'

He looked at me as if I was a difficult elderly relative who was always changing their mind.

'Do you definitely want to go there?' he asked slowly.

'YES! Take me there. Take me to Le fucking Méridien.'

His brother shrugged, and then wordlessly went back into his hotel, closing the door behind him.

I climbed back into the car, and pulled the door shut behind me. The driver begrudgingly got back into his seat, shut his door and then fired the ignition.

'Le Méridien,' I said quietly. 'Take me to Le Méridien.'

He said nothing, but executed a U-turn, and then floored the accelerator.

*

When we finally pulled up outside the correct hotel, he turned around again.

'Here we are. Méridien. Bad hotel.'

'Well, I'm staying here anyway.'

'Is four hundred.'

'I've already paid you.'

He squinted, as if I was deliberately misunderstanding him. 'Yes, yes. Four hundred.'

'I've paid. I paid you when you picked me up. I gave you five hundred. You owe me. You owe me change.'

He shook his head, and then shrugged. 'I have no change.'

I was furious now. I didn't care about cultural differences. I didn't care about economic disparity. All I cared about was that this man was a dishonest bastard who was trying to fleece me. I got out of the car, and slammed my passenger door shut and then went around to the boot to get my suitcase out. I then slammed that shut too. And then I went round to his passenger window and, just for good measure, called him a fucking cunt.

I checked into the hotel, and then went and drank a whisky in a bar on the top floor, still seething about the bastard driver. Then I retired to my ridiculously luxuriant room, but was far too tired to enjoy any of its charms. Instead I spent an age tottering about the room, furiously trying to work out how to turn off all the lights, before finally climbing into the large, soft bed. I let out an enormous sigh, and then fell into a deep, deep sleep.

*

The next morning I boarded a flight to Nagpur to find a complimentary local newspaper on my seat. At the bottom of the front page was a headline that immediately caught my eye. It said 'ENGLISH NATIONAL ARRESTED IN PRESS BOX AT CHANDIGARH'. I was intrigued. Who could it be? Had Geoffrey Boycott become so angry about something that he'd gone mad and removed his trousers? Perhaps Mr Who The Fuck's That? had punched someone?

No, it turned out. The actual story that I read both amazed and terrified me. The paper described how towards the end of the second Test, an English national had been arrested at the Punjab Cricket Association for the crime of attempting to gain entry to the press box by using a press pass that he was not entitled to possess. That is exactly what I had just done for three days until I was struck by the lethal combination of a brutal case of the shits and confronted by a distinct sense of my own failure. If I hadn't suffered my tummy troubles and miniature breakdown at the moment that I had, then I too would have been at the ground on the final day of the game. And if I had been there on the day when they really scrutinised everybody's passes then maybe I could have been arrested too for being in possession of a pass that so clearly wasn't my own.

According to the paper, the man in question had turned up at the ground in Chandigarh the day before the game, falsely claimed that he was a freelance journalist and then been issued with some sort of alternative or temporary pass. That particular detail annoyed me intensely. How come it had been so easy for him to get a pass? I'd had an absolute nightmare.

But it was another detail of the story that made me feel so distinctly uneasy. It was the fact that he had been described as being arrested 'whilst attempting to gain access'. If he had not been arrested in the press box itself, therefore, that could mean that the other journalists hadn't seen the incident happen and thus wouldn't know who it was. The first that they might have heard of it would have been reading the local papers as I was now. All they would read, therefore, was a story about a pretend journalist being arrested, just as I suddenly disappeared from the tour. They could all have been reading an article like this one and thinking, 'That must have been that bloody bloke...'

Then an even more horrible thought struck me. What if the person who had turned up to the match was in fact the genuine owner of my pass? What if he had turned up at the ground to find that his official press pass was no longer available, and so he had improvised something to enable him to get on with his job? At Chandigarh, as I had found to my cost, they could some-times be super-strict about freelancers. Maybe they had got so fed up with requests for access from freelancers that they had suddenly got super-tough about it all and this poor fellow was simply the straw that broke the camel's back. But it was me that had got the camel in that condition in the first place. Arrest seemed a bit harsh, but even so. I started to panic about the possibility that a man might have been arrested because I had his official press pass.

And so it was with this on my conscience that I carried on my way to Kipling Camp. The man who sat beside me on my flight to Nagpur was a gentleman in his fifties, anxious to know where I was from and exactly what I was doing in India. He told me of his love of English comedy, and I agreed with him that it was amongst the best the world had to offer. Alas, it turned out to be the *Carry On* films in particular that he so admired, and he spent a great deal of time explaining in excruciating detail various sequences from the film *Carry On Camping*. I could understand little of what he was saying, and it was rather difficult to concentrate during some of his longer and more involved descriptions. He himself was not totally clear on all of the plot points, and would sometimes break off from the narrative. 'No, no. Hang on. That is quite wrong. I beg your pardon. No, at this moment it was the man and not the lady who was holding up the tent pole.' I spent a proportion of my teens acquiring bronze, silver and gold Duke Of Edinburgh Awards, and so I think I've probably encountered most of the double entendres that pitching a tent can provide, but nevertheless he was a kind and friendly man and so I laughed uproariously throughout like a polite guest on a panel show.

Upon landing at Nagpur, I nipped into the lavatory for what turned out to be a much lengthier visit than I had reckoned for, and finally left the cubicle to find the airport almost totally abandoned. I made my way to the luggage carousel only to find it empty and stationary. I asked various airport staff where I might reasonably expect to find my suitcase, and on each occasion was directed further and further away from the carousel, until eventually I followed the trail to a far-flung office where a man in a crisp white shirt sat behind an almost empty desk apparently doing nothing. In front of his desk stood my suitcase.

'Hello, sir?'

'Hi there. That's my suitcase. Is it all right if I take it?' I asked.

'Sir?'

'That suitcase. It's mine.'

'This one?'

He pointed to the only piece of luggage that was in his line of vision.

'That's right.'

'This luggage is lost property.'

'Well, it was lost. But now it's found. It's mine.'

'It's yours?' He looked doubtful about this.

'That's right.'

'Can you prove this, please?'

There was a label attached to the suitcase's handle that contained a barcode, a flight number and my name.

'Here we are. "M JUPP". That's me.'

He pushed his chair back slowly, and gradually rose from it, using the flimsy armrests as levers until he had finally prised himself into an upright position. Then he walked around to the front of the desk and looked at the label I was holding.

'Ah yes. M Jupp.'

'Exactly.'

'How do I know this is your name?'

He didn't ask this question in a surly manner, more as if he was asking for guidance. I showed him my passport.

'There. That's my name. Miles Jupp. It matches.'

He examined the passport, and then the name on the label again.

'Miles Jupp. M Jupp.'

'Yes.'

'You are saying that the "M" is for "Miles"?'

'Yes.'

'Hmmm.'

He walked back round to his chair, and then slowly lowered himself into it again.

'Can I take the suitcase?' I asked.

'It's not really enough proof,' he said. 'But...' He raised his palms as if surrendering, and then he exhaled without opening his mouth so that his lips vibrated and he made a sound like a horse who had been severely inconvenienced.

'It's okay to take it?' I checked.

He raised his palms again and shook his head, and then made a face as if to say, 'Oh what does it matter who takes the suitcase? What does anything matter? What are any of us really here for?'

And so I wheeled the suitcase out of his office and back through the empty departure hall, and out into the fierce morning sun, where a lone man was standing next to a lone car.

'You are looking for a car? You are Miles?'

'That's right. Hello.'

'Hello, sir. You are going to Kipling?'

'Yes, please.'

As we eased out of the airport car park and into the traffic, he called over his shoulder to me. 'You look tired.'

'I am.'

'Well, don't worry. You can have a good sleep now,' he said before suddenly jamming on the brakes and beeping his horn.

An hour outside of Nagpur, I did finally manage to fall asleep. But then I was awoken by the driver shouting. I opened my eyes in time to see a lorry on our side of the road heading straight towards us having attempted to overtake a cart being pulled by a cow whilst going around a corner. I started to let out a shout, and braced myself for impact, but my driver skilfully swerved off the road, allowing the lorry to squeeze between us and the cart, and then careered back onto the road in time to avoid us hitting a rock. It was an incredible manoeuvre. He may even, although I could be wrong about this, momentarily have touched the brake. I was wide awake for the remaining four-hour journey to the camp.

We travelled east from Nagpur at first, past Bhandara and almost to the edge of Maharashtra. We then headed north up into Madhya Pradesh, past Gondia, Waraseoni and Balaghat. We drove through big towns, and then small towns and then villages, along straight main roads, and then narrow winding ones and then finally off tarmac altogether and along dirt tracks. All the time I stared out of the window, watching the changing landscape, and the changing colours. And all the time I felt as if I was escaping.

Chapter Fourteen

To leave the press corps behind for a while and then spend some time in Kanha National Park was an experience akin to swimming underwater. If you have a mask on you suddenly realise that you are surrounded by completely different colours and sounds. Sound and light both travel differently through water, and nothing is the size that you imagined it would be. Going underwater and being able to see what is there is like visiting another world.

The camp is a collection of huts in a clearing, built around a roofed central dining area called the Shamiana. I checked in at one of the huts, and was then taken to the Shamiana where I found Alan sitting in an armchair, reading a book about tigers and dressed, as always, in an Australian rugby top.

We had three amazing days there. In the mornings we would go off on safaris in jeeps, and saw an astonishing array of animals; langurs, sambar, peacocks, wild boar, jungle cockerels, jackals, spotted deer, barking deer, barasingha, serpent eagles, kingfishers and Indian bison.

In the afternoons we would follow Tara down to the river where she and her mahout would play together before she would lie down on one side and a crowd of us would gather round and help scrub her skin with stones.

At the slightest sign of movement we would leap back and give her space to get up and then lie down again on her other side. I leapt back particularly far at these points, much to the derision of Tom, a volunteer at the camp. Tara weighed two tonnes, for goodness' sake, but clearly in the wild it didn't do to show your fear. After being scrubbed, Tara liked to invest a little time blowing water at us all as we feebly attempted to splash her back. It seems that no matter how hard you try, you cannot beat an elephant in a water fight. At night the staff, volunteers and guests would all eat and drink together and discuss the day's sightings. We shared huge, glorious curries, and drank beer.

There was a public holiday on one of the days and so the park was closed. It rained heavily all morning, so we loitered on our hut's veranda and called each other names. After lunch it stopped raining and we played cricket with some of the camp's staff. As we returned from our game, we were passed by Tara who was carrying two loud Americans on her back. We followed them at a distance down to the river, and were rewarded by the sight of Tara and her mahout bathing and frolicking. The two Americans sat watching from the bank but Alan and I bounded into the water and helped the mahout to scrub her skin with stones and then watched as they played together. The Americans headed back to the camp before the sun began to set, but we stayed in the river swimming and splashing about. At one point I swam across the wide river to climb up onto the opposite bank and sat there for a moment, taking in the view.

'This is the reason that people should travel,' I thought. 'It's not about hotels for the business traveller and air conditioning, but about moments like this: a murky river, a setting sun, an elephant.' But of course being outside the train station in Delhi, being bullied and shoved by taxi drivers whilst tripping over people in the gutters and looking helplessly into the sad eyes of a beggar lady and feeling flustered and guilty; that was the point of travel too.

In the company of the press corps, I felt nervy and on edge. Sitting on the bank of a murky river watching the sunset in the company of an elephant, I felt something I hadn't felt for weeks: I was relaxed.

*

The highlight of the visit was our final morning. It was the third safari that we had ventured out on with our guides and naturalists Neil and Sidat. At half past seven we discovered that a tiger had been seen making a kill by a group of mahouts on their elephants, and so we set off to find it. There were, we were told, 126 tigers in Kanha National Park, but that wouldn't necessarily mean that you would see one whenever you ventured out. No guest at the camp had seen one since we had been there, but an hour later we heard that it had been spotted again, and we were driven to the edge of some undergrowth where the elephants and their mahouts were waiting and we climbed from the jeeps onto the elephants' saddles so that they could lead us from the tracks and through the undergrowth.

And there we came across the tiger. It was an astonishing sight. Not only was he a staggering size, but he also looked so unbelievably calm and relaxed as he dozed in the sun. But then, what does a tiger have to worry about? In the complete wild he might fret about poaching and extinction, but in a national park he has no such fears. Just like Tara, he played to the camera beautifully.

Later in the morning we came across him again, when he crossed the track about two jeeps in front of us. A moving tiger is a different proposition altogether, and there was a real sense of fear when he appeared to be heading straight towards us. In the end, he changed his mind and headed off into the undergrowth to go about the business of being a tiger in private, and leaving us all desperately hoping that our cameras had been working properly.

Before leaving the camp we went to one of the cabins to check out. Alan, it emerged, did not have quite enough money to pay for his stay, and so he asked if I might lend him a little more. We then took a car, which I paid for, all the way back to Nagpur so that we could catch our flights, which I had also paid for, to Mumbai.

*

'What are you going to do when we get to Mumbai?' asked Alan, as we sat in the spartan departure lounge at Nagpur.

And what would I do? We would arrive in Mumbai in time for the final Test in the series, but I really wasn't all that sure if I wanted to see any more cricket. I had left Chandigarh feeling fed up with the game, and also fed up with being part of the press corps. Everybody, though, had been emphasising what an amazing hotel the Taj Mahal in Mumbai was. And I had seven nights booked there, for which I had paid an astronomical amount. I had looked it up on the Internet before I set off for India, and I knew that it was an astonishingly large hotel; large enough for me to stay at without necessarily having to bump into any of the press corps or indeed the teams, who would also be staying there. Kipling Camp had afforded me a wonderful opportunity to see a bit of India that I wouldn't have if I was just following the tour. I could use the Taj Mahal as a base from which to explore Mumbai, and try and make up for the fact that I had seen almost nothing of Nagpur or Chandigarh.

'I don't know,' I said. 'Maybe a bit of sightseeing? The thing I'm most looking forward to is the hotel, to be honest.'

'Oh, that's right,' said Alan. 'You've already got a hotel booked there, haven't you?'

'Yes.'

'Mmm.'

'You not organised anything, Alan?'

'Well actually, I was going to ask you about that. I mean, seeing as you've got a place booked, do you reckon I could stay there?'

I had thought that this might happen. I didn't begrudge lending Alan the money at all. I had had more luck than him since leaving university, and was glad that he'd not been embarrassed to ask for the loan in the first place. He had also just been something of a saviour in my hour of need. But I was also worried that the whole lending thing was getting a little out of control. At what point in our lives was he planning to pay it all back? It was just the flights to India that he asked to borrow the money for, originally, but I'd also subbed him for a large chunk of his bill at Kipling, and then covered the taxi and the cost of this flight. This was beginning to turn into a really substantial amount of money, and my new choice of career was not yet proving particularly profitable. Or indeed at all profitable. If I had succeeded in becoming any sort of cricket journalist at all, then it was a redundant one.

'I don't know, Alan...'

'Just for tonight. I could find myself a hostel tomorrow. But for tonight. It will be really late when we get there. And I've never been before. I wouldn't know where to go.'

This was certainly true. I couldn't pay for a man to go to Mumbai and then just abandon him on the streets outside the airport.

'I suppose so,' I said. 'I'm sure that one night would be all right.'

'I could give you a bit of money or something, maybe pay for a meal? Is it an expensive hotel?'

'It's one of the most expensive in India apparently. About three hundred pounds a night, I think.'

'Fuck,' said Alan, and then chewed this over for a while. 'Well, it would be a really good meal.'

'It's fine,' I said. 'Don't worry about it.'

'Just one night,' Alan repeated.

*

The domestic airport is in north Mumbai, and the Taj is in the Apollo Bunder area of south Mumbai, a distance of a little under 14 miles. This is not an enormous undertaking. But it turns out that if two ex-English public schoolboys climb into your taxi in a multi-storey car park a little after midnight and ask to be taken to the most expensive hotel in your city, then the rules of your business will tell you that the only allowable response you can make is to take them for 'a fucking ride'.

We were in that cab for nearly an hour and a half, shouting our heads off at a man who, despite making a number of calls on his mobile, appeared unable to hear us above the sound of his engine while he drove us around Rock Beach and Jogeshwari and Kurla. If you look at a map of Mumbai, you will see – unless Mumbai has the most confusing one-way system that has been imposed anywhere in the world – the extent to which this man decreed that we deserved to be fleeced. In retrospect it was almost admirable.

Alas, when he finally jammed on the brakes at half past one in the morning, having travelled for well over an hour, that was still not the end of our journey. We had not pulled up outside Mumbai's most splendid hotel. We hadn't pulled up outside anything that even closely resembled splendour. We were on a long, straight and dark road that at first sight looked as if it was in the heart of Mumbai's badlands.

'Where are we?' I asked.

'I can go no further,' said our driver, who was at last able to hear us now that he had turned off his engine.

'What do you mean?' asked Alan.

'I have driven enough now,' he said, as if taxi drivers in that part of the world were members of a strict trade union that forced them to stop working at half past one on the dot, regardless of whether they were still carrying passengers or not.

Alan and I exchanged confused glances.

'What happens now?' I asked.

'We wait.'

'What do we wait for?'

'We wait...for a friend of mine.'

The next glances that Alan and I exchanged were nervous ones. What was this guy up to? Was he a gangster? Perhaps the 'friend' of his that we were waiting for was the gangster. Our driver's job was merely to deliver gullible Englishmen to this part of town in exchange for a cut of our possessions after we'd been robbed and our bodies dumped.

I looked ahead and then turned around to see through the rear windscreen, but I could not see the lights of any other cars. I couldn't see any lights at all, in fact. Nor could I see any people.

'Do you think we should run for it?' Alan asked me in a whisper.

'Maybe we should,' I replied, feeling my whole body tense.

When you're the only person in a situation that is terrifying it somehow seems manageable. You wonder if you are just imagining the reasons behind your terror. But when you discover that somebody else is just as scared as you are, then your fears are suddenly justified and real. But what good would making a run for it achieve? We had no idea where we were, and where we would run to. And would we try and escape with our belongings, or leave them behind in the boot?

I gently tried the catch on my door to see if it would open or not, unsure as to how I would respond to either outcome. The catch opened easily and the door started to swing open.

'What are you doing?' said the driver.

'I'm just...' I started to answer and then stopped. I didn't know what I was doing.

'Everything is okay?'

'I'm not sure,' I said.

'It's better to have door shut. Is safer.'

'How do you mean?' Alan asked.

'Is just safer. Here. This place. Better to be shut.'

The driver sounded scared too, but I wasn't sure if that was a reason to relax or not.

Then, far ahead along the street, we saw the headlights of another car appear in the distance. They came slowly towards us, the driver saying nothing.

'Is this your friend?' said Alan.

'I don't know.'

Alan and I looked back and forth at each other and then at the oncoming headlights until the other car eventually pulled alongside us, and we heard someone exit, open their boot and then come and open the boot of our taxi behind us and begin removing its contents.

Alan and I exchanged one final look, and then he shouted, 'Go! Go! Go!'

I yanked open my door, and Alan and I bundled out of the taxi as fast as we could, and then stood crouched there, breathless, ready to do battle with whoever or whatever we found.

What we found was possibly the smiliest man I had ever seen, in the process of loading my suitcase into the boot of his gleaming yellow taxi.

'Hello!' he beamed. 'I am going to take you to The Taj Mahal! Please! Get in! You will be comfortable!'

And indeed comfortable we were, even if the smiliest man I had ever seen also had one of the worst and most persistent coughs that I have ever heard. Endearingly, though, he also had the most tremendous desire to apologise for it.

All the final 20 minutes to the Taj we could just hear 'Karr-fleurgh! Please excuse me, gentlemen. Kaaaarr-*flleuurhgh*!!! I am sorry about this. Yes. I have a cough. Sorry.'

We were dropped outside the Taj a little before two, paid something extortionate, and were then ushered inside by a polite, slightly sleepy-looking, doorman.

*

The Taj is truly a place of wonder. It was built at the turn of the twentieth century by Jamsetji Tata and stands directly opposite the Gateway Of India on the waterfront, through which the last of the British troops to leave India finally processed on 28 February 1948. It has always been a hotel. It now has a staggering 565 rooms and is full of grand, sweeping staircases, and beautiful tiled corridors. I could not appreciate any of this at two in the morning, however. I simply wanted to be shown to a bed and to sleep.

We were ushered into a high-ceilinged, dark-panelled room in order to check in, and sat on two delicately carved wooden chairs at a deep polished table, across which sat a handsome Indian gentleman in a beautiful suit, who was as charming as can be.

'What name is your reservation in?'

'Jupp.'

'Ah yes,' he said as he opened a leather-bound folder, and ran his finger down a list of neatly typed names.

'Mr M Jupp. Seven nights. We did not know if we were going to receive you tonight.'

'Yes, I'm sorry we're so late. We got rather a late flight from Nagpur.'

'From Nagpur? Then you should have landed here a little before midnight, yes?' he said with a smile.

'We did, yes.'

He glanced up at the clock on the wall beside him. 'Then I think you must have experienced some difficulty with your taxi.'

'We did. Yes,' I said, chuckling as if we'd just been stuck in a little bit of traffic, rather than parked up in a deserted part of town frightened for our lives.

The man smiled politely, and then returned to the paper-work. 'Your booking is...for one.'

'That's right, yes,' I said.

'Would I be able to stay as well?' asked Alan.

'You would like a room too, sir?'

'Oh no. I'll just stay in his.'

'If you are happy for this, sir?'

'It's fine,' I said. 'It's just for one night.'

'Certainly. I'll arrange for a camp bed to be sent up to your room.'

'Great. If you can let us know about any extra charge for that, that would be great,' I said, looking at Alan. Alan busied himself with a mark on his Australian rugby top.

'Just sign here, here, here, here and here. Date here. And sign there,' said the man, indicating all with a flourish.

I did as I was told.

'And this gentleman will show you to your room.'

Behind us stood a porter who had silently loaded our luggage onto a trolley. The gentleman stood up from behind the desk, and handed the keys to the porter.

'Have a wonderful stay,' he said. 'And sleep well.'

'Oh we will,' I assured him.

*

Upstairs the porter delivered us and our luggage to a sumptuous room, and as he was showing us around it two other men arrived with a camp bed, which they unfolded and set up underneath the window. Alan thanked everybody profusely as they left and I tipped them. I demanded first use of the bathroom, and was just in the middle of brushing my teeth when I heard the phone ring and Alan answer it.

'Great news!' he said as I emerged from the bathroom.

'Yes?'

'That was the man from the reception. He said he's checked

with his supervisors and I can stay in the room for the whole week! At no extra cost!'

*

I slept deeply, but not for long, my body perhaps already conditioned by the succession of early starts that we had made in order to go on our safaris. I had not shut the curtains before crashing out, and the morning Mumbai light flooded the room. I climbed out of my expensive bed, and tiptoed around the free version that Alan was still sprawled out on to look out of the window. What was meant to be my room, but was now our room, overlooked the hotel's central courtyard and swimming pool. It was not yet seven in the morning, but already there were plenty of swimmers doing lengths and figures stretching by the side. I showered and dressed, and then slipped out of the room to find some breakfast and to take a proper look at this amazing hotel. Our room was at one end of a long and wide corridor, with marble black and white flooring. I could hear the flip-flopping of my flip-flops gently reverberating as I slowly walked along, taking in the sheer wonderment of the place. I stopped and leant against a gallery rail to look down at similar floors below, and then craned forward and looked up to see yet more floors, the whole building towering above me as if I was standing on the hull floor of a mighty ship. I made my way down a grand staircase, and then across a hallway and out into the courtyard. Even though I was standing in the shade, I could already feel the heat of the sun, and there was a glare caused by it reflecting off the glasses on the tables that had been laid out for those wanting to eat their breakfast outside.

Despite the pool being busy, and the clinking of knives and forks against plates by a few couples enjoying breakfast under huge white parasols, there was a beautiful calm about the place. A few waiters in white uniforms scuttled past me with trays, and nodded at me silently, as if we were in the cloisters of a monastery.

The sound of the hectic city that sprawled beyond these walls was muffled by them. It was as if everything was filtered. A light breeze blew through the palm trees and across the tops of beautifully manicured bushes, carrying with it only the lightest scent of the city and the sea. It had the feeling of a sanctuary. We had come a long way in 24 hours. This time the day before we would still have been getting hurled around the back of a 4x4 as we searched the jungles of central India for a tiger. Now all I hunted was a cooked breakfast.

I walked out of the shade and into the sun, just to feel its heat for a moment. As I did so I shielded my eyes, and it was only then that I recognised the figures in and around the pool. It was the England team; the very people who I had come to India to follow and to watch.

I hadn't seen them for several days now, and had spent those days not thinking about cricket at all. I had arrived in Mumbai not knowing how I would spend my time here other than to explore and to luxuriate. But now, seeing our team all looking happy, unified and focused ahead of the final Test, I became incredibly, almost feverishly excited about the prospect of watching them play again. The misery and disappointments of Chandigarh were suddenly a world away. England had gone away, regrouped and come back to fight again. And so had I. This match was their final chance to scrap for a victory to save the series. It was also my last chance to try and achieve any of my ambitions. I would go to the ground, I decided, and I'd try and get back into the press box, and once I had done that I would pitch more stories to the *Western Mail* and to BBC Scotland. I would find a Welsh angle. I would find a Scottish angle. And then I would scour the city for other stories and I would pitch them too.

Refreshed and energised by my surroundings, I felt as positive about the idea as I had for weeks.

*

I breakfasted hurriedly at the next table to a South African gentleman, whom I immediately assumed to be Kevin Pietersen's father. He turned out, of course, to be the father of Andrew Strauss. Then I rushed back to the room to get my journalism kit together and to dig out the press pass. This caused me some nerves as I headed up the stairs. What if it was the rightful owner of my pass who had been arrested? Would his name be on some sort of blacklist? Or would passes be checked much more thoroughly as a result of whoever it was that had made it into the Chandigarh press box? I could still wear a hat and sunglasses, of course, but I no longer had the beard that had played such a prominent part in my disguise. Were the other journalists aware of the full story in Chandigarh anyway? Perhaps they still believed that it was me who had been arrested. It didn't matter, I decided. This was my last chance, and I was going to take it.

Alan had just woken up when I got into the room, and was sitting on the edge of the camp bed sleepily flicking through a guidebook.

'I can't believe where that driver must have taken us last night,' he said. 'Anyway, you were up early.'

'Yeah, I had a look around the hotel. It's amazing. And so is breakfast.'

'Oh, is breakfast included?' he asked, trying to sound casual.

'I don't know,' I said as I opened up my suitcase and started rummaging around for the press pass. 'Can you check before having any?'

'Yes, sure.'

'Because if it isn't then it's likely to be really expensive here.'

'Okay.'

'Or maybe, rather like with your sleeping arrangements, you can get a free camping equivalent. Perhaps you can have some freeze-dried egg cooked up for you in a mess tin.'

'You don't mind me staying here, do you?'

'Well...'

'I mean, I'm not in the way or anything?' said Alan, sitting in a bed that blocked off access to the mini bar.

'No. Well, perhaps a little. The only thing is...I'm here to work. I'm going to be busy here.'

'Oh? I was just looking up some things that we could do in the guidebook.'

'Well, I've got lots of work to do. Writing. Journalism.'

'I thought that had all just...gone to shit?'

'Well it hasn't been great. But this is my last chance. I'm going to go for it,' I said, slinging my laptop case over my shoulder and pocketing the pass.

'Are you going to the ground now?'

'Yes.'

'Oh right. Well, I'll see you this evening then. Good luck.'

'Thanks.'

'Call me if you get bored.'

'Will do.'

*

There was a queue of taxis waiting outside the hotel's main lobby, and I jumped into the first one. I wanted to get there in good time for the start of the game, get myself a good place in the box and catch up on everything that had been going on. Then I could send a few ideas to the *Western Mail* and BBC Scotland before play got under way.

The Wankhede stadium is across the other side of the jutting promontory on which South Mumbai lies, between the MK Road and Ocean Drive. Fifty rupees was enough to take me there, and I was dropped off at the south side of the ground. If the grounds had been far from full at the other two venues, there was no chance that this could happen here. The streets all around the ground were full of fans of both teams, and I joined a bottleneck of people that had formed to pass through the scrappy-looking Vinoo Mankad gate.

Soldiers and police were checking tickets and passes, and pulling some fans aside to check the contents of their bags. I put on my hat and sunglasses and when I got near the front I held up the pass and flashed it at a policeman. When he saw it he reached over the people in front of me and grabbed hold of me by the arm.

'You. Come here, please.'

He pulled me through the crowd, and then I stood next to him nervously as he inspected the pass again. Had they been asked to look out for anyone using this pass?

'You are journalist?'

'That's right.'

'You know where you're going?'

'I don't.'

'This way.'

He pointed me in the direction of a grimy white building ahead of me at the far end of the tarmac stretch that ran between the gate and the edge of the first of the stands. There was a narrow doorway there, with two more policemen standing outside it.

'Is this the media enclosure?' I asked.

One of them glanced at the pass, and ushered me through wordlessly. Fantastic. The pass worked here just as well as it had in Chandigarh. If anything, people here were inspecting it even less thoroughly.

On the other side of the door I encountered Rod Gilmour, who was typically carrying a huge bundle of kit.

'Hi, Miles. What happened to you at Chandigarh?'

'Oh I got a bit ill. And then I went off for a few days. I saw a tiger.'

'A tiger?'

'Yeah. Have you been up to much?'

'Well, I've been busy, but I haven't seen a tiger.'

What I wanted to know about, though, was the man who had been arrested. Clearly Rod didn't think it was me, as he hadn't said, 'Oh my God, you got arrested.'

It turned out that the fellow who had been arrested was not the rightful owner of my pass. But it was someone who, like me, had been using a press pass he was not entitled to. He was also, like me, only posing as a journalist. However, unlike me, he had been turning the situation to his advantage.

The man was a gambler. He had worked out that if he could get into the press box, then he could have access to the Internet. And if he had access to the Internet and had a good view of the cricket, then he could log on to British gambling sites and gamble on the outcome of the next delivery.

The other people who were using and running these websites would all have been in Britain, and all of them would have been getting their information from the television. But what happened on the field in Chandigarh didn't appear on television screens in Britain for 15 seconds. Our friend was using this 15-second delay to place bets on the outcomes of deliveries that he had already seen with his own eyes. It was a very clever scam. He couldn't lose. Unfortunately for him it was also illegal, and, rather more unfortunately, a number of the journalists in the press box worked out what he was doing and informed the authorities.

*

Rahul Dravid won the toss, and to the surprise of most people, asked England to bat. Alastair Cook had come down with some sort of stomach bug, however, and so his place in the team was taken by Owais Shah, and Ian Bell stepped up to open the batting. The line-up of the whole team had changed rather markedly, in fact. The 37-year-old Shaun Udal had come into the team to partner Monty Panesar in the spin department and James Anderson was added to the pace attack.

Right from the start, the game was a war of attrition. Bell and Strauss put on 52 runs for the first wicket, Ian Bell batting for 100 painstaking minutes for 18 runs before suddenly slicing a short and wide ball from Sreesanth to Harbhajan Singh at point. At lunch we were 63–1.

By tea, we had moved on to 158–1, the new batsman Shah having scored a half-century from 91 deliveries, and Strauss looking in his best form of the tour on 88 not out. And by the close of play we were 272–3. After five and a half hours Strauss had finally edged one through to the keeper, having made 128 beautiful, valuable runs. Shah retired hurt after tea with his score still exactly 50, as if he was playing in a benefit game. Cramp in the fingers was the reason given for his absence and he didn't appear again until the next day. Kevin Pietersen got himself set up for a lengthy stay, but then drove hard at a swinging delivery from Sreesanth and was caught behind for 39. Flintoff and Collingwood batted out time at the end of the day. We had made extremely steady progress, and not exactly piled on the agony, but we had certainly done enough to make Dravid regret his decision to make us bat first.

We made it to 400 exactly in the end. There was a flurry of wickets after Collingwood and Flintoff's obdurate partnership of 86 was broken and we were 356–8 at one stage. But Anderson stuck around, and Shah returned and scored another 38 runs to take us to what amounted to an imposing score in the circumstances. Hoggard then had Sehwag caught at slip, and then Jaffer caught down the leg side to leave India 24–2. The noise that erupted from the crowd when Tendulkar emerged from the pavilion was one of the loudest and most excited cheers I have ever heard; the groan when he was dismissed by Anderson 20 minutes later was one of the most disappointed. Yuvraj Singh and Rahul Dravid, however, then fought their way to a 50 partnership from 90 deliveries. India were 89–3 by the close of play.

Singh did not last long the next morning, adding only five more to his score before chasing a wide ball from Flintoff into the hands of Jones the Keeper. But Dravid was irritatingly obdurate, and guided India to 142–4 before trying to flick Anderson down the leg side and clipping the ball to Jones, who took a stunning catch, flinging himself full-stretch to his left and then performing a series of ecstatic tumbles.

At lunch, then, they were 153–5 and England were in a dominant position. By tea they had fought their way to 217–8, largely owing to an innings of 64 from Dhoni that had been unusually watchful until the last four deliveries he faced, which were bowled by Flintoff. The first he spanked off his legs, the second he carved over point, the third he edged through the slips – and all to the boundary. But off the fourth delivery he bunted one towards midwicket and set off for a ridiculous run, only for James Anderson to gather the ball and throw down the stumps at the bowler's end.

The ninth-wicket partnership was worth an infuriating 55 runs, Sreesanth and Kumble bringing up 50 off just 67 balls. Panesar finally trapped Kumble in front for 30, and then Anderson yorked Munaf Patel. England looked disappointed with the way the Indian innings had finished as they trudged off the pitch, but they had earned a lead of 121. We had extended it by a further 31 by the close of play although for the loss of Strauss and Bell, both of whom had edged full deliveries through to the keeper.

The fourth day was one of the slowest days of cricket I have ever seen; so slow in fact that at times it almost looked the way that people who don't like cricket imagine every day must be. We had added just 107 runs by teatime for the loss of three wickets. And 138 for 5 represented a fight-back. When Shah had run himself out for 38 after two and three-quarter hours at the crease, England were reeling (albeit slowly) at 85–5. The 19 runs Flintoff had scored by tea took him 84 deliveries. When Collingwood was finally dismissed for 32 – caught brilliantly by Harbhajan Singh off his own bowling, diving one-handed to his left – he had faced 118 balls and failed, or perhaps not even tried, to score from 101 of them.

That left us on 151–6, and heightened the atmosphere by several notches. 'India! India!' roared the Indian fans. 'Barmy Army! Barmy Army' roared the Barmy Army, who had already been busy in Mumbai. Prior to the Test they organised a cricket match and also a sponsored one-mile run through the city streets, all to raise money for Sport Relief. They had been in fine voice throughout the game, and had brought with them a brass band, who let rip periodically, especially to signify bowling changes. Whenever Freddie Flintoff came on to bowl they would play 'Meet The Flintstones'. Rather more whimsically, Yorkshireman Matthew Hoggard was greeted with the theme from *Last Of The Summer Wine*.

The tempo was not upped by the shift in atmosphere, however. Geraint Jones joined in the blocking, but survived 21 balls before it all got too much and he tried to pull the twenty-second, a shortish ball from Singh, and succeeded in top edging it, so that it ballooned somewhere behind square leg and was caught by a sprinting Irfan Pathan. Hoggard's arrival at the crease prompted not only the aforementioned musical accompaniment, but also some shots from Flintoff. They managed a partnership of 26, of which Hoggard contributed six, before, having tried a number of wild and unsuccessful sweep shots, he attempted his least successful of the innings that resulted in him being LBW to Kumble. That partnership, though, took England's lead past the 300 mark – a feat accomplished by Flintoff swinging Singh over square leg for a six.

Drinks were taken after Hoggard's dismissal and Flintoff left the field, presumably to have a quick tactics chat with coach Duncan Fletcher. He returned with instructions for the new batsman James Anderson. These appeared to be to lunge at and miss the first two deliveries he faced and then connect with a drive off the final ball of the over and hastily run two. These instructions he followed to the letter.

Flintoff made it to a half-century off 145 deliveries. But he went down the wicket to the 146th, took a mighty heave, missed it and was stumped. He had been out there for 209 minutes. Anderson played a few shots before edging Kumble to Dravid at slip, to leave England all out with a lead of 313.

But such statistics do not tell the whole story. The going may have been slow, and I have certainly never seen more defensive shots played in my life. We may have scored just 191 runs in the innings at an archaic rate of a tickle over two runs an over. But they were vital runs. And they were runs scored in the most difficult and gruelling of circumstances. Mumbai was without doubt the hottest of the three Test venues that we had encountered on the tour. It was staggering. We may have been right next to the sea, but there was simply no way that any breeze could find its way into the cauldron-like atmosphere of the Wankhede stadium. I was in the shade for the whole day, and sweated throughout. Runs had come at a trickle throughout, but by keeping the innings going for as long as they could, with Flintoff as the main architect, the team had fought us into a strong position. And by the close of play, we were in an even stronger one. India were 18–1, Anderson having bowled stand-in opener Irfan Pathan for just six. At the start of the final day of the series, India needed to score 295 to win. England needed to take nine wickets.

*

But I did not watch much of that cricket from the vantage point that I had expected to. After discovering the truth about that man that had been arrested from Rod, I had sought out the press box itself, which was a tall glass affair with steeply raked rows of seats and desks that fanned out from the front. As I climbed the steps that led up to the entrance near the back of the box, I felt both excited and anxious about returning to the press corps. It was now the best part of a week since I had seen the majority of its inhabitants, and I did not know how my return to the box would be met. Some people would inevitably have forgotten all about me, if they had ever noticed that I was there at all. Others would have formed firmer, perhaps more negative, opinions of me. The news that I was not a journalist at all but a former children's television actor, would presumably have travelled further around the group.

But when I walked into the box a strange thing happened. Various journalists looked up and said, 'Hello, Miles.' Mr Who The Fuck's That? came over and shook my hand. 'We wondered where you'd got to,' he said cheerily.

So I found myself an empty seat, sat down in it and began to take out my bits and pieces ready to resume my journalism career. The seat that I had chosen was easily the best I had yet had at any of the venues. I had a fantastic view overlooking the whole of the ground. And not only could I see all of the playing area, but because we were positioned high up, I was able to see nearly all of the crowd. And everybody appeared to be there. All of the press corps were in the box. Behind us were the BBC commentary positions, and just away to our left were the ones for Sky. Immediately in front of us was a box that contained the players' families.

Although people were still pouring into the ground, there was an already far larger crowd than either of the other games had attracted, and it was packed with fans, and colour and anticipation. Amidst all the flags and banners on display there were even a few Welsh ones, perhaps brought by people who like me had travelled to India expecting to see Simon Jones.

I switched on my laptop, and connected to the Internet. And then I wrote an email to my contact at BBC Scotland describing the scene in front of me exactly as I saw it; a cauldron bubbling with expectation. 'Indian crowds are the liveliest in the world,' I wrote. 'They fizz.' I even wrote to the *Western Mail* explaining that Simon Jones may not have made it to the third Test, but his supporters had. And then the game got under way. India won the toss, asked England to bat again, and the series burst back into life.

As our opening pair walked out to bat the crowd roared, they chanted, they clapped and they sang. In our box, however, a clock ticked, a fan whirred, and nobody in the place said a word. I couldn't believe it. There I was, sitting in the press box: the place that I dreamt of getting into, the place that I had lied and fibbed to get into – the place, crucially, that I had managed to get into. And I realised that it was full of people hunched over laptops, sharpening pencils, and muttering about the Wi-Fi. I looked out at the crowd – screaming and singing and clapping and being happy. And I thought: 'I don't want to be in here. I want to be out there.'

I felt this so strongly that I acted almost without thought. I didn't even look around the box. I just turned off my laptop, packed up my things and I walked out. I walked back down the stairs, out of the entrance to the media enclosure, and instead walked around to an entrance to one of the stands. I climbed up into the stand, and I sat near the back surrounded by India fans and I started to watch the game from there. Instantly everything felt different.

It felt right.

I clapped, and I shouted and I cheered, all things that you can never do in the press box.

The press box could never be like that because it is a place of work. All of those people in the press box were working. Its inhabitants worked the whole time. They couldn't celebrate when we took wickets; they had to make notes. They couldn't cheer when we scored boundaries, because they were too busy writing it up. And they had to be neutral and objective all the time.

I simply hadn't been at work. I had just been playing at it. The objectives that I had set myself at the beginning of the tour seemed modest at the time. But I had not made a single radio broadcast; I had not made it into print; I hadn't earned myself a penny, and I had got no other work. When I had switched on my laptop in the press box, the one email that I'd received from my potential employers was from someone at the *Western Mail* saying that they were happy with the 'blog experiment'. 'It has been read by twenty-two people!'

Yes, I had chatted to heroes. I had got along with some people, and not with others. And I couldn't blame them. I had been lying to them, and been there on false purposes. I had done the equivalent of getting dressed up in a suit and tie, marching into a random boardroom and just asking people to budge up a bit. Of course people were annoyed. Of course they were suspicious. They were right to be.

If I tried to be a journalist I would always be the boy in the dinner hall, standing there with his tray and a panicked expression wondering where to sit. And if I couldn't see somewhere I'd quietly put my tray on the racks and walk out again.

I just wanted to go back to cricket being as it was, when it was simpler. If England won, I would be happy. If they didn't, then I would not. And that was why, I realised, I had done this whole thing. That was why I was now sitting on a filthy bench in a raucous stand surrounded by strangers, and over 5,000 miles from home. I was there because I love cricket. Lots of people can't bear it, and lots of people can't understand its appeal. But I didn't come to love cricket through reason or debate. Love is like belief. It happens by instinct, and then you make a leap.

I love cricket in exactly the same way that some people love Bob Dylan or the Beatles; in the same way that people love the Romantic poets, or the Bilbao Guggenheim, or the Fibonacci sequence. I love it in the same way some people love the feeling of sunlight on their eyelids or that others love beekeeping. I love it, it pains me to admit, in exactly the same way that some people must love football.

*

And so it was in a packed stand that Alan and I were sitting to watch the fifth day. Flintoff and Hoggard opened the bowling, and it was the latter who made the first breakthrough, trapping the night watchman Kumble in front to leave India 21–2. But this brought Rahul Dravid in, who instantly looked at his most stubborn and resilient. He was still there at lunch, nearly two hours later, with just nine runs to his name. Wasim Jaffer looked just as entrenched, adding only six runs to his overnight score in an hour before he was dismissed by Flintoff. At 33–3, India looked to be in trouble, but at lunchtime they were 75–3 and all three results looked possible. Tendulkar had come to the crease and looked in his best touch of the series, racing to 34 not out by the interval. Dravid, by contrast, had celebrated his seventy-seventh minute at the crease by running Hoggard down to the third-man boundary, doubling his score in the process.

Again, the response to Sachin's arrival at the wicket was astonishing. Alan and I did not even see his approach from the pavilion as our view was obscured by a sea of flags. 'Sachin! Sachin!' roared the crowd. When the noise had finally settled down, I leant forward and tapped the man in front of me on the shoulder. 'What's the name of the new batsman?' I asked. He looked horrified for a moment before he realised that I was joking. Then I noticed that the replica India shirt he was wear-
~~hore Sachin's signature. 'Sachin's wife is a family friend,' he
~~e. 'I have been to his house.'

'What's he like?'

'He is humble.'

*

So when play resumed after the lunch interval (a lunch interval in which I had encountered, bizarrely, Stephen Fry. I asked him to pose for a photograph holding my press pass), India needed 238 to win with seven wickets in hand. But England were just astonishing. Dravid was the first to go, in the first over, edging Flintoff to Geraint Jones without adding to his score.

Shaun Udal had bowled just two overs of his off-spin before lunch. The day before I had sat listening as some Indian spectators berated and mocked a long list of England off-spinners. But that day Udal was the unexpected punchline to their joke, and it was delivered beautifully. Tendulkar prodded forward to Udal's third ball of the afternoon session only for it to spin, take the inside edge and then carry to Ian Bell fielding under the helmet. India 76–5.

Five overs later, Anderson replaced Flintoff and with only his second delivery got the ball to reverse into Sehwag and trap him LBW for a duck. India 77–6. 'We'll be back at the pool by three,' said Alan.

Yuvraj Singh hit two straight fours off Anderson's next over, and then oddly, given that there had been only nine overs of play since lunch, there was a drinks interval. With the score on 89–6, Owais Shah put down a low, hard chance at slip off Anderson. At the start of the next over, though, Monty Panesar was given a much easier chance to catch and failed to even get a hand on it. Dhoni came down the wicket to Shaun Udal and took the most almighty swing at a full, looping delivery only to get an edge on it, and for the ball to climb high into the air over long off. I did not follow the flight of the ball, but instead watched Monty move a little to his right and settle into a catching position. So I was extremely surprised to then see the ball hit the ground over a metre from where Monty had positioned himself. It was one of the worst attempts to take a catch the international game has ever seen.

Three balls later, though, Dhoni tried an identical shot and this time Monty made no mistake. India 92–7. Harbhajan Singh hit a screaming boundary past point off the bowling of Anderson, but then top edged a sweep shot off Udal which was held by Hoggard at fine leg. Flintoff returned to the attack to bowl round the wicket to the left-handed Yuvraj Singh, who was still battling away after an hour in the middle. His fourth ball swung away, took the outside edge and carried to Collingwood at third slip. India 99–9. The last man, Patel, then brought up the hundred with a driven single off the final ball of Flintoff's over.

That left him to face Shaun Udal, a 37-year-old man playing just his fourth Test match and who had started the game with a Test average of 92.23. Patel swung at the second ball of the over, it took a top edge, and it flew down to the fine-leg boundary just in front of where we were sitting. Hoggard sprinted around the boundary, jumped up and held the catch with both hands above his head. India 100 all out. England had won by 212 runs. And at the moment that I knew that Hoggard had held on to that catch, I leapt up onto the bench that I was sitting on, with my arms aloft, and I shouted 'Yeeeeeeeeeeeeees!!' And I knew that on that bench was where I belonged.

*

After the game there was a presentation ceremony. And so I used my pass for the final time to step out onto the pitch. I didn't want to get too close to the presentation itself, but instead wandered out around the boundary, and looked up at all the English fans cheering in the stands. The Indian fans might have lost the game, but they were cheering too.

Back at the hotel, the celebrations began. Players and journalists and their families mingled freely around the pool. Backs were slapped and photos were taken. That night Alan and I went out to a restaurant to celebrate England's victory, and some good news that Alan had received during the day: he had been offered a place to study at RADA. We returned in time to encounter a rather drunk-looking *Test Match Special* team. Out by the pool the England team, or those of them who were still standing, were singing 'I love you baby' into someone's mobile phone.

*

The next morning all of the team's kit was piled high in the lobby, and there were a number of journalists about, ready to set off to follow the one-day series. David Gower was sitting on a sofa looking relaxed. He smiled at me.

'Are you succeeding?' he asked. I laughed.

I said goodbye to Simon and Kevin, and then went over to speak to Andrew Walpole, who appeared to be overseeing England's departure. He had his children with him.

'Thanks very much for everything, Andrew.'

'Oh, my pleasure. Sorry it's been a bit difficult for you at times.'

'No, no. It's been great.'

'What are you up to now then?'

'I'm going home tomorrow.'

'Well, it's been nice to meet you. Perhaps we'll see you during the summer.'

'Maybe, Andrew. Maybe.'

We shook hands. Just as I was walking away, I heard one of his children say, 'Daddy? Wasn't that man from…?' but I hurried around the corner.

Alan and I said goodbye in front of the Gate Of India, and he gave me a replica India shirt before climbing aboard a ferry, and heading off to stay at a fishing village further along the coast. I watched and waved until he was just a speck in the distance.

Then I climbed aboard a different ferry to spend the day looking around Elephanta Island, which lies about six miles to the south-east.

The ferry took an hour or so, and I had a gentle time there, wandering about on my own admiring the extraordinary temples carved into the rock, taking photos of monkeys and buying gifts for my friends and family. When I'd had enough, I walked back down the steep path to catch a ferry back to the Gate Of India.

It was late afternoon, and there were few other passengers aboard. Mumbai, as we approached, looked terrific, and so I tried to go onto the upper deck to get a better view. A crewman stopped me at the foot of the stairs. To go onto the upper deck would cost me ten more rupees, but I had no more rupees left. So instead I got as far forward on the lower deck as I could, plonked my legs further apart so that I wouldn't lose my balance, and took in the view from there. The wind was blowing through my hair, and the spray from the sea splashed over me as I stood watching an orange sun go down behind the Gate Of India and the Taj behind it. Music was playing gently over the boat's tannoy system. I took out my camera to take a photo of one of the most stunning views that I had ever seen, but its battery had run out. I would just have to remember it all: the setting sun, the jolly music, the gentle bobbing and the sea breeze. If it had been a film then at this point the camera would have panned out and out and out, until I and then the boat became just specks as the credits slowly began to roll. As it was I just stood there, squinting into the sun and grinning like an idiot.

Post Script

A few weeks after I returned from India, I moved to north London. That summer I joined a cricket club. It was rather a fancy club, and the standard was far too high for me. But I had little else to do, and plenty of time to devote to playing regularly for a team.

I tended to play for one of the 'friendly' Sunday teams, and every Wednesday evening we would have net sessions. Some people were there without fail, and others were there sporadically. Every now and then a total newcomer would turn up.

One Wednesday night a new man came along. He was very neatly turned out, and looked like a useful bowler. He bowled seam up with a whippy action. As we were queuing to bowl, we began chatting and I asked him what he did for a living.

'I've got my own business,' he said cryptically.

That could mean anything. He could run a fleet of luxury cars, or he could be a hit man.

'What do you mean?' I said. 'What sort of business?

'Well, actually I'm a professional gambler.'

'That's amazing,' I said. 'I've never met a professional gambler before. Although I did hear about this fantastic scam recently. I was in India earlier this year following the cricket. And this guy got into the press box during the game at Chandigarh, hooked up to the Internet there and then started gambling on British betting sites. They're usually working off a fifteen-second delay, but he was watching it live, obviously, and so he could beat the system. Very clever. He got found out though. They arrested him.'

I hadn't been looking at him while I spoke; I was keeping my eye on the batsmen in the nets. So only when I'd finished my tale did I look up and see the expression on this man's face. His face was ashen, and he was standing with his arms folded, staring at the ground. And I just knew, instantly, that it was him that I was talking about.

'Oh my God,' I said. 'It was you.'

He looked up, embarrassed but saying nothing.

'It was you, wasn't it?' I repeated. 'You were the man they arrested at Chandigarh.'

I knew that I was making a massive leap, but I was completely, almost weirdly, confident that I was right.

He still said nothing.

'Please. Tell me. Were you out there? Was it you? In March? At Chandigarh? I just need to know.'

'Look,' he said eventually. 'I was in India in March. That's all I can tell you.'

He waited for his turn to bowl, and then, having done so, he quietly packed up his bags and he left. He never came back to the club. Which was a shame. As I said, he looked like a very useful bowler.

I saw him once again, at the Twenty20 Final day at Trent Bridge in Nottingham. I was sitting at the top of the pavilion with a friend who is a member there, and suddenly there he was, walking past me and carrying a laptop.

I called his name out, and he looked back and caught my eye. A look of panic crossed his face, and he turned away again and carried on walking.

*

Some months after that, something else happened. I logged onto my email, and there in the inbox was, finally, a message from Mary Macfarlane at BBC Scotland. It said:

Dear Miles,

I'm so sorry not to have replied to any of the many messages you sent from India. The fact of the matter is that I became ill not long after we spoke and was off work from then until now. It's a real shame as much of it sounded fascinating, and I would have absolutely loved you to make some broadcasts for us.

Yours,

Mary Macfarlane.

I stared at the screen for some minutes in disbelief. If she hadn't been ill, then they might have carried my reports. I would have been working as a real journalist. Everything could have turned out so very differently.

And yet reading the message I didn't feel wistful. Instead I felt strangely glad that everything had happened in exactly the way that it did. It couldn't have unfolded like this for anyone who was truly meant to be a cricket journalist.

I sent a reply:

Dear Mary,

Very nice to hear from you. I'm glad that you are feeling better. That's very kind of you to say, but please don't worry about India or my cricket reports! I only asked if you'd be interested in some journalism from me on the off chance. It's not as if I'm a proper journalist anyway.

I'm just a fan of the game.

Yours,

Miles Jupp

Acknowledgements

I would like to thank my beautiful wife Rachel for her love, support and encouragement. Nothing means anything without you and what you do. Nye and Eliza, neither of you can read yet but I hope you know how much Daddy loves you. Mum, Dad, Ed and Sam: you can all read and I love you too. And you, Jamie.

I owe an enormous amount of gratitude to Peter Searles who directed the stage show of *Fibber* and without whose exhortations, experience and bloody-mindedness this whole story would still only exist as drunken stories I'd tell and wild scribblings on scraps of paper in a box under my bed. My 'Shakespeare From Below The Waist' workshop is coming on leaps and bounds.

Thanks to Richard Bucknall, Georgie Donnelly and Rob Sandy, who all did so much hard work to organise and promote the Edinburgh run and subsequent tour of the stage show. Claire Walker and Chris Robinson really are damn fine at what they do. And smashing people.

The office of my agent Tavistock Wood is the coolest place I ever go. Thanks for introducing me to those Bond girls, and for letting me raid the leftovers from all the famous people's goody bags. Molly Wansell, you really are terrific. Angharad, Charles and Milly: I'll see you at the movies.

I would like to thank and/or apologise to anyone who is mentioned in the book (and a few who aren't) who were on the tour of India. I genuinely have a huge amount of respect for you and the job that you do. Simon Mann and Kevin Howells were great company in India and have continued to be so ever since.

Simon also read an early draft of this book and may well have prevented me from getting sued. Steve Coverdale got me in touch with the right people in the first place, and then listened to me go on about it afterwards. Andrew Walpole is an absolute gentleman and showed this liar kindness I simply did not deserve. The *Western Mail* and BBC Scotland are both marvellous institutions. And Charles Boase is a splendid father-in-law, grandfather and subeditor.

My ushers: Ed, Will Medvei, James Mitchell, Oli Bevan and George Nisbet. I know it was a while ago but I'm not sure I've ever thanked you properly. Great job, guys. And you all looked terrific.

I am most grateful to Jake Lingwood for being such an encouraging and understanding editor, even though he does like exclamation marks too much. He should also be grateful to me for not sacking him the night he drunkenly told me, 'I'm not really an editor. I think of myself as a DJ.'

Since I started out in this moderately crazy business there are a number of people who have either encouraged me, influenced me, been my friends, given me confidence, offered me paid work or indeed a combination of any or all of these things. Sam Kelly, Frankie Boyle, Dougie Anderson, Tom Wrigglesworth, Jane Berthoud, Peter Cattaneo, Sam Michell, Sarah Crowe, Hannah Pescod, Pete Graham, Richard Melvin, Iain Gillie, Mairi Daimer, Richard Wilson, Juliet Cadzow, Owen Lewis, Maggie Service, Matthew Justice, Selina Cadell, Armando Iannucci, Sam Collins, Tommy Sheppard, Kenton Allen, Nick Findlay-Coulson, Simon Munnery, Dave Smith, Stewart Lee, Humphrey Ker, Thom Tuck, David Reed, Chris Brand, Paul Sneddon and Will Smith: you have all made a difference.